Microsoft SharePoint 2010 and Windows PowerShell 2.0: Expert Cookbook

50 advanced recipes for administrators and IT Pros to master Microsoft SharePoint 2010 and Microsoft PowerShell 2.0 automation

Yaroslav Pentsarskyy

BIRMINGHAM - MUMBAI

Microsoft SharePoint 2010 and Windows PowerShell 2.0: Expert Cookbook

First published: November 2011

Production Reference: 1071111

Published by Packt Publishing Ltd.
Livery Place
35 Livery Street
Birmingham B3 2PB, UK.

ISBN 978-1-84968-410-1

www.packtpub.com

Cover Image by John Green (iguana@cogeco.ca)

Credits

Author

Yaroslav Pentsarskyy

Reviewers

Muhammad A. Piracha

Ravikanth C

Acquisition Editor

Stephanie Moss

Development Editor

Maitreya Bhakal

Technical Editor

Manasi Poonthottam

Project Coordinator

Kushal Bhardwaj

Proofreader

Joel T. Johnson

Indexer

Monica Ajmera Mehta

Production Coordinator

Melwyn D'sa

Cover Work

Melwyn D'sa

About the Author

Yaroslav Pentsarskyy has been involved in SharePoint solution architecture and implementation since 2003. He has been a Microsoft MVP since 2009 and keeps in close contact with the SharePoint product team. Yaroslav frequently presents at technical events worldwide as well as online. You can always find a fresh bit of SharePoint information on his blog: `http://www.sharemuch.com`. To learn everything Yaroslav knows about SharePoint, check out his two new books *Top 60 Custom Solutions built on SharePoint 2010* and *SharePoint 2010 branding in practice*.

About the Reviewers

Muhammad A. Piracha is a senior Software Engineer at Bamboo Solutions Corporation, which is based in Reston, Virginia. Bamboo Solutions is a leading provider of software solutions for the Microsoft SharePoint platform. Muhammad has over 15 years of experience in building document management software applications using various Microsoft products. He has experience in a variety of capacities, including architecting, designing, and developing software for SharePoint technologies since its release in 2003. When he is not on a computer writing code, he enjoys spending time with his family and outdoor activities.

Ravikanth C has more than 10 years of experience in the IT industry. In the beginning of his career, he worked at Wipro Infotech managing Windows, Solaris servers, and Cisco network equipment. He currently works at Dell Inc. as a lead engineer in the SharePoint solutions group. As a part of his work, he has authored several whitepapers on MOSS 2007 and SharePoint 2010 that provide guidance around infrastructure elements of a SharePoint deployment. His work also involves performance testing and sizing of SharePoint workloads on Dell servers and storage. Ravikanth is passionate about automation and outside of work he writes regularly on his blog, `http://www.ravichaganti.com/blog`, about topics related to Windows PowerShell, Microsoft SharePoint, and Windows Server virtualization.

In 2010, Ravikanth received Microsoft's Most Valuable Professional (MVP) award in Windows PowerShell. You can also hear him speak regularly at BITPro (`http://bitpro.in`) user group meetings and other in-person events at Bangalore, India.

www.PacktPub.com

Support files, eBooks, discount offers, and more

You might want to visit www.PacktPub.com for support files and downloads related to your book.

Did you know that Packt offers eBook versions of every book published, with PDF and ePub files available? You can upgrade to the eBook version at www.PacktPub.com and as a print book customer, you are entitled to a discount on the eBook copy. Get in touch with us at service@packtpub.com for more details.

At www.PacktPub.com, you can also read a collection of free technical articles, sign up for a range of free newsletters and receive exclusive discounts and offers on Packt books and eBooks.

http://PacktLib.PacktPub.com

Do you need instant solutions to your IT questions? PacktLib is Packt's online digital book library. Here, you can access, read and search across Packt's entire library of books.

Why Subscribe?

- ▶ Fully searchable across every book published by Packt
- ▶ Copy and paste, print and bookmark content
- ▶ On demand and accessible via web browser

Free Access for Packt account holders

If you have an account with Packt at www.PacktPub.com, you can use this to access PacktLib today and view nine entirely free books. Simply use your login credentials for immediate access.

Instant Updates on New Packt Books

Get notified! Find out when new books are published by following @PacktEnterprise on Twitter, or the *Packt Enterprise* Facebook page.

Table of Contents

Preface

PowerShell is tightly integrated with SharePoint 2010, demonstrating an important alliance between the fastest growing collaboration and web publishing platform, and the latest task automation framework. The advantages of PowerShell and SharePoint integration help administrators and infrastructure specialists achieve everyday enterprise tasks more efficiently, and this book will ensure you get the most out of SharePoint configuration and management.

When it comes to custom SharePoint 2010 solution configuration, creating robust PowerShell scripts is the best option for saving time and providing a point of reference to when changes are made in the server environment. This practical expert cookbook translates the most commonly found scenarios into a series of immediately usable recipes, allowing you to get up and running straight away with writing powerful PowerShell scripts for SharePoint.

Microsoft SharePoint 2010 and Windows PowerShell 2.0: Expert Cookbook focuses on a range of distinct areas of SharePoint administration, with expert recipes targeting unique business examples.

You will learn exactly how solutions were achieved for managing SharePoint list settings with PowerShell, PowerShell configuration of SharePoint FAST Search, and more. You will also learn how to tailor the recipe to your own business needs.

With this advanced cookbook in hand, you will be fully equipped with the source code as a starting point for creating your scripts in order to take advantage of the integration between SharePoint and PowerShell.

What this book covers

Chapter 1, PowerShell Scripting Methods and Creating Custom Commands: Go further with PowerShell to create your own PowerShell commands (CmdLets) and snap-ins and share them with your team.

Chapter 2, Enterprise Content Deployment and Provisioning using PowerShell: Automate your SharePoint 2010 custom solution deployment by using a robust PowerShell script.

Chapter 3, Performing Advanced List and Content Operations in SharePoint using PowerShell: Master the management of SharePoint lists and list settings with PowerShell.

Chapter 4, Managing External Data in SharePoint and Business Connectivity Services using PowerShell: Get to the bottom of administering Business Connectivity Services (BCS) in SharePoint.

Chapter 5, Managing SharePoint 2010 Metadata and Social Features using PowerShell: Learn all about performing the most common configurations around SharePoint taxonomy features and user profile services.

Chapter 6, Managing SharePoint Search and FAST Search with PowerShell: Configure SharePoint FAST Search using PowerShell including audience targeting and improving search results.

Chapter 7, Managing SharePoint Site Content in Bulk using PowerShell: Configure content on SharePoint pages including bulk provisioning and configuration publishing pages, content types and web parts.

Chapter 8, Managing Documents and Records in SharePoint with PowerShell: Get the most out of document and records management in SharePoint 2010 by automating configuration.

Chapter 9, Administrating Web Application and Server Administration in SharePoint with PowerShell: Simplify SharePoint server management by using PowerShell for tasks like web application settings, configuration and monitoring, sandbox features, and more.

What you need for this book

To complete the tasks in this book, you will need a system with SharePoint 2010 Server Standard installed. Some areas of the book will require FAST Search to be installed and configured. We recommend downloading and installing 2010 Information Worker Demonstration and Evaluation Virtual Machine (RTM) Virtual Machine environment if you do not have a compatible system set up. The most current link to download the virtual environment can be retrieved by searching for the 2010 Information Worker Demonstration and Evaluation Virtual Machine (RTM). By downloading the preceding environment, you will ensure all of the configurations and setups have been performed and your system is ready for using PowerShell with SharePoint.

Who this book is for

If you are a SharePoint administrator or IT Pro who wants to extend your knowledge of PowerShell automation, this book is a must have. You should have a solid grasp of working with SharePoint and PowerShell.

Conventions

In this book, you will find a number of styles of text that distinguish between different kinds of information. Here are some examples of these styles, and an explanation of their meaning.

Code words in text are shown as follows: " Set the filename of the script to `ManageSandbox.ps1`."

A block of code is set as follows:

```
$QuotaTemplate.UserCodeMaximumLevel = 200
$QuotaTemplate.UserCodeWarningLevel = 100
$AdminService.Update()
```

When we wish to draw your attention to a particular part of a code block, the relevant lines or items are set in bold:

```
$SPSite.WebApplication.Update()

  Write-Host "Web application configuration complete"
  }
$SPSite.Dispose()Any command-line input or output is written as
follows:

PS C:\Users\Administrator\Desktop> .\ WebApplicationThrottling.ps1
```

New terms and **important words** are shown in bold. Words that you see on the screen, in menus or dialog boxes for example, appear in the text like this: "Click **File | Save** to save the script to your development machine's desktop."

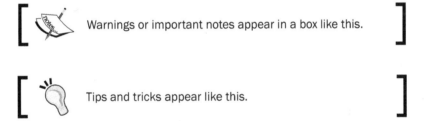

> Warnings or important notes appear in a box like this.

> Tips and tricks appear like this.

Reader feedback

Feedback from our readers is always welcome. Let us know what you think about this book—what you liked or may have disliked. Reader feedback is important for us to develop titles that you really get the most out of.

To send us general feedback, simply send an e-mail to `feedback@packtpub.com`, and mention the book title via the subject of your message.

If there is a book that you need and would like to see us publish, please send us a note in the **SUGGEST A TITLE** form on www.packtpub.com or e-mail suggest@packtpub.com.

If there is a topic that you have expertise in and you are interested in either writing or contributing to a book, see our author guide on www.packtpub.com/authors.

Customer support

Now that you are the proud owner of a Packt book, we have a number of things to help you to get the most from your purchase.

Downloading the example code

You can download the example code files for all Packt books you have purchased from your account at http://www.PacktPub.com. If you purchased this book elsewhere, you can visit http://www.PacktPub.com/support and register to have the files e-mailed directly to you.

Errata

Although we have taken every care to ensure the accuracy of our content, mistakes do happen. If you find a mistake in one of our books—maybe a mistake in the text or the code—we would be grateful if you would report this to us. By doing so, you can save other readers from frustration and help us improve subsequent versions of this book. If you find any errata, please report them by visiting http://www.packtpub.com/support, selecting your book, clicking on the **errata submission form** link, and entering the details of your errata. Once your errata are verified, your submission will be accepted and the errata will be uploaded on our website, or added to any list of existing errata, under the Errata section of that title. Any existing errata can be viewed by selecting your title from http://www.packtpub.com/support.

Piracy

Piracy of copyright material on the Internet is an ongoing problem across all media. At Packt, we take the protection of our copyright and licenses very seriously. If you come across any illegal copies of our works, in any form, on the Internet, please provide us with the location address or website name immediately so that we can pursue a remedy.

Please contact us at `copyright@packtpub.com` with a link to the suspected pirated material.

We appreciate your help in protecting our authors, and our ability to bring you valuable content.

Questions

You can contact us at `questions@packtpub.com` if you are having a problem with any aspect of the book, and we will do our best to address it.

1
PowerShell Scripting Methods and Creating Custom Commands

In this chapter, we will cover:

- ► Setting up your Virtual Machine and running a test script
- ► Authoring, debugging, and executing script accessing farm settings with PowerGUI and PowerShell ISE
- ► Accessing advanced SharePoint 2010 functionality with external libraries
- ► Creating a custom PowerShell command (CmdLet)
- ► Creating a custom PowerShell Snap-In

Introduction

PowerShell as a scripting language will execute actions on your target environment. Scripting is not a new concept and PowerShell is definitely not a new language. However, PowerShell and SharePoint 2010 integrate very well. This integration allows administrators and developers to access not just a limited set of commands, but also to connect to SharePoint objects and libraries to take advantage of additional capabilities of SharePoint as a platform. To ensure that we are on the same page while reading this book and trying out various recipes, we'll start by setting up your environment and verifying the setup by running a test script. After all, SharePoint relies on components, most of which we're going to be directly interacting with, and having a consistently configured environment will help in reducing any potential integration issues.

Although we can author our PowerShell scripts in Notepad and execute them in a PowerShell command-line environment, you can experience more advantages from authoring and debugging your scripts by using rich authoring environments, such as PowerGUI or PowerShell ISE. In this chapter, we'll see exactly what the benefits of using those environments are.

Whether you are creating a PowerShell script in a professional scripting environment or calling an existing script from a command line, you'll quickly notice that a default set of commands is definitely not enough to manage and work with your SharePoint system. When you have the need to author scripts accessing various other aspects of SharePoint functionality, you will need to use the additional libraries available to facilitate custom or out-of-the-box functionality required. This is a very common scenario for developers when building custom solutions for a variety of platforms. PowerShell, as a scripting language, really takes advantage of this concept allowing you to call functions from SharePoint and third-party libraries. In this chapter, we'll take a look at exactly how you can access advanced SharePoint 2010 functionality using external libraries.

As you become more familiar with authoring PowerShell scripts, you will realize that you can create a collection of reusable functionality which can be shared with others. That's when you can take advantage of sealing your custom functionality in a portable and sharable way. We'll take a look at how you can package your custom scripts as custom PowerShell CmdLets, as well as how to create a custom PowerShell Snap-In.

Setting up your Virtual Machine and running a test script

In this recipe, we'll ensure your development environment is configured properly.

Getting ready

To complete the recipes in this book, it's assumed you're running a system with SharePoint 2010 Server Standard installed. If not, it is recommended you download and install the 2010 Information Worker Demonstration and Evaluation Virtual Machine (RTM) Virtual Machine environment, if you do not have a compatible system set up. For the most current link to download this virtual environment, search Microsoft Download Center with the keyword **2010 IW demo RTM**.

By downloading the preceding environment, you will ensure all of the configurations and setups have been performed and your system is ready for using PowerShell with SharePoint. Whether you're using your own or a downloaded Virtual Machine, let's ensure PowerShell is enabled in your environment.

How to do it...

Let's see how you can get your virtual environment configured and run your first script using the following steps:

1. On the target Virtual Machine, ensure you are logged in with an administrator's role.

2. Click **Start | All Programs | Microsoft SharePoint 2010 Products | SharePoint 2010 Management Shell**.

3. Input `Get-ExecutionPolicy` and press *Enter* on your keyboard. PowerShell may return a value of `Restricted`.

4. Input `Set-ExecutionPolicy Unrestricted` and hit *Enter*.

 Ensure this policy is reverted back on your production environments to avoid the risk of malicious script execution.

5. Input the following command in the window:

   ```
   Get-SPSite | Where-Object {$_.Url -eq "http://intranet.contoso.com"}
   ```

6. You should see a result that looks similar to the following screenshot:

```
Administrator: SharePoint 2010 Management Shell                        _ □ ×
PS C:\Users\Administrator> Get-SPSite | Where-Object {$_.Url -eq "http://intrane
t.contoso.com"}

Url
---
http://intranet.contoso.com
WARNING: More results were found in Get-SPSite but were not returned.  Use
'-Limit ALL' to return all possible results.

PS C:\Users\Administrator> _
```

How it works...

On Windows 2008 Server, PowerShell script execution policy is set to restrict script execution by default. As an administrator, you can choose to allow script execution by calling the `Set-ExecutionPolicy Unrestricted` command.

For more information on options available for script execution policy and how it affects your environment, search TechNet with the keyword **Set-ExecutionPolicy**.

Once script execution is not restricted, we run a PowerShell command enumerating all of the SharePoint sites with the `http://intranet.contoso.com` URL. This assumes you have an existing site collection with such a URL. If you're using the downloadable environment from above, the site collection will be already set up for you. If you're running a site collection with a different URL, feel free to replace the value in this example.

There's more...

In this example, we assumed you were running a Virtual Machine downloaded from the Microsoft download site with all of the pre-set options. In this case, you may see that the execution policy has already been set to `unrestricted`. In this case, you don't need to set the value again.

Authoring, debugging, and executing script accessing farm settings with PowerGUI and PowerShell ISE

As you can see from the previous recipe, authoring and executing a PowerShell script is a simple task that can be done right from the command line. In this recipe, we'll take a look at how you can author and debug your PowerShell scripts using two of the most popular tools: **PowerShell ISE** and **PowerGUI**. Using these tools, we'll execute a script accessing farm settings of the SharePoint site.

Getting ready

First, let's ensure you have installed PowerShell ISE:

1. On the target Virtual Machine, click **Start | Administrative Tools | Server Manager**.
2. On the left-hand side panel of the **Server Manager** window, click the **Features** node.
3. In the main window of the Server Manager, click **Add Features**.
4. From the **Add Features** Wizard, ensure **Windows PowerShell Integrated Scripting Environment (ISE)** is selected. If it is selected and grayed out, as seen in the following screenshot, skip to Step 6 in this sequence.

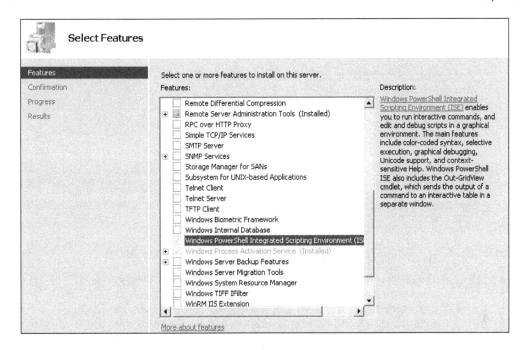

5. Click **Next** and **Install** on the following window to install the feature.

6. Upon installation completion, close the **Server Manager** window.

Let's now install PowerGUI:

1. Navigate to `http://www.powergui.org` or search the Internet with **PowerGUI**.

2. Download the latest version of PowerGUI installer.

3. Run the installation package on your development environment and install the PowerGUI tool using the default installation options.

Now that you have all of the tools installed, let's use PowerShell ISE and PowerGUI to author, debug, and execute our new script.

How to do it...

Let's see how PowerShell ISE and PowerGUI can help with your script authoring.

1. On your development environment, click **Start | All Programs | Accessories | Windows PowerShell | Windows PowerShell ISE**.

2. In the PowerShell ISE window's top section, type in the following script:

```
$siteUrl = "http://intranet.contoso.com"

$snapin = Get-PSSnapin | Where-Object {$_.Name -eq 'Microsoft.
SharePoint.Powershell'}
if ($snapin -eq $null) {
Write-Host "Loading SharePoint Powershell Snapin"
Add-PSSnapin "Microsoft.SharePoint.Powershell"
}

$site = Get-SPSite | Where-Object {$_.Url -eq $siteUrl}
$site.WebApplication.QueryFeatures("00BFEA71-EC85-4903-972D-
EBE475780106")
```

Downloading the example code

You can download the example code fles for all Packt books you have purchased from your account at `http://www.PacktPub.com`. If you purchased this book elsewhere, you can visit `http://www.PacktPub.com/support` and register to have the fles e-mailed directly to you.

3. Press *F5* on your keyboard.

4. Take a note of the results returned by the script which will contain multiple instances in the following format:

```
DefinitionId          : 00bfea71-ec85-4903-972d-ebe475780106
Parent                : My
Properties            : {}
Definition            : SPFeatureDefinition
Name=FeatureDefinition/00bfea71-ec85-4903-972d-ebe475780106
Version               : 3.0.0.0
FeatureDefinitionScope : Farm
```

5. Now let's see the result with PowerGUI. On your development environment, click **Start | All Programs | PowerGUI | PowerGUI Script Editor**.

6. In the top section of the PowerGUI editor, insert the same code we used in step 2 of this sequence:

```
$siteUrl = "http://intranet.contoso.com"

$snapin = Get-PSSnapin | Where-Object {$_.Name -eq 'Microsoft.
SharePoint.Powershell'}
if ($snapin -eq $null) {
Write-Host "Loading SharePoint Powershell Snapin"
Add-PSSnapin "Microsoft.SharePoint.Powershell"
```

```
}

$site = Get-SPSite | Where-Object {$_.Url -eq $siteUrl}
$site.WebApplication.QueryFeatures("00BFEA71-EC85-4903-972D-
EBE475780106")
```

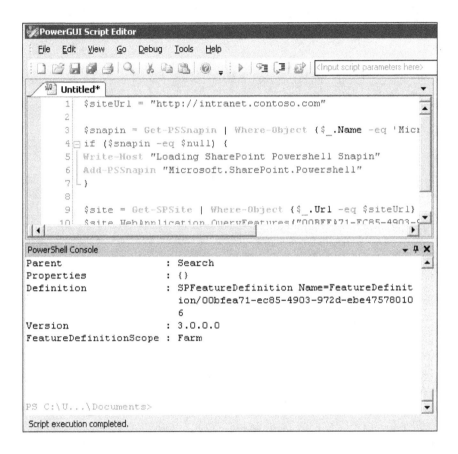

7. Press *F5* to execute your script.

8. Take a note of the same result set in the PowerShell Console window right below the editor, seen in the previous image.

9. Switch back to the script editor section of the screen and set your cursor on the last line of the code.

10. Press *F9* to set the breakpoint on the last line of the code.

11. Press *F5* to execute the script up to the breakpoint.

12. Take a note of the script editor window when the script has been executed up to the breakpoint. Your PowerGUI editor will look similar to the following screenshot:

```
PowerGUI Script Editor

File   Edit   View   Go   Debug   Tools   Help

                                                      <Input script parameters here>

  Untitled*

   1   $siteUrl = "http://intranet.contoso.com"
   2
   3   $snapin = Get-PSSnapin | Where-Object ($_.Name -eq 'Microsoft.SharePoint.Power
   4   if ($snapin -eq $null) {
   5   Write-Host "Loading SharePoint Powershell Snapin"
   6   Add-PSSnapin "Microsoft.SharePoint.Powershell"
   7   }
   8
   9   $site = Get-SPSite | Where-Object ($_.Url -eq $siteUrl)
  10   $site.WebApplication.QueryFeatures("00BFEA71-EC85-4903-972D-EBE475780106")


PowerShell Console
Version              : 3.0.0.0
FeatureDefinitionScope : Farm



WARNING: More results were found in Get-SPSite but were not returned.   Use '-Limit ALL'
to return all possible results.

[DBG]: PS C:\Us...\Documents>

Executing script...
```

13. At this point you can press *F5* on your keyboard to continue execution.

How it works...

We launched the PowerShell ISE to execute our custom script. The first thing our script is going to do is load the PowerShell cmdlet library for SharePoint. This extension library holds various PowerShell functions allowing us to work with SharePoint objects from within PowerShell. Once the library is loaded, our script connects to our SharePoint site, http://intranet.contoso.com, and gets a hold of the current site. Further, the script calls a function which enumerates all of the SharePoint sites and their basic details which have a specified featured ID active in them, as seen in the following screenshot

```
PowerShell Console
Version                   : 3.0.0.0
FeatureDefinitionScope    : Farm

DefinitionId              : 00bfea71-ec85-4903-972d-ebe475780106
Parent                    : Marketing
Properties                : {}
Definition                : SPFeatureDefinition Name=FeatureDefinit
                            ion/00bfea71-ec85-4903-972d-ebe47578010
                            6
Version                   : 3.0.0.0
FeatureDefinitionScope    : Farm

DefinitionId              : 00bfea71-ec85-4903-972d-ebe475780106
Parent                    : New Products
Properties                : {}
Definition                : SPFeatureDefinition Name=FeatureDefinit
                            ion/00bfea71-ec85-4903-972d-ebe47578010
                            6
Version                   : 3.0.0.0
FeatureDefinitionScope    : Farm

DefinitionId              : 00bfea71-ec85-4903-972d-ebe475780106
Parent                    : Projects
Properties                : {}
Definition                : SPFeatureDefinition Name=FeatureDefinit
                            ion/00bfea71-ec85-4903-972d-ebe47578010
                            6
Version                   : 3.0.0.0
PS C:\Users\Administrator\Documents>

Script execution completed.
```

This function can be pretty handy when you're trying to locate problem features, or determine which site will be affected by the planned feature upgrade.

Our PowerShell script has been executed first in PowerShell ISE to see what capabilities you have in this Integrated Scripting Environment (ISE).

We then used PowerGUI to see how the same script can be executed and debugged. As you can see, PowerGUI has a few more features facilitating the script authoring process.

The debug option available in the script editor is particularly handy when your script doesn't quite yet work to your standards, and you want to figure out potential problems in it. If you're a developer, you already know all about debugging and its benefits.

Once you're satisfied with the script, you can execute it and run it on the current environment.

There's more

Let's take a look at how we can author and execute scripts with PowerGUI.

Script authoring with PowerGUI

One of the other advantages to PowerGUI is the ability to see values of variables in your script as it executes. The **Variables** panel is, by default, on the right-hand side of your **PowerGUI** window as seen here:

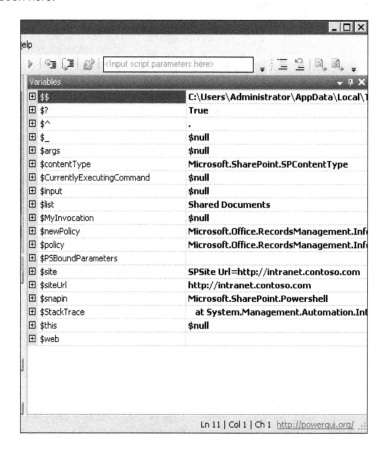

Without this panel, if you wanted to list the variable value, you would typically need to call it in a command line. If the variables in question are complex objects, you get to see the value of all the properties too, as shown in the following screenshot:

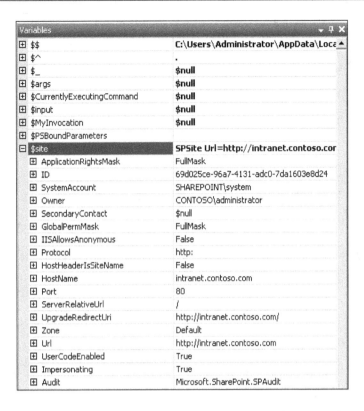

Also, to aid you with script authoring, PowerGUI has a collection of handy snippets which you can access with the **Edit | Insert Snippet** option.

For more tips on working with PowerGUI user interface and features, check out http://www. Powergui.org. For more tips on PowerShell ISE, search TechNet for Windows PowerShell Integrated Scripting Environment.

Accessing advanced SharePoint 2010 functionality with external libraries

In the previous recipe, we looked at some of the functionalities available to you in the PowerShell library, designed to help you access basic features in SharePoint. By using those features, you can access SharePoint objects and manipulate their properties. But what if you need to access the object model beyond what's available to you from the PowerShell snap-in for SharePoint? In this recipe, we'll take a look at how you can access more advanced features in SharePoint by referencing SharePoint assemblies and associated methods in those libraries.

Getting ready

In this example, we'll be using PowerGUI to execute our script. So log in to your environment with administrative privileges and launch PowerGUI.

How to do it...

The following steps will demonstrate how you can use some of the advanced SharePoint functions by referencing external assemblies in your PowerShell script:

1. Navigate to the test site URL: `http://intranet.contoso.com` and click on the **Shared Documents** library to access the library.

2. In the ribbon click **Library | Library Settings**.

3. Under **Permissions and Management** click **Information management policy settings as seen in the following screenshot:**.

```
List Information

Name:            Shared Documents
Web Address:     http://intranet/Shared Documents/Forms/AllItems.aspx
Description:     Share a document with the team by adding it to this do


General Settings                    Permissions and Management

Title, description and navigation   Permissions for this document
                                    library
Versioning settings
                                    Manage files which have no
Advanced settings                   checked in version

Validation settings                 Workflow Settings

Column default value settings       Enterprise Metadata and
                                    Keywords Settings
Manage item scheduling
                                    Generate file plan report
Rating settings
                                    Information management policy
Audience targeting settings         settings

Metadata navigation settings        Record declaration settings

Per-location view settings

Form settings
```

4. Select **Document** from the list of available content types.

5. Take note that none of the policies have been defined for this document library.

6. Switch to your PowerGUI scripting editor and enter the following script:

```
$siteUrl = "http://intranet.contoso.com"

$snapin = Get-PSSnapin | Where-Object {$_.Name -eq 'Microsoft.
```

```
SharePoint.Powershell'}

if ($snapin -eq $null) {
Write-Host "Loading SharePoint Powershell Snapin"
Add-PSSnapin "Microsoft.SharePoint.Powershell"
}

$site = Get-SPSite | Where-Object {$_.Url -eq $siteUrl}
$web =  $site.OpenWeb();
$list = $web.Lists["Shared Documents"];

$policy = [Microsoft.Office.RecordsManagement.InformationPolicy.
ListPolicySettings]($list);
if ($policy.ListHasPolicy -eq 0)
{

$policy.UseListPolicy = "true";
$policy.Update();
}

$contentType = $list.ContentTypes["Document"];
[Microsoft.Office.RecordsManagement.InformationPolicy.Policy]::
CreatePolicy($contentType, $null);

$newPolicy = [Microsoft.Office.RecordsManagement.
InformationPolicy.Policy]::GetPolicy($contentType);

$newPolicy.Items.Add(
"Microsoft.Office.RecordsManagement.PolicyFeatures.Expiration",
"<Schedules nextStageId='3'>" +
"<Schedule type='Default'>" +
"<stages>" +
"<data stageId='1' stageDeleted='true'></data>" +
"<data stageId='2'>" +
"<formula id='Microsoft.Office.RecordsManagement.PolicyFeatures.
Expiration.Formula.BuiltIn'>" +
"<number>1</number>" +
"<property>Created</property>" +
"<period>years</period>" +
"</formula>" +
"<action type='action' id='Microsoft.Office.RecordsManagement.
PolicyFeatures.Expiration.Action.MoveToRecycleBin' />" +
"</data>" +
"</stages>" +
"</Schedule>" +
```

```
"</Schedules>");

$newPolicy.Update();
```

7. Press *F5* to execute the script, and then wait until the script executes.

8. Switch back to the policy setting page we accessed in step 5. Take note of the new policy added to the **Retention policy** where expiration has been enabled on the document library items, as seen in the following screenshot:

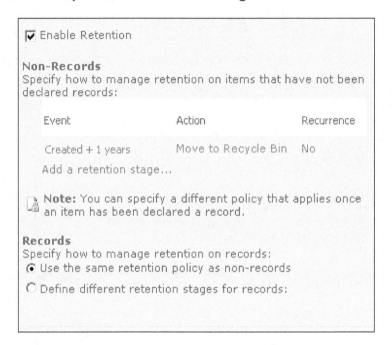

How it works...

The preceding code demonstrates how to take advantage of SharePoint class libraries to access functionality and methods available in those class libraries, and not directly available as PowerShell SharePoint script extensions. Although methods used here are discussed in detail in *Chapter 8, Managing Documents and Records in SharePoint with PowerShell*, this recipe demonstrates basics behind accessing SharePoint object model using PowerShell. In this example, we created a new expiration policy on the document library of the team site on the development environment downloaded from Microsoft's download site http://intranet.contoso.com.

We started by accessing the site which we are interested in by using the PowerShell Get-SPSite method. We then accessed the current site at which the **SharePoint Documents** document library is hosted.

Next, we got hold of the current policy on the library in order to add a new instance of a policy.

We used the `CreatePolicy` method available in the `[Microsoft.Office.RecordsManagement.InformationPolicy.Policy]` namespace to create a policy for the library. This part demonstrates how the function is not available in the PowerShell syntax, but is available in the SharePoint library, and can be called in order to access some of the advanced functions in SharePoint.

The rest of the preceding code adds the definition of the policy we're trying to create on the library and adds the new policy object to the list of available policies.

When you execute this script, the newly defined policy will be added to the library on the site.

There's more

Let's take a look at how you can access external SharePoint libraries to execute more advanced PowerShell commands.

Accessing other SharePoint libraries and related functions

In this example, we looked at how you can create an expiration formula on the library, but there is plenty more you can do. To access functions in SharePoint libraries, you need to identify the object class and namespace those functions belong to so you can reference them in PowerShell.

If you search for the policy function class on TechNet you will find: `Microsoft.Office.RecordsManagement.InformationPolicy.Policy`. From there you can also determine various functions available to be called.

To call any of the functions, you would use the method we used in the preceding source code and reference the namespace first, followed by the class and function names.

Let's look at another example where we use PowerShell to connect to the current site and then change the status of features on the site.

1. Open PowerGUI, click **File | New** to create a new script.

2. Add the following code to the script window:

```
$siteUrl = "http://intranet.contoso.com"

$snapin = Get-PSSnapin | Where-Object {$_.Name -eq 'Microsoft.
SharePoint.Powershell'}
if ($snapin -eq $null) {
Write-Host "Loading SharePoint Powershell Snapin"
Add-PSSnapin "Microsoft.SharePoint.Powershell"
}
```

```
$site = Get-SPSite | Where-Object {$_.Url -eq $siteUrl}
$features = $site.FeatureDefinitions;
$features.get_Item("CustomFeature").Status = "Offline"
```

3. Run the script from within PowerGUI by pressing *F5*.

4. Verify the status of our `CustomFeature` which should be `Offline`.

Note that we did not have direct access to the `features` object but rather to its parent. Yet, by using PowerShell, we were able to call function on a child object allowing us to change the status of the feature on the site.

In this case, we set the feature to be `Offline`. Among other available options related to a feature status, we could choose the following: `Online`, `Disabled`, `Offline`, `Unprovisioning`, `Provisioning`, `Upgrading`.

As you can see, this method is handy when you need to disable defective features across many sites in your environment.

This example demonstrates how you can access other available libraries in SharePoint and even your own custom libraries to call functions from within them.

Creating a custom PowerShell command (CmdLet)

In this chapter, previous recipes have tackled accessing custom functions in other SharePoint libraries, and using those functions to perform various operations in our script. It's now time for us to see how we can create our own custom function executing some custom logic. Once the command has been created, it will be accessible from within PowerShell for users to call.

This is particularly handy when you're creating a collection of functions which perform frequent administrative tasks on your server.

Another example where you might want to create your own CmdLet is when you're planning to package those as custom offering for your customers to download and use on their environments.

Getting ready

To create a custom CmdLet, we will be using Visual Studio 2010 Professional. If you're using the virtualized environment we downloaded in the recipe, *Setting up your Virtual Machine and running a test script*, Visual Studio 2010 Professional will already be installed on your system. Otherwise, ensure you at least have the Professional version installed to continue with this recipe.

How to do it...

Let's take a look at how you can create your own CmdLet using the following steps:

1. From within your Visio Studio 2010, click **File | New | Project ....**

2. From **Installed Templates** select **Visual C# | Class Library**.

3. Leave the default name for the project as **ClassLibrary1** and click **OK**.

4. In the **Solution Explorer**, right-click **References | Add Reference** to add the following references:

   System.Management.Automation, *which can be found in a list of assemblies in the* **.NET** *tab.*

5. Also add a reference to **Microsoft.SharePoint**. *The reference can be found in the* **SharePoint** *tab as seen here:*

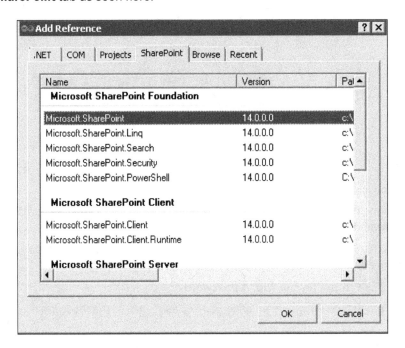

6. In the **Solution Explorer**, pick the **Class1.cs** and rename the file to **PowerShell Cmdlet1.cs**.

7. Replace the contents of the **PowerShell Cmdlet1.cs** with the following code:

```
using System.Management.Automation;
using Microsoft.SharePoint;

namespace PowerShellCmdlet1
{
```

```
[Cmdlet(VerbsCommon.Set, "WebTitle")]
public class PowerShell_Cmdlet1 : Cmdlet
{
    [Parameter()]
    public string siteUrl;

    [Parameter()]
    public string newTitle;

    protected override void ProcessRecord()
    {
        base.ProcessRecord();

        using (SPSite site = new SPSite(siteUrl))
        {
            using (SPWeb web = site.OpenWeb())
            {
                web.Title = newTitle;
                web.Update();
                WriteObject("New Title: " + web.Title);
            }
        }
    }
}
```

8. Right-click the project name **ClassLibrary1** and select **Properties**.

9. From the **Properties** page, pick the **Signing** tab and check the check mark titled **Sign the assembly**.

10. From the drop-down entitled **Choose a strong name key file**, pick **New** and provide key filename of your choice, which usually is safe to call **key.snk**.

11. Uncheck **Protect my file with a password** and click **OK**.

12. Your project will now have an assigned key as shown in the following screenshot:

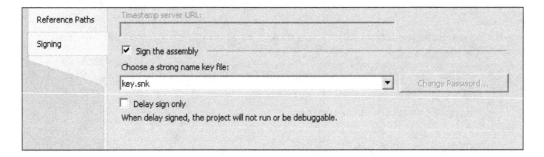

13. At this point, your Visual Studio **Solution Explorer** tree will look as in the following screenshot:

How it works...

At this stage, we have created a new class representing our CmdLet with Visual Studio solution. Visual Studio will produce an assembly file as an output of the solution once built.

Our solution has only one CmdLet functionality which is defined in `PowerShell_Cmdlet1`. You will notice the `[Cmdlet(VerbsCommon.Set, "WebTitle")]` part of the code defines the type of the command and the name of it.

If you noticed, all of the PowerShell commands we have called so far have a naming convention of a `[Verb]-[Action]`. The verb in this case is either `Get` or `Set`. In fact, for the full list of available verbs, in your command let code, place the cursor over `VerbsCommon.Set` and press *F12*. Visual Studio will display all of the available verbs allowing you to find the one appropriate to the CmdLet you're creating.

The second part of the CmdLet declaration is the action of your function, which can be titled according to your preference.

The best practice here is to name the command something descriptive to the action executed by it.

The actual functionality of the CmdLet is defined right below the CmdLet declaration, in our case, in the `PowerShell_Cmdlet1` class.

We started with a parameter declaration, which is an optional piece but often used. Since most PowerShell commands contain a reusable set of instructions to be performed on the object, it's very common when authoring a new script to accept parameters specifying an object. For PowerShell scripts interacting with SharePoint, this will be a URL of the site or list name, and so on. In our case, we'll capture the URL and the new title of the SharePoint site. The following function will use the parameters we supplied to connect to the URL we have identified, and rename the site title to the one defined.

The logic defined in `ProcessRecord` of our code handles all of the functionality our CmdLet will execute, and this is where you can code the functionality of your own CmdLet.

Finally, once the logic of our CmdLet has been created, we're prepared to make the functionality available in the PowerShell command line. Details of the CmdLet installation process are described in the *Creating a custom PowerShell Snap-In recipe*.

Due to the nature of CmdLet, before installing it on the system, we need to make sure the output DLL is signed with a strong name.

The purpose of signing the assembly with the strong name is to ensure the assembly can be dropped into the **Global Assembly Cache (GAC)**, where it can be consumed by the installation process.

See also

Creating a custom PowerShell Snap-In recipe in this chapter.

Creating a custom PowerShell Snap-In

As we've seen in the *Creating a custom PowerShell command (CmdLet)* recipe, the creation of PowerShell CmdLet is a process of defining the functionality you want to expose to the user, and sealing it as a .NET assembly. In this recipe, we'll take a look at how you install your custom CmdLet which directly involves the creation of a **PowerShell Snap-In.**

We have already used the PowerShell Snap-In when we referenced a set of SharePoint Set earlier in this chapter. In this case, we called the following command:

```
Add-PSSnapin "Microsoft.SharePoint.Powershell"
```

In this example, we'll use similar approach to call our custom Snap-In.

Getting ready

As trivial as it sounds, to create a Snap-In, you will need to create another class in the Visual Studio solution you created earlier to define your CmdLet. Your Snap-In solution doesn't need to contain both a Snap-In and a CmdLet. In fact, you can have them created in two separate solutions as long as your Snap-In references the CmdLet. In this example we'll add a Snap-In class to the existing CmdLet solution, which is very common when creating PowerShell CmdLet libraries.

How to do it...

We'll take a look at how you can create your own PowerShell Snap-In.

1. Switch to the Visual Studio 2010 solution you used to create a CmdLet earlier.

2. From the **Solution Explorer**, right-click the project name, **PowerShellCmdlet1** and select **Add | Class ....**

3. In the **Solution Explorer,** pick the **Class1.cs** and rename the file to **PowerShell Cmdlet1.cs**

4. Rename the newly created class to **PowerShellCmdlet SnapIn1.cs**.

5. Open the class file created and replace the contents of the **PowerShellCmdlet SnapIn1.cs** with the following code:

```
using System.Collections.ObjectModel;
using System.ComponentModel;
using System.Management.Automation;
using System.Management.Automation.Runspaces;

namespace PowerShellCmdlet1
{
    [RunInstaller(true)]
    public class PowerShellCmdlet_SnapIn1 : CustomPSSnapIn
    {
        private Collection<CmdletConfigurationEntry> _cmdlets;

        /// <summary>
        /// The description of powershell snap-in.
        /// </summary>
        public override string Description
        {
            get { return "A Description of MyCmdlet"; }
        }

        /// <summary>
        /// The name of power shell snap-in
```

```
        /// </summary>
        public override string Name
        {
            get { return "MyCmdlet"; }
        }

        /// <summary>
        /// The name of the vendor
        /// </summary>
        public override string Vendor
        {
            get { return ""; }
        }

        public override Collection<CmdletConfigurationEntry>
Cmdlets
        {
            get
            {
                if (null == _cmdlets)
                {
                    _cmdlets = new Collection<Cmdlet
                    ConfigurationEntry>();
                    _cmdlets.Add(new CmdletConfigurationEntry
                        ("Set-WebTitle", typeof(PowerShell_Cmdlet1),
"Set-WebTitle.dll-Help.xml"));
                }
                return _cmdlets;
            }
        }

    }
}
```

6. Right-click the project name **PowerShellCmdlet1** and select **Build**.

7. Right-click the project name **PowerShellCmdlet1** and select **Open Folder in Windows Explorer**.

8. In the folder opened, open the bin\Debug folder and locate the PowerShellCmdlet1.dll.

9. Click **Start** | **Run** on your development environment and open the Global Assembly Cache by typing c:\windows\assembly.

10. Drag-and-drop the PowerShellCmdlet1.dll to the assembly folder.

11. Open a PowerShell command line from **Start | All Programs | Accessories | Windows PowerShell | Windows PowerShell**.

12. Type in the following command to install our newly added Snap-In assembly. Ensure the path to your assembly is correct. In this example, our path is `C:\ Users\Administrator\Documents\visual studio 2010\projects\ PowerShellCmdlet1\PowerShellCmdlet1\bin\Debug`:

    ```
    PS> set-alias installutil $env:windir\Microsoft.NET\Framework\
    v2.0.50727\installutil
    ```

    ```
    PS> cd "C:\Users\Administrator\Documents\visual studio 2010\
    projects\PowerShellCmdlet1\PowerShellCmdlet1\bin\Debug"
    ```

    ```
    S> installutil PowerShellCmdlet1.dll
    ```

13. Now that our Snap-In has been installed, let's open our SharePoint test intranet site, `http://intranet.contoso.com`. Take note of the current site title.

14. Switch back to the PowerShell command-line window and register the new Snap-In:

    ```
    PS> Add-PSSnapin "MyCmdlet"
    ```

15. Let's change the title of the site by executing our custom CmdLet:

    ```
    PS> Set-WebTitle -siteUrl "http://intranet.contoso.com" -newTitle
    "Test Title"
    ```

16. Switch back to `http://intranet.contoso.com` and take note of the changed title.

How it works...

Since we have already created the actual CmdLet, we reused the same Visual Studio solution to add a Snap-In class. The Snap-In class will perform the role of installer. As you can see, the contents of the class declare the name and description on the CmdLet as well as a reference to CmdLet class. This information will further be used to identify your custom CmdLet.

Once the solution has been built and the solution library has been generated, we copied the library to GAC. We used `InstallUtil` to install and uninstall server resources by executing the installer components in our CmdLet library. By executing the `InstallUtil` command we will actually make the Snap-In available in the PowerShell command line.

Once installed, we can add the Snap-In and execute our custom CmdLet.

As you will notice, due to the fact that our custom Snap-In library will be placed into the GAC, the custom code executed will have access to most of the server resources. Because of the level of access, when downloading custom Snap-Ins ensure they come from a trusted source.

There's more

Let's take a look at how you can uninstall your Snap-In from the system as well as how Visual Studio templates can help you with Snap-In authoring.

Uninstalling a Snap-In from your system

Previously, we looked at how you can install the Snap-In so it's available to be called from the command line. You can also uninstall the Snap-In by using the uninstall key of the `InstallUtil` command. Here is a sample uninstall syntax for our Snap-In:

```
PS> installutil /u PowerShellCmdlet1.dll
```

It's quite common to need to uninstall the Snap-In. One common scenario includes the CmdLet authoring process. As you author your CmdLet and discover problems with it or would like to add more functionality, to have the new version available you would need to re-install the Snap-in on the environment.

Visual Studio CmdLet and Snap-In item templates

In this example, we looked at how you can install a custom PowerShell Snap-In by adding code to a Visual Studio solution. Since this is a fairly common task, there are a few templates available online which you're welcome to use to create core CmdLet and Snap-In code automatically. The core functionality will be your starting point which you can add your customizations to.

One of the templates you can try is available at *CodePlex*. The project is called PowerShell Visual Studio 2008 templates and recently was hosted at this URL: `http://psvs2008.codeplex.com`.

Although the version of this package is specifically designed for Visual Studio 2008, it is also compatible with Visual Studio 2010.

Once you download the package, open it on the development environment where you have Visual Studio installed, and install all of the suggested components, as seen in the following screenshot:

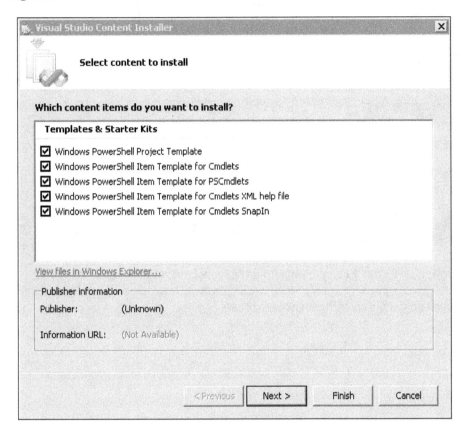

Once installed, to add a new instance of a template for CmdLet and Snap-In, simply right-click on the project name in **Solution Explorer**, and select **Add | New Item**.

From here, you need to pick the appropriate Snap-In or CmdLet template and click **Add** to create an initial version of the file, as seen in the following screenshot:.

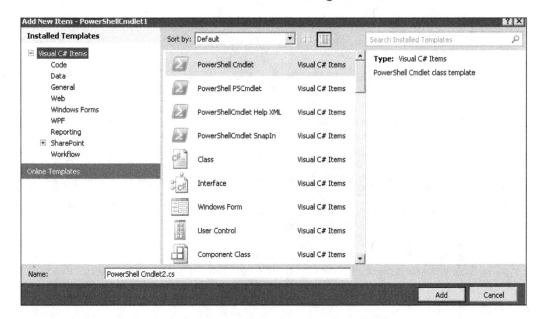

Whether you will be using components from the preceding template, or creating your own CmdLet classes, search MSDN with the keyword *Cmdlet Development Guidelines* for some handy tips and details on authoring your CmdLets.

2
Enterprise Content Deployment and Provisioning Using PowerShell

In this chapter, we will cover:

- ▶ Provisioning site hierarchy during solution deployment
- ▶ Installing features on the site and managing existing site features
- ▶ Creating permission levels and security groups that use them
- ▶ Managing site templates and their availability on sites
- ▶ Associating features to existing site templates
- ▶ Managing SharePoint workflow association using PowerShell
- ▶ Configuring site themes and user interface artifacts

Introduction

As we've seen in *Chapter 1, PowerShell Scripting Methods and Creating Custom Commands*, the strength of PowerShell lies in its ability to access and manipulate complex objects in SharePoint. In this chapter, we'll take a look at many more PowerShell capabilities and usage scenarios targeting enterprise content provisioning and deployment.

When setting up a new solution in your environment, you are likely to want to set it up on a test environment before rolling it out to production. In more complex scenarios, customers require the same solution to be deployed to testing, quality assurance, staging, and production environments. If your solution requires site hierarchy to be provisioned to many environments on the target system, it might be a very time consuming and error-prone task. In this chapter, we'll take a look at how you can create a reusable deployment script with PowerShell to automate your site hierarchy provisioning and solution deployment.

As your SharePoint environment is set up and used in production, periodically you will need to upgrade or install additional functionality. In this chapter, we'll cover how you can activate a set of features across multiple site collections allowing you to streamline your upgrade and solution maintenance process.

Quite often, an out-of-the-box site template is all you need for your SharePoint sites. Over time, your users request additional functionality which they would like to see in subsequent instances of their SharePoint sites. We'll take a look at exactly what's involved in automatically triggering customizations on your custom and out-of-the-box site templates. We'll also look at how you can leverage PowerShell to limit the availability of templates on your SharePoint site.

Many corporate intranets make use of workflows to manage business processes on the site. Whether you are using SharePoint or custom workflows on the site now, or planning to use it in the future, we'll see how you can associate existing workflow templates to lists and libraries within your site.

Finally, we'll see how you can automate managing the look and feel of the site using a PowerShell script.

Provisioning site hierarchy during solution deployment

In this recipe, we'll give full attention to one of the most common tasks administrators and developers need to perform together when a new solution is deployed to client environments: provisioning of site hierarchy. To keep this recipe within the scope of actual site provisioning and not custom site template development, we will be provisioning a site hierarchy of team sites. In your scenario, you are very likely to need to provision site hierarchy of sites deriving from a custom site template. The template will be developed separately and the PowerShell script we'll create here will not change regardless of the templates we're provisioning.

In fact, the PowerShell script we'll create is going to use an XML file where developers will specify the order of the site provisioning and site template used, as well any features activated on the site once it's created.

At the end of this recipe, you will have a reusable script which you can use on many other projects, as well as being able to extend it to facilitate any additional deployment needs you may have.

Getting ready

We'll assume you have already set up your virtual development environment as described in *Chapter 1, PowerShell Scripting Methods and Creating Custom Commands*. We'll also assume you're comfortable with using tools we discussed in the chapter. For this recipe, we'll be using PowerGUI to author the script.

How to do it...

Let's take a look at how site and content provisioning can be accomplished with the script in this recipe:

1. On the target Virtual Machine, ensure you are logged in with an administrator's role.
2. Click **Start | All Programs | PowerGUI | PowerGUI Script Editor**.
3. In the main script editing window of PowerGUI, add the following script:

```
# Defining script variables
[xml]$SiteStructure = get-content SiteStructure.xml
$WebAppUrl = $SiteStructure.Setup.Attributes.Item(0).Value
$SiteCollectionUrl = $SiteStructure.Setup.SiteCollection.
Attributes.Item(1).Value
$SiteUrl = $WebAppUrl + $SiteCollectionUrl

# Loading Microsoft.SharePoint.PowerShell
$snapin = Get-PSSnapin | Where-Object {$_.Name -eq 'Microsoft.
SharePoint.Powershell'}
if ($snapin -eq $null) {
Write-Host "Loading SharePoint Powershell Snapin"
Add-PSSnapin "Microsoft.SharePoint.Powershell"
}

# Deleting existing site found at target URL
$targetUrl = Get-SPSite | Where-Object {$_.Url -eq $SiteUrl}
if ($targetUrl.Url.Length -gt 0) {
  Write-Host "Deleting existing site at" $SiteUrl
  Remove-SPSite -Identity $SiteUrl -Confirm:$false
}


# Creating site structure
```

```
$SiteCollectionName = $SiteStructure.Setup.SiteCollection.
Attributes.Item(0).Value;
$SiteCollectionOwner = $SiteStructure.Setup.SiteCollection.
Attributes.Item(2).Value;
$SiteCollectionTemplate = $SiteStructure.Setup.SiteCollection.
Attributes.Item(3).Value;

Write-Host "Creating new site collection at" $SiteUrl
$NewSite = New-SPSite -URL $WebAppUrl$SiteCollectionUrl -
OwnerAlias $SiteCollectionOwner -Template $SiteCollectionTemplate
-Name $SiteCollectionName
$RootWeb = $NewSite.RootWeb

Write-Host "Site collection created successfully"
Write-Host "Title:" $RootWeb.Title -foregroundcolor Green
Write-Host "URL:" $RootWeb.Url -foregroundcolor Green
Write-Host "-----------------------------------"

for ($i=1; $i -lt $SiteStructure.Setup.SiteCollection.ChildNodes.
Count; $i++ )
  {
   $childsite = $SiteStructure.Setup.SiteCollection.ChildNodes.
Item($i);
   $WebName = $childsite.Attributes.Item(0).Value
   $WebUrl = $childsite.Attributes.Item(1).Value
   $WebTemplate = $childsite.Attributes.Item(2).Value
   Write-Host "Creating new web at" $SiteUrl/$WebUrl
   $NewWeb = New-SPWeb $SiteUrl/$WebUrl -Template $WebTemplate -
Addtotopnav -Useparenttopnav -Name $WebName
   Write-Host "Web created successfully"
   Write-Host "Title:" $NewWeb.Title -foregroundcolor Green
   Write-Host "URL:" $NewWeb.Url -foregroundcolor Green
   Write-Host "-----------------------------------"
  }
start-process -filepath iexplore -argumentlist $SiteUrl
```

4. Click **File** | **Save** to save the script to your development machine's desktop. Set the filename of the script to `setup.ps1`.

5. Click **File** | **New** in PowerGUI application.

6. Add the following code in the newly opened file window:

```
<Setup WebAppUrl="http://intranet.contoso.com">
 <SiteCollection Name="Root Site" Url="/sites/rootsite"
OwnerAlias="contoso\administrator" Template="STS#0">
  <Site Name="Child 1" Url="child1" Template="STS#0"/>
```

```
    <Site Name="Child 2" Url="child2" Template="STS#0"/>
    <Site Name="Child 3" Url="child3" Template="STS#0"/>
  </SiteCollection>
</Setup>
```

7. Save the file on your desktop by clicking **File** | **Save** providing the following filename: `SetupStructure.xml`.

8. Open the PowerShell console window and call `setup.ps1` using the following command:

   PS C:\Users\Administrator\Desktop> .\setup.ps1

9. As a result, your PowerShell script will create a site structure as shown in the following screenshot:

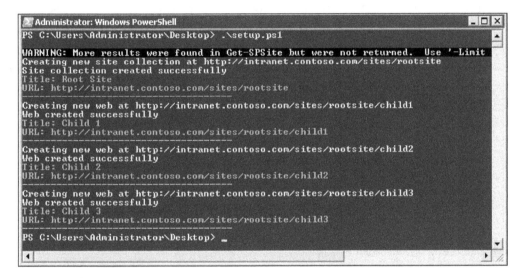

10. Observe the Internet Explorer window opening and navigate to our newly created site collection with URL: `http://intranet.contoso.com/sites/rootsite`.

How it works...

The automated site provisioning process we created above consists of two parts: a PowerShell script executing the commands, and the XML defining our site structure.

Let's take a look at the XML containing the site structure definition. The top element, `<Setup/>`, defines the web application URL which is used to connect to the site and create new site collection.

<SiteCollection/> is the next node in the XML which defines parameter values required for the script to create a new site collection on the specified web application.

The last item in the XML definition is the <Site/> node defining the sites which are going to be created under the site collection. Some of the other parameters required for the site creation are also captured here. These parameters include the URL, name, and the template. In our recipe example, we're using the STS#0 template which is a **Team Site.**

Let's take a look at the actual PowerShell provisioning script. First, the script gets a hold of the XML file defining provisioning variables we just looked at. The structure of the XML is parsed to extract the variables from SiteStructure.xml.

Once the PowerShell snap-in has been loaded, the script proceeds in creating a site collection defined in the <SiteCollection/> node. The existing site collection with the same URL will be deleted. This may not be the behavior you would like to implement to avoid site deletion in error, in which case remove the following code:

```
# Deleting existing site found at target URL
$targetUrl = Get-SPSite | Where-Object {$_.Url -eq $SiteUrl}
if ($targetUrl.Url.Length -gt 0) {
   Write-Host "Deleting existing site at" $SiteUrl
   Remove-SPSite -Identity $SiteUrl -Confirm:$false
}
```

By removing this code, if an existing site collection exists on the URL provided, the provisioning of the site collection will fail.

Once site collection has been provisioned, any associated sites under the site collection will be provisioned.

As a result, when the provisioning is complete, the following is the resulting site collection with child sites created in it: http://intranet.contoso.com/sites/rootsite, as seen in the following screenshot:

See also

The *Installing features on the site and managing existing site features* recipe in this chapter.

Installing features on the site and managing existing site features

In the last recipe, we became familiar with how to create a script to provision your projects' site hierarchy. It's quite common for any site template to use custom or out-of-the-box SharePoint features. Those features give site templates consistent functionality once the instance of the site has been created.

In this recipe, we'll take a look at what's involved in activating site features on sites using PowerShell.

We'll also see how the functionality from this recipe can be incorporated in the script we created in last recipe.

Getting ready

In this recipe, we'll use PowerGUI to add extra functionality to the script we discussed in the *Provisioning site hierarchy during solution deployment* recipe.

How to do it...

Let's see how you can provision site hierarchy using the following steps:

1. On the target Virtual Machine, ensure you are logged in with an administrator's role.
2. Click **Start | All Programs | PowerGUI | PowerGUI Script Editor**.
3. In the main script editing window of PowerGUI add the following script:

```
# Defining script variables
[xml]$SiteStructure = get-content SiteStructure.xml
$WebAppUrl = $SiteStructure.Setup.Attributes.Item(0).Value
$SiteCollectionUrl = $SiteStructure.Setup.SiteCollection.
Attributes.Item(1).Value
$SiteUrl = $WebAppUrl + $SiteCollectionUrl


# Loading Microsoft.SharePoint.PowerShell
$snapin = Get-PSSnapin | Where-Object {$_.Name -eq 'Microsoft.
SharePoint.Powershell'}
if ($snapin -eq $null) {
Write-Host "Loading SharePoint Powershell Snapin"
Add-PSSnapin "Microsoft.SharePoint.Powershell"
}


# Deleting existing site found at target URL
$targetUrl = Get-SPSite | Where-Object {$_.Url -eq $SiteUrl}
if ($targetUrl.Url.Length -gt 0) {
  Write-Host "Deleting existing site at" $SiteUrl
  Remove-SPSite -Identity $SiteUrl -Confirm:$false
}



# Creating site structure

$SiteCollectionName = $SiteStructure.Setup.SiteCollection.
Attributes.Item(0).Value;
$SiteCollectionOwner = $SiteStructure.Setup.SiteCollection.
Attributes.Item(2).Value;
$SiteCollectionTemplate = $SiteStructure.Setup.SiteCollection.
Attributes.Item(3).Value;

Write-Host "Creating new site collection at" $SiteUrl
$NewSite = New-SPSite -URL $WebAppUrl$SiteCollectionUrl -
OwnerAlias $SiteCollectionOwner -Template $SiteCollectionTemplate
-Name $SiteCollectionName
$RootWeb = $NewSite.RootWeb
$features = $SiteStructure.Setup.SiteCollection.Features
```

```
   if($features.Feature.Length -gt 0)
  {
    foreach ($SiteColFeature in $features.Feature)
    {
      $ActivatedFeature = Enable-SPFeature $SiteColFeature -url
$RootWeb.Url
      Write-Host "Enabled Feature:" $SiteColFeature -
foregroundcolor Green
    }
  }

Write-Host "Site collection created successfully"
Write-Host "Title:" $RootWeb.Title -foregroundcolor Green
Write-Host "URL:" $RootWeb.Url -foregroundcolor Green
Write-Host "-----------------------------------"

for ($i=1; $i -lt $SiteStructure.Setup.SiteCollection.ChildNodes.
Count; $i++ )
 {
  $childsite = $SiteStructure.Setup.SiteCollection.ChildNodes.
Item($i);
  $WebName = $childsite.Attributes.Item(0).Value
  $WebUrl = $childsite.Attributes.Item(1).Value
  $WebTemplate = $childsite.Attributes.Item(2).Value
  Write-Host "Creating new web at" $SiteUrl/$WebUrl
  $NewWeb = New-SPWeb $SiteUrl/$WebUrl -Template $WebTemplate -
Addtotopnav -Useparenttopnav -Name $WebName
  Write-Host "Web created successfully"
  Write-Host "Title:" $NewWeb.Title -foregroundcolor Green
  Write-Host "URL:" $NewWeb.Url -foregroundcolor Green
  $features = $SiteStructure.Setup.SiteCollection.ChildNodes.
Item($i)
  if($features.Feature.Length -gt 0)
  {
    foreach ($WebFeature in $features.Feature)
    {
      $ActivatedFeature = Enable-SPFeature $WebFeature -url
$NewWeb.Url
      Write-Host "Enabled Feature:" $WebFeature -foregroundcolor
Green
    }
  }
  Write-Host "-----------------------------------"
 }
start-process -filepath iexplore -argumentlist $SiteUrl
```

4. Click **File** | **Save** to save the script to your development machine's desktop. Set the filename of the script to `setup.ps1`.

5. Click **File** | **New** in the PowerGUI application.

6. Add the following code in the newly opened file window:

```
<Setup WebAppUrl="http://intranet.contoso.com">
 <SiteCollection Name="Root Site" Url="/sites/rootsite"
OwnerAlias="contoso\administrator" Template="STS#0">
 <Features>
  <Feature>ContentTypeSyndication</Feature>
 </Features>
 <Site Name="Child 1" Url="child1" Template="STS#0"/>
 <Site Name="Child 2" Url="child2" Template="STS#0"/>
 <Site Name="Child 3" Url="child3" Template="STS#0"/>
 </SiteCollection>
</Setup>
```

7. Save the file on your desktop by clicking **File** | **Save**, providing the following filename: `SetupStructure.xml`.

8. Switch back to your browser and navigate to our SharePoint test site: `http://intranet.contoso.com/sites/rootsite`.

9. Click **Site Actions** | **Site Settings** | **Site Collection Administration** | **Site collection features**.

10. Take note that the **In Place Records Management** feature, seen below, should not be set to **Active**.

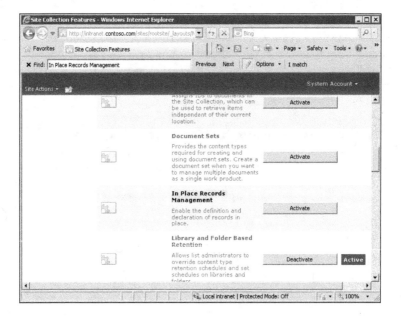

11. Open the PowerShell console window and call `setup.ps1` using the following command:

```
PS C:\Users\Administrator\Desktop> .\setup.ps1
```

12. As a result, your PowerShell script will create a site structure and activate the **In Place Records Management** feature as shown in the following screenshot:

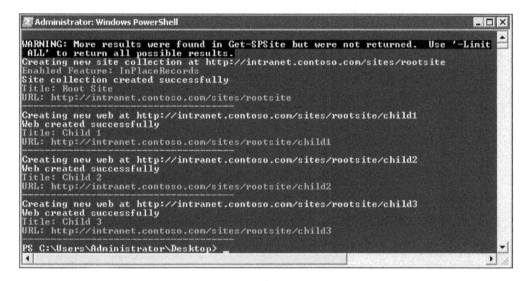

13. From the SharePoint site, click **Site Actions | Site Settings | Site Collection Administration | Site collection features**.

14. Take note that the **In Place Records Management** feature is now set to **Active**.

How it works...

Similar to the _Provisioning site hierarchy during solution deployment_ recipe, the provisioning process consists of two parts: the PowerShell script executing the provisioning, and the XML defining our site structure and other parameters.

The additional node, `<Features/>`, specifies any of the feature names that will be activated on the site collection.

If there are features to be activated at the site collection level, the `<Features/>` node will contain each feature folder name defined in the following format:

```
<Features>
    <Feature>Feature 1 Folder Name</Feature>
    <Feature>Feature 2 Folder Name</Feature>
</Features>
```

To find out the name of the folder for a particular installed feature on your site, from the development machine, navigate to: `C:\Program Files\Common Files\Microsoft Shared\Web Server Extensions\14\TEMPLATE\FEATURES`. This is where SharePoint holds all of the installed features, each of which has its own respective folder. In our example, we have activated the **In Place Records Management** feature by calling out the **InPlaceRecords** feature, as shown in the following screenshot:

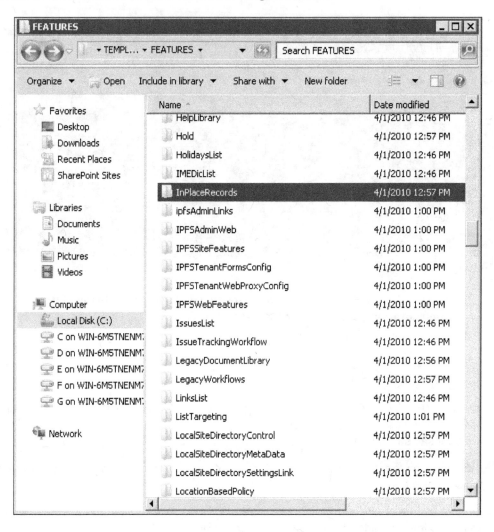

Similar to the `<SiteCollection/>` node, the `<Site/>` node defines sites to be created under the site collection. Here, we can also define SharePoint features to be enabled.

The features for the site need to be scoped for the site
level and not the site collection.

Let's take a look at our PowerShell provisioning script.

At first, the script gets a hold of the XML file which defines common provisioning variables.

Once the PowerShell snap-in has been loaded, the script proceeds to create the site collection
with details defined in the `<SiteCollection/>` node. If features are to be enabled on the
site collection level, the following script will enumerate all of the nodes representing features
and enable them sequentially:

```
$features = $SiteStructure.Setup.SiteCollection.Features
  if($features.Feature.Length -gt 0)
  {
    foreach ($SiteColFeature in $features.Feature)
    {
      $ActivatedFeature = Enable-SPFeature $SiteColFeature -url
$RootWeb.Url
      Write-Host "Enabled Feature:" $SiteColFeature -foregroundcolor
Green
    }
  }
```

Once site collection has been provisioned, any associated sites under the site collection are
now provisioned. If site nodes have features specified on them, those are also enabled after
the site has been created.

The following portion of the script enables site features associated to the site:

```
$features = $SiteStructure.Setup.SiteCollection.ChildNodes.Item($i)
  if($features.Feature.Length -gt 0)
  {
    foreach ($WebFeature in $features.Feature)
    {
      $ActivatedFeature = Enable-SPFeature $WebFeature -url $NewWeb.
Url
      Write-Host "Enabled Feature:" $WebFeature -foregroundcolor Green
    }
  }
```

When the provisioning is complete, the site structure with associated features gets
provisioned to your SharePoint system.

Creating permission levels and security groups that use them

SharePoint permission architecture allows for site administrators and owners to assign various types of access to site users. Permissions assigned will be used by various parts of the system to determine whether a particular user has access to a certain feature or not.

The creation of custom permission levels and groups which will use those permission levels, is as important as the site hierarchy definition. After all, our PowerShell script created in the *Provisioning site hierarchy during solution deployment* recipe already creates site hierarchy, so defining your custom permissions on the site will be a nice add-on for our automated site deployment script.

Getting ready

In this example, we'll use PowerGUI to execute our script, so you'll need to log into your environment with administrative privileges and launch PowerGUI.

How to do it...

In the following sequence, we'll take a look at how you can provision permission levels and security groups using PowerShell:

1. Click **Start | All Programs | PowerGUI | PowerGUI Script Editor**.

2. In the main script editing window of PowerGUI, add the following script:

```
# Defining script variables

$SiteUrl = "http://intranet.contoso.com"
$RoleName = "Contso Read"
$RoleDescription = "Can open items and forms in SharePoint"
$RoleAccess = "OpenItems, Open, ViewPages, ViewListItems,
ViewVersions, ViewFormPages"

$GroupName = "Contoso Readers"
$GroupOwner = "contoso\administrator"

# Loading Microsoft.SharePoint.PowerShell
$snapin = Get-PSSnapin | Where-Object {$_.Name -eq 'Microsoft.
SharePoint.Powershell'}
```

```
if ($snapin -eq $null) {
Write-Host "Loading SharePoint Powershell Snapin"
Add-PSSnapin "Microsoft.SharePoint.Powershell"
}

$SPSite = Get-SPSite | Where-Object {$_.Url -eq $SiteUrl}
  if($SPSite -ne $null)
  {
    # Provisioning new role to the site
    $RootWeb = $SPSite.RootWeb
    $NewRoleDefinition = New-Object Microsoft.SharePoint.
SPRoleDefinition
  $NewRoleDefinition.Name = $RoleName
  $NewRoleDefinition.Description = $RoleDescription
  $NewRoleDefinition.BasePermissions = $RoleAccess

  $RootWeb.RoleDefinitions.Add($NewRoleDefinition)
    Write-Host "Provisioned" $RoleName "at" $RootWeb.Url

  # Creating a security group
  $RootWeb.SiteGroups.Add($GroupName,$RootWeb.
AllUsers[$GroupOwner], $null, $GroupName)
  Write-Host "Created" $GroupName "at" $RootWeb.Url

  # Assigning new permission level to the group
  $NewGroup = $RootWeb.SiteGroups[$GroupName]
  $RootWeb.Roles[$RoleName].AddGroup($NewGroup)
  Write-Host "Assigned" $RoleName "to" $NewGroup "at" $RootWeb.Url
  }

Write-Host "------------------------------------"
```

3. Save the file on your desktop by clicking **File | Save**, providing the following filename: SetSecurity.ps1.

4. Switch back to your browser and navigate to our SharePoint test site: http://intranet.contoso.com.

5. Click **Site Actions | Site Permissions** and take note of the list of available security groups, as shown in the following screenshot:

Name	Type	Permission Levels
Adam Barr (CONTOSO\adamb)	User	Limited Access
Approvers	SharePoint Group	Approve
Contoso Administrator (CONTOSO\administrator)	User	Full Control, Limited Access
Designers	SharePoint Group	Design, Limited Access
Hierarchy Managers	SharePoint Group	Manage Hierarchy
Restricted Readers	SharePoint Group	Restricted Read
Style Resource Readers	SharePoint Group	Limited Access
Team Site Members	SharePoint Group	Contribute
Team Site Owners	SharePoint Group	Full Control

6. On the ribbon, under the **Manage** group, select **Permission Levels** and take note of the list of available permission levels on the site, as shown in the following screenshot:

Add a Permission Level | ✕ Delete Selected Permission Levels

Permission Level	Description
Full Control	Has full control.
Design	Can view, add, update, delete, approve, and customize.
Contribute	Can view, add, update, and delete list items and documents.
Read	Can view pages and list items and download documents.
Limited Access	Can view specific lists, document libraries, list items, folders, or documents when given permissions.
View Only	Can view pages, list items, and documents. Document type with server-side file handlers can be viewed in the browser but not downloaded.
Approve	Can edit and approve pages, list items, and documents.
Manage Hierarchy	Can create sites and edit pages, list items, and documents.
Restricted Read	Can view pages and documents, but cannot view historical versions or user permissions.

7. Open the PowerShell console window and call `SetSecurity.ps1` using the following command:

   PS C:\Users\Administrator\Desktop> .\SetSecurity.ps1

   As a result, your PowerShell script will create permission levels and security groups with the command-line output results as shown in the following screenshot:

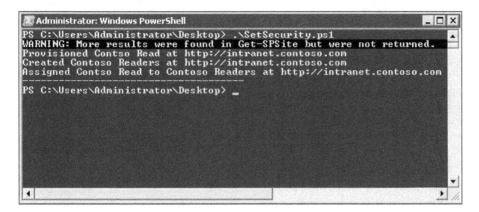

8. Switch back to your browser and navigate to our SharePoint test site: http://intranet.contoso.com.

9. Click **Site Actions | Site Permissions** and take note of the list of a newly available security group: **Contoso Readers**.

10. On the ribbon, under the **Manage** group, select **Permission Levels,** and take note of the list of newly available permission level: **Contoso Read**.

How it works...

As always, in the first part of our script, we assigned the variables further consumed in the script. In this recipe, the main variables we've been working with include role name, permission access, as well as the SharePoint security group name and owner's username.

We loaded the SharePoint PowerShell snap-in and connected to our test site collection: http://intranet.contoso.com.

Once connected, we created a new role definition by using PowerShell command `New-Object Microsoft.SharePoint.SPRoleDefinition`. We assigned the name and the description for the role as well as the permission access our role will have on the site. Permission access specifies the list of capabilities that members of the role will have access to. The detailed list of available options can be retrieved from the MSDN when searching for *SPBasePermissions Enumeration*.

In our case, our access permission includes: `OpenItems`, `Open`, `ViewPages`, `ViewListItems`, `ViewVersions`, `ViewFormPages`.

Once the role is created on the root site collection, it's available to be used in security groups or when a user is directly added to the securable object. For example, if we add our user directly to the document library, the newly created role will be available for the administrator or site manager to be picked from. When our user accesses the site, they will inherit the level of access a particular role has.

In our case, we go one step further and create a security group which uses the role. This allows for multiple users to be added to the security group and will inherit the level of access the group has been given. When the group is given an access to a securable object, everyone in that group will have equal access to the securable object with the level of access the group has been assigned. In our case, the group named **Contoso Readers** has been created and **contoso\administrator** has been chosen as a group owner.

The last step was to associate the group with the role. This has been accomplished with the following command: `$RootWeb.Roles[$RoleName].AddGroup($NewGroup)`. Here, the role has been given a name of the newly provisioned group which assigns a permission level to the group.

The approach described here can be used for automated permission provisioning, similar to the one described for SharePoint sites in the *Provisioning site hierarchy during solution deployment* recipe.

Managing site templates and their availability on sites

As with many other features on SharePoint sites, you can define your own custom site templates and then specify whether those templates are going to be available for users to use. You can also define whether users can create an instance of the site based on chosen out-of-the-box site templates.

In most scenarios, site owners in your organization will not need access to all of the site templates available in SharePoint out of the box. One of the most common reasons is the fact that the custom branding your organization may be using has not been designed for all site templates. When such ad-hoc sites are created, they will not follow the envisioned corporate look and feel as well as functionality.

In this recipe, we'll take a look at how you can define the set of specific site templates which are allowed to be created below the hierarchy of the root site. By using PowerShell for this scenario, we'll dramatically decrease the time required to perform this configuration as well as provide more consistent configuration steps.

Getting ready

In this example, we'll use PowerGUI to execute our script so log into your environment with administrative privileges and launch PowerGUI.

How to do it...

In the following sequence, we're going to see how you can select which site templates are going to be available to users:

1. Click **Start | All Programs | PowerGUI | PowerGUI Script Editor**.

2. In the main script editing window of PowerGUI, add the following script:

```
# Defining script variables

$SiteUrl = "http://intranet.contoso.com"

# Loading Microsoft.SharePoint.PowerShell
$snapin = Get-PSSnapin | Where-Object {$_.Name -eq 'Microsoft.
SharePoint.Powershell'}
if ($snapin -eq $null) {
Write-Host "Loading SharePoint Powershell Snapin"
Add-PSSnapin "Microsoft.SharePoint.Powershell"
}


$SPSite = Get-SPSite | Where-Object {$_.Url -eq $SiteUrl}
  if($SPSite -ne $null)
  {

    # Enabling selected web templates
    $RootWeb = $SPSite.RootWeb
  $ExistingWebTemps = $RootWeb.GetAvailableWebTemplates(1033) |
Where-Object {$_.IsHidden -eq 0}
   $NewWebTemps = New-Object System.Collections.ObjectModel.
Collection[Microsoft.SharePoint.SPWebTemplate]

   $BlogTemplate = $ExistingWebTemps | Where-Object {$_.Title -
ccontains "Blog"}
   $NewWebTemps.Add($BlogTemplate);

   $RootWeb.SetAvailableWebTemplates($NewWebTemps, 1033);
   $RootWeb.Update();

    Write-Host "Updated available templates to inlcude"
```

```
$NewWebTemps "at" $RootWeb.Url


    }


    Write-Host "------------------------------------"
```

3. Click **File** | **Save** to save the script to your development machine's desktop. Set the filename of the script to `SetSiteTemplates.ps1`.

4. Switch back to your browser and navigate to our SharePoint test site: `http://intranet.contoso.com`.

5. Click **Site Actions** | **Site Settings** | **Look and Feel** | **Page layouts and site templates**.

6. Take note that the current **Subsite Templates** setting is set to **Subsites can use any site template,** as seen in the following screenshot:

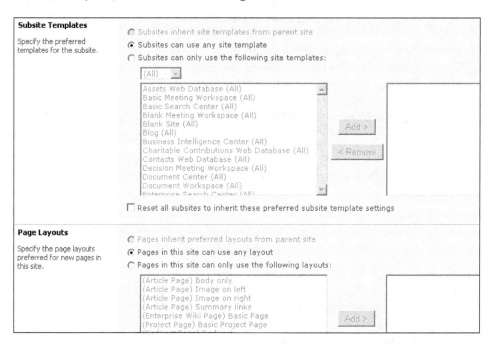

7. Open the PowerShell console window and call `SetSiteTemplates.ps1` using the following command:

```
PS C:\Users\Administrator\Desktop> .\ SetSiteTemplates.ps1
```

As a result, your PowerShell script will execute the script with the results similar to the following screenshot:

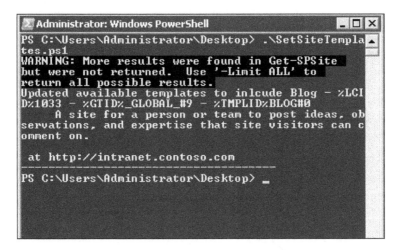

8. Switch back to your browser and navigate to our **Team Site**: `http://intranet.contoso.com`.

9. Click **Site Actions | New Site**. Take note that the only available sub-site to be created is of a **Blog** template, as seen in the following screenshot:.

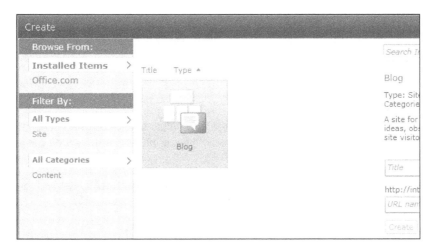

How it works...

Restricting site templates available on the site eliminates confusion among content authors who maintain the site.

As always, our script starts with setting of the initial variables. In this case, we're setting the site URL to our SharePoint site: `http://intranet.contoso.com`.

Once the connection to the desired site collection has been established, we proceed to accessing the list of site templates:

```
$SPSite = Get-SPSite | Where-Object {$_.Url -eq $SiteUrl}
```

You can retrieve the current list of available site templates on the site by executing:

```
$RootWeb.GetAvailableWebTemplates(1033) | Where-Object
{$_.IsHidden -eq 0}
```

In this case, `$RootWeb.GetAvailableWebTemplates(1033)` retrieves all site templates with **English-US** locale ID, which is `1033`.

The additional filter `Where-Object {$_.IsHidden -eq 0}` specifies that the templates retrieved are to be with the property of `Hidden` set to `false`. This is a fairly common technique which allows script authors to quickly filter the collection of objects based on the defined parameter.

Once we retrieve site templates which are not hidden on our root site, we create a new blank collection of templates. This collection of templates will be used to define a new set of allowed templates on the site:

```
New-Object System.Collections.ObjectModel.Collection[Microsoft.
SharePoint.SPWebTemplate]
```

In this recipe, we're going to allow content authors to only create sites of a `Blog` site template. This is achieved by filtering the collection of available site templates to include the ones with the `Blog` as the title:

```
$BlogTemplate = $ExistingWebTemps | Where-Object {$_.Title -ccontains
"Blog"}
```

Once the collection has been updated with the new set of allowed templates, we set this collection to be used on the site:

```
$RootWeb.SetAvailableWebTemplates($NewWebTemps, 1033);
```

Once our script has executed, we can see the results right away by the list of available site templates on the site. We can also verify the list of available site templates on the site settings page by navigating to: **Site Actions** | **Site Settings** | **Look and Feel** | **Page layouts and site templates,** which is shown in the following screenshot:

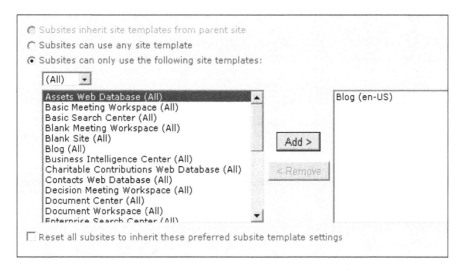

The approach outlined here will greatly reduce the maintenance effort when new site templates are deployed to the site and need to be automatically available on various levels across the enterprise SharePoint environment.

Associating features to existing site templates

The out-of-the-box set of templates available in SharePoint are made to be very comprehensive. However, it's quite challenging to make an adjustment to the SharePoint features being used on the particular site template.

In this recipe, we'll take a look at how you can attach an out-of-the-box feature to be provisioned into the site template which didn't originally have this feature.

This method is incredibly powerful when your SharePoint site has been around for a while and you'd now like to upgrade new sites to include new functionality requested by your business users.

By using PowerShell for this purpose, you will be able to make quick and un-intrusive changes to your new site templates.

Getting ready

In this example, we'll use PowerGUI to execute our script so log into your environment with administrative privileges and launch PowerGUI.

How to do it...

The following steps will demonstrate how you can associate features to site templates using a script:

1. On the target Virtual Machine, ensure you are logged in with an administrator's role.

2. Click **Start | All Programs | PowerGUI | PowerGUI Script Editor**.

3. In the main script editing window of PowerGUI, add the following script:

```
# Loading Microsoft.SharePoint.PowerShell
$snapin = Get-PSSnapin | Where-Object {$_.Name -eq 'Microsoft.
SharePoint.Powershell'}
if ($snapin -eq $null) {
Write-Host "Loading SharePoint Powershell Snapin"
Add-PSSnapin "Microsoft.SharePoint.Powershell"
}


# Get SharePoint Features folder
$FeaturesFolder = [Microsoft.SharePoint.Utilities.SPUtility]::GetG
enericSetupPath("Template\Features")


# Create a new Feature
New-Item $FeaturesFolder"\StapleFeature" -type directory


# Copy Feature definition files
Copy-Item feature.xml $FeaturesFolder"\StapleFeature\feature.xml"
Copy-Item stapling.xml $FeaturesFolder"\StapleFeature\stapling.
xml"


Install-SPFeature -Path $FeaturesFolder"\StapleFeature\feature.
xml"
Write-Host "Team Site definition updated to include Group Lists"


Write-Host "-----------------------------------"
```

4. Click **File | Save** to save the script to your development machine's desktop. Set the filename of the script to `AssociateFeatures.ps1`.

5. Click **File | New** in PowerGUI application.

6. Add the following code in the newly opened file window:

```xml
<?xml version="1.0" encoding="utf-8" ?>
<Feature Id="B9486E41-09A0-48A5-8619-4278B9511B6D"
        Title="Feature Stapling Sample"
         Description="Staples features to site definition."
         Version="1.0.0.0"
         Scope="Farm"
         Hidden="FALSE"
         xmlns="http://schemas.microsoft.com/sharepoint/">
  <ElementManifests>
  <ElementManifest Location="stapling.xml" />
</ElementManifests>
</Feature>
```

7. Save the file on your desktop by clicking **File | Save** and providing the following filename: `feature.xml`.

8. Click **File | New** in PowerGUI application.

9. Add the following code in the newly opened file window:

```xml
<Elements xmlns="http://schemas.microsoft.com/sharepoint/">
    <FeatureSiteTemplateAssociation Id="9C03E124-EEF7-4DC6-B5EB-
86CCD207CB87" TemplateName="STS#0" />
</Elements>
```

10. Save the file on your desktop by clicking **File | Save** and providing the following filename: `stapling.xml`.

11. Open the PowerShell console window and call `AssociateFeatures.ps1` using the following command:

```
PS C:\Users\Administrator\Desktop> .\ AssociateFeatures.ps1
```

12. As a result, your PowerShell script will create site structure as shown in the following screenshot:

13. Navigate to your SharePoint test site: http://intranet.contoso.com.

14. Click **Site Actions | New Site**. Pick **Team Site** from the selection of sites.

15. Provide a new name and URL for the site, for example **NewSite**, and click the **Create** button.

16. Once the site is created, you will see a **Team Site** with an additional list created under the **Lists** in **Quick Launch** called **Phone Call Memo,** as seen in the following screenshot.

How it works...

To associate a new out-of-the-box feature to the site template of our choice, we need to create and install a custom **SharePoint Feature** which will define such association.

We start by creating a `feature.xml` file which contains basic information about our custom SharePoint Feature, such as name, ID, and description, as well as the location to the actual feature manifest file.

The feature manifest file, in our case named `stapling.xml`, is the file that will define the actual association.

> The manifest associates an out-of-the-box feature with an ID of
> `9C03E124-EEF7-4DC6-B5EB-86CCD207CB87` to a site template with
> ID `STS#0` denoting a **Team Site**.

The preceding manifest code associates the out-of-the-box SharePoint Feature, which is a **Group Lists** feature, to the site definition of a **Team Site**. As a result, when provisioned, each new instance of the **Team Site** will contain an instance of **Group Lists** which is a set of lists including **Phone Call Memo** list.

Next, we provision our feature using a PowerShell script. In our script, we determine the directory path which is used by SharePoint to host all of its features.

The directory path is saved in a variable $FeaturesFolder. Next, we create a new folder, called StaplingFeature, in the SharePoint Feature's directory and copy feature.xml and staple.xml to it. Lastly, we use the Install-SPFeature command to install the feature and complete the association of our **Group List** feature to the **Team Site** template.

To test the functionality, we can either navigate to our site and see whether the new lists have been created, or see whether the feature is activated in the site settings or not.

To verify the feature from **Site Settings**, navigate to our newly created site with the new associated feature: http://intranet.contoso.com/NewSite. Once on the site, click **Site Actions | Site Settings | Manage Site Features** and ensure the **Group Work Lists** feature is set to **Active** as shown in the following screenshot:

There's more

To disassociate the feature from the template, you would need to deactivate our custom association feature, named **StaplingFeature**, by calling the following command in the PowerShell command line:

```
UnInstall-SPFeature -Identity StapleFeature
```

After the confirmation below, your feature will be deactivated as shown with the command-line output:

```
Confirm

Are you sure you want to perform this action?

Performing operation "Uninstall-SPFeature" on Target

"FeatureDefinition/4af9999a-0517-4224-9ed3-d2f9f87d92e2".

[Y] Yes  [A] Yes to All  [N] No  [L] No to All  [S] Suspend  [?] Help
(default is "Y"): Y

PS C:\Users\Administrator\Desktop>
```

Managing SharePoint workflow association using PowerShell

SharePoint workflows allow business users to execute a custom set of instructions on SharePoint objects. Workflows are deployed to site instances and can be associated to a particular list or site to facilitate the business need.

Just as many organizations realize the need for custom and out-of-the-box features to be added to their site templates, workflows are often needed and associated to a list.

When a new business process is introduced in an organization, one of the most crucial tasks is the ability to introduce it to your SharePoint portal quickly and effectively.

 Workflow instance management shown in this recipe is very handy when you need to standardize business processes available on various sites as your business users request custom or out-of-the-box capabilities.

In this recipe, we'll take a look at how you can associate an instance of the workflow to one of the existing libraries. We'll also see how you can disassociate an instance of the workflow from the library.

Getting ready

In this example, we'll use PowerGUI to execute our script so log into your environment with administrative privileges and launch PowerGUI.

How to do it...

The following sequence will demonstrate how you can associate a SharePoint workflow to a library:

1. Click **Start | All Programs | PowerGUI | PowerGUI Script Editor**.

2. In the main script editing window of PowerGUI, add the following script:

```
# Defining script variables

$SiteUrl = "http://intranet.contoso.com"
$List = "Shared Documents"
$WorkflowTemplateTitle = "Approval - SharePoint 2010"

# Loading Microsoft.SharePoint.PowerShell
$snapin = Get-PSSnapin | Where-Object {$_.Name -eq 'Microsoft.
SharePoint.Powershell'}
if ($snapin -eq $null) {
Write-Host "Loading SharePoint Powershell Snapin"
Add-PSSnapin "Microsoft.SharePoint.Powershell"
}

# Setting site themes on sites and sub sites
$SPSite = Get-SPSite | Where-Object {$_.Url -eq $SiteUrl}
```

```
if($SPSite -ne $null)
{
   $RootWeb = $SPSite.RootWeb;
$SPList =$RootWeb.Lists[$List];

   $Culture = New-Object System.Globalization.CultureInfo("en-US");
   $Template = $RootWeb.WorkflowTemplates.GetTemplateByName($Workfl
owTemplateTitle,$Culture);
   $TaskList = $RootWeb.Lists["Workflow Tasks"];
   $HistoryList = $RootWeb.Lists["Workflow History"];
   $Association=[Microsoft.SharePoint.Workflow.
SPWorkflowAssociation]::reateListAssociation($Template,"Approval",
$TaskList,$HistoryList);

   $SPList.WorkflowAssociations.Add($Association);
   $SPList.Update();
   }

Write-Host "Workflow has been associated to "$List
Write-Host "-------------------------------------"
```

3. Click **File** | **Save** to save the file on the desktop of your environment. Name the file AddWorkflow.ps1.

4. Open the PowerShell console window and call AddWorkflow.ps1 using the following command:

    ```
    PS C:\Users\Administrator\Desktop> .\ AddWorkflow.ps1
    ```

5. As a result, your PowerShell script will connect to the site and associates the **Approval** workflow instance to the **Shared Documents** library. The output of the command line will look similar to the following screenshot:

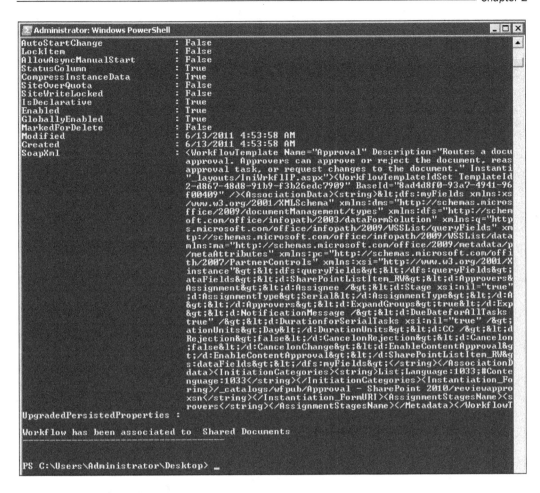

6. Switch to our SharePoint site: `http://intranet.contoso.com`.

7. Click **Shared Documents** on the quick launch of the site and select **Library** from the ribbon.

8. From the **Library** tab in the ribbon, select the **Workflow Settings** fly out option as shown in the following screenshot:

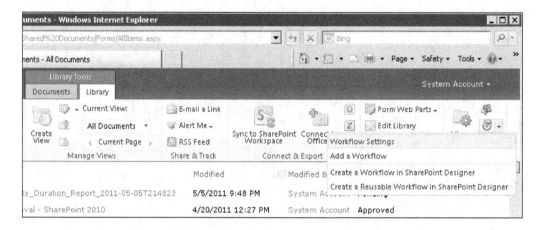

9. Take note of the newly associated **Approval** workflow to the library:

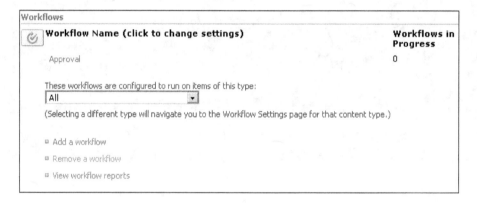

Workflow templates installed on SharePoint 2010 will become available for site owners and administrators to be associated to libraries and lists. When a custom workflow template is created and installed on the server, you can use the following command to get a hold of the workflow template object:

$RootWeb.WorkflowTemplates.GetTemplateByName($WorkflowTemplateTitle,$Culture);

Here, the `WorkflowTemplates` property contains the available workflow templates installed on the SharePoint web. By providing the `title` of the workflow template and the culture ID, you can get an object representing a template to further create an instance of it.

To successfully create a new instance of a workflow template, we get a hold of the **Workflow Tasks** and **Workflow History** lists which are integral for ensuring our workflow functions properly. The workflow task list will store all of the tasks associated with the workflow, and the workflow history list will log out-of-the-box and custom events as your workflow instance runs.

Next, we create a workflow association object representing a new workflow template, task, and history lists, as well as the name of the workflow instance:

```
$Association = [Microsoft.SharePoint.Workflow.SPWorkflowAssociation]::
CreateListAssociation($Template,"Approval",$TaskList,$HistoryList);
```

Once the association has been created, it can be added to the list by using the following command:

`$SPList.WorkflowAssociations.Add($Association);`

Only after being added to the list will an association execute on list items according to defined rules.

There's more

Similar to adding an association, you can remove it by using the following command:

`$SPList.WorkflowAssociations.Remove($Association);`

Configuring site themes and user interface artifacts

Custom branding and design artifacts are integral parts of any site. As developers create solution packages which are going to deliver branding artifacts to the site, those changes must be applied to the site in a traceable fashion so they can be reversed or backed up. Also, as your SharePoint site goes through a branding upgrade, the design artifacts must be applied on existing sites without much intrusion to site operation.

This recipe focuses on updating SharePoint managed theme references automatically by using PowerShell. Using this approach, you will be able to update any of your existing sites to use the new theme.

Getting ready

Ensure the site you are using for testing, in our case http://intranet.contoso.com, has several sub-sites created under it.

If the root site doesn't have sites created under it, create them manually using the SharePoint user interface, or follow the steps in the *Provisioning site hierarchy during solution deployment* recipe in this chapter.

How to do it...

Let's see how we can automate branding configurations with PowerShell using the following sequence:

1. Ensure that you're logged into your development environment with administrative privileges.

2. Click **Start | All Programs | PowerGUI | PowerGUI Script Editor**.

3. In the main script editing window of PowerGUI, add the following script:

```
# Defining script variables

$SiteUrl = "http://intranet.contoso.com"
$NewTheme = "Azure"


# Loading Microsoft.SharePoint.PowerShell
$snapin = Get-PSSnapin | Where-Object {$_.Name -eq 'Microsoft.
SharePoint.Powershell'}
if ($snapin -eq $null) {
Write-Host "Loading SharePoint Powershell Snapin"
Add-PSSnapin "Microsoft.SharePoint.Powershell"
}


# Setting site themes on sites and sub sites
$SPSite = Get-SPSite | Where-Object {$_.Url -eq $SiteUrl}
  if($SPSite -ne $null)
  {
    $themes = [Microsoft.SharePoint.Utilities.ThmxTheme]
::GetManagedThemes($SiteUrl);
    foreach ($theme in $themes)
    {
      if ($theme.Name -eq $NewTheme)
      {
       break;
      }
    }
    foreach ($SPWeb in $SPSite.AllWebs)
    {
    $theme.ApplyTo($SPWeb, $true);
      Write-Host "Set" $NewTheme "at :" $SPWeb.Title "
(" $SPWeb.Url ")"
    }
  }

Write-Host "Site theme update complete"
```

```
Write-Host "URL:" $SPSite.Url -foregroundcolor Green
Write-Host "------------------------------------"
```

4. Click **File** | **Save** to save the file on the desktop of your environment; let's name the file SetThemes.ps1.

5. Open the PowerShell console window and call SetThemes.ps1 using the following command:

   PS C:\Users\Administrator\Desktop> .\ SetThemes.ps1

6. As a result, your PowerShell script will connect to the site and apply the new theme to it as shown in the following screenshot:

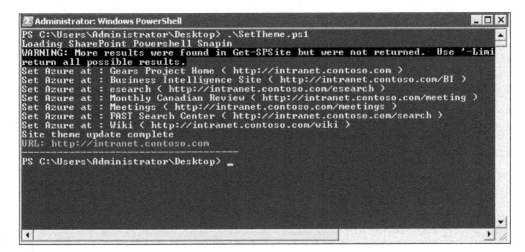

7. Switch to the SharePoint site you have identified in the script variable of this recipe: http://intranet.contoso.com.

8. Click **Site Actions** | **Site Settings** | **Look and Feel** | **Site Theme**.

9. Ensure the **Current Theme** is set to **Azure**, as you can see in the following screenshot:

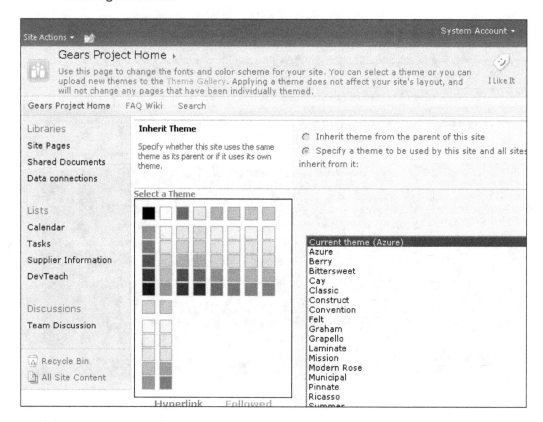

How it works...

In SharePoint 2010, the theme engine allows developers and designers to provision site themes right into the designated SharePoint library where all of the themes are stored. The themes can be added or removed directly from the library. Once provisioned or updated, themes would need to be manually set on the site.

In our PowerShell script, we start by setting variables specifying the URL of the site where we need to update the theme and the name of the current theme.

The theme doesn't need to be an out-of-the-box theme. It can very well be a custom theme which has been deployed manually or programmatically.

To find the list of available themes on your current site:

1. While logged into your SharePoint site, click **Site Actions | Site Settings | Look and Feel | Site Theme**.

 You can call the following method to get the list of available themes using PowerShell: `[Microsoft.SharePoint.Utilities.ThmxTheme]::GetManagedThemes([server url])`.

2. Pick the theme of your choice and note its name.

The name of the theme is later specified in the script variable.

By using the `[Microsoft.SharePoint.Utilities.ThmxTheme]` library and its method `GetManagedThemes()`, we connect to the site collection where the theme has been deployed.

Next, we enumerate all of the available themes and find the one we're looking for. We save the object representing the chosen theme and pass it on to the next loop. The loop will go through the URL we have specified, in our case `http://intranet.contoso.com`, and its sub-sites and apply the new theme to each of the sites.

One of the ways you can identify whether the theme has been applied or not is simply by accessing the site. Another method is to navigate to the theme settings page to see what the current theme is.

Since the theme provisioning process takes a few seconds, depending on the performance of your environment, when executing the preceding theme provisioning script, ensure you wait until the script execution has completed and you have received a confirmation message from PowerShell.

There's More

Let's take at look how the new masterpage can be assigned to the site using PowerShell.

Assigning a new masterpage to the SharePoint site

One of the other design artifacts often used in SharePoint 2010 is the **site masterpage**. The masterpage will define the look and feel of the site just as themes do. Additionally, masterpages will drive the structure of the page parts.

As your SharePoint site goes through its life cycle, your design team may give you a new masterpage which better fits business needs. In such cases, the masterpage will be provisioned to the masterpage gallery. Just as in the scenario with themes, the masterpage needs to be set at the site level in order to be used.

PowerShell provides an easy mechanism for updating the masterpage of the site assuming it's already deployed to the site.

1. Ensure you're logged into your development environment with administrative privileges.

2. Click **Start | All Programs | PowerGUI | PowerGUI Script Editor**.

3. In the main script editing window of PowerGUI, add the following script:

```
# Defining script variables

$SiteUrl = "http://intranet.contoso.com"
$NewMasterUrl = "_catalogs/masterpage/newmaster.master"

# Loading Microsoft.SharePoint.PowerShell
$snapin = Get-PSSnapin | Where-Object {$_.Name -eq 'Microsoft.
SharePoint.Powershell'}
if ($snapin -eq $null) {
Write-Host "Loading SharePoint Powershell Snapin"
Add-PSSnapin "Microsoft.SharePoint.Powershell"
}

# Setting site themes on sites and sub sites
$SPSite = Get-SPSite | Where-Object {$_.Url -eq $SiteUrl}
  if($SPSite -ne $null)
  {
    foreach ($SPWeb in $SPSite.AllWebs)
    {
    $SPWeb.MasterUrl = $NewMasterUrl;
    $SPWeb.Update()
      Write-Host "Set" $NewMasterUrl "at :" $SPWeb.Title "("
$SPWeb.Url ")"
    }
  }

Write-Host "Site masterpage update complete"
Write-Host "URL:" $SPSite.Url -foregroundcolor Green
Write-Host "-----------------------------------"
```

4. Click **File | Save** to save the file on the desktop of your environment; let's name the file SetMasterpage.ps1.

5. Open PowerShell console window and call SetMasterpage.ps1 using the following command:

```
PS C:\Users\Administrator\Desktop> .\ SetMasterpage.ps1
```

Provided the masterpage has been deployed, it will be applied to the specified site and its sub-sites.

See also

The *Provisioning site hierarchy during solution deployment* recipe of this chapter.

3

Performing Advanced List and Content Operations in SharePoint using PowerShell

In this chapter, we will cover:

- ▶ Creating lists of custom structure
- ▶ Setting SharePoint list item validation with PowerShell
- ▶ Setting list item security
- ▶ Setting list relationships
- ▶ Customizing list views
- ▶ Managing the use of content types in lists

Introduction

Lists and libraries are heavily used in any SharePoint site. In this chapter, we'll see how you can use PowerShell to define lists based on a custom structure and deploy them on to various levels of your SharePoint site. We'll see how you can define validation rules on items created in lists.

We'll also take a look at how you can automate provisioning of custom security on the list items.

Since many lists in your custom SharePoint solution may be dependent on data coming from other lists, we'll see how you can define lists with referential relationships as well as define rules around referential integrity between list items.

Most of the time, the business users of SharePoint sites interact with lists using one or more list views. In this chapter, we'll see how you can meet this need and create an automated script which provisions list views into the list, as well as defines the behavior and the structure of the view.

Lastly, we'll take a look at how you can assign lists to use a specific content type. This method will allow your organization to standardize on types of business content and assign specific lists to store only the defined set of that content.

Creating lists of custom structures

As business users in any organization use their company's SharePoint site, they often like to add new types of data to specific SharePoint sites or across all of the sites in the farm. For example, you may be asked to create a calendar list on each project site. This may sound like a simple request, but there may be over 100 project sites, and each one now needs to contain a new calendar list. The manual implementation of such a request may be a cumbersome process.

In this recipe, we'll learn exactly what's involved in creating a PowerShell script which provisions a custom SharePoint list and defines its fields. Once the fields are provisioned, we'll add a few test items to the list to see it in action.

At the end of this recipe, you will be able to work with SharePoint lists and create instances of them as well as define their structure and fields.

Getting ready

Considering you have already set up your virtual development environment as described in *Chapter 1, PowerShell Scripting Methods and Creating Custom Commands*, we'll get right into authoring our script. In this recipe, we'll be using PowerGUI to author the script, which means you will be required to be logged in with an administrator's role on the target Virtual Machine.

How to do it...

1. Click **Start | All Programs | PowerGUI | PowerGUI Script Editor**.

2. Add the following script in the main script editing window of PowerGUI:

```
# Defining script variables

$SiteUrl = "http://intranet.contoso.com"
$ListTitle = "Custom List"
$ListDescription = "Custom List"

# Loading Microsoft.SharePoint.PowerShell
$snapin = Get-PSSnapin | Where-Object {$_.Name -eq 'Microsoft.
SharePoint.Powershell'}
if ($snapin -eq $null) {
Write-Host "Loading SharePoint Powershell Snapin"
Add-PSSnapin "Microsoft.SharePoint.Powershell"
}

$SPSite = Get-SPSite | Where-Object {$_.Url -eq $SiteUrl}
  if($SPSite -ne $null)
  {
    # Creating an instance of a custom list
    $RootWeb = $SPSite.RootWeb
    $NewListTemplate = $RootWeb.ListTemplates["Custom List"]
    $NewListInstance = $RootWeb.Lists.Add($ListTitle,
$ListDescription, $NewListTemplate)

  # Display list on quick launch
  $SPList = $RootWeb.Lists[$NewListInstance]
  $SPList.OnQuickLaunch = $true
  $SPList.Update()

  # Add few other fields to the list
  $ListFields = $SPList.Fields;
   $TextField = $ListFields.Add("TextField", [Microsoft.
SharePoint.SPFieldType]::Text, $false);
   $TextFieldInstance = $ListFields.GetField($TextField)
   $DateField = $ListFields.Add("DateField", [Microsoft.SharePoint.
SPFieldType]::DateTime, $false)
  $DateFieldInstance = $ListFields.GetField($DateField)
  $SPList.Update()

  # Add new fields to a default view
  $ListView = $SPList.DefaultView
   $ListViewFields = $ListView.ViewFields
   $ListViewFields.Add($TextFieldInstance)
  $ListViewFields.Add($DateFieldInstance)
```

```
    $ListView.Update();

    # Add a new list item
    $SPListItem = $SPList.Items.Add()
    $SPListItem["Title"] = "New Item Title"
    $SPListItem["TextField"] = "Text Fields Value"
    $SPListItem["DateField"] = [System.DateTime]::Now
    $SPListItem.Update()

    Write-Host "Created list" $ListTitle "of template"
$NewListTemplate.Name "at" $RootWeb.Url
    }

    Write-Host "-------------------------------------"
```

3. Click **File | Save** to save the script to your development machine's desktop. Set the filename of the script to `CreateList.ps1`.

4. Open the PowerShell console window and call `CreateList.ps1` using the following command:

    PS C:\Users\Administrator\Desktop> .\ CreateList.ps1

5. As a result, your PowerShell script will create a site structure as shown in the following screenshot:

6. Now, in your browser, let's switch to our SharePoint test site: `http://intranet.contoso.com/`.

7. On the **Quick launch** menu of your site, under the **Lists** section locate the list titled **Custom List**.

8. Open the list and ensure the test list item has been created in it as shown in the following screenshot:

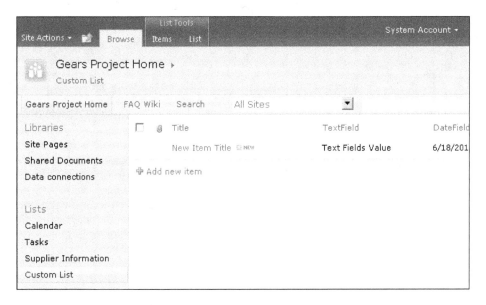

How it works...

First, we defined the script variables used in our script. In this recipe, the variables include: a site URL, a list title, and a description.

Once a PowerShell snap-in has been loaded, we connect to the root site of our SharePoint site collection and access the list template representing a **Custom List**:

```
$NewListTemplate = $RootWeb.ListTemplates["Custom List"]
```

Next, we used the Add function of our list collection property of the site to add a new list:
$RootWeb.Lists.Add.

The result from the Add function is the **ID** of the newly created list which we then used to connect to an instance of our list:

```
$SPList = $RootWeb.Lists[$NewListInstance]
```

Once we have an object representing an instance of our list, we specified the property to show our list on the **quick launch** menu of the site.

So far, we have created the list and have it visible on the **quick launch**. However, the only field in our list was the out-of-the-box **Title** field. To add a few custom fields to our list, we defined them in our list field collection:

```
$ListFields = $SPList.Fields;
$TextField = $ListFields.Add("TextField", [Microsoft.SharePoint.
SPFieldType]::Text, $false)
```

In here, [Microsoft.SharePoint.SPFieldType] defines the type of SharePoint field we've created. Our fields were: a text-type field and a date-type field.

 To find out what other types of fields are available out there, reference *MSDN* with the keyword **SPFieldType**.

Having our additional fields added to the list has now made them available in the default view of the list. To allow users to see our newly added list fields, we connected to the default view of the list and enabled new fields to be shown in the view.

Lastly, we added a test item to the list to demonstrate how our new items can be automatically populated in the list, if the need be. To do that, we created a new list item object and then populated fields of the new list item:

```
$SPListItem = $SPList.Items.Add()
$SPListItem["Title"] = "New Item Title"
```

Once complete, our list has been created with a defined set of fields as well as test items.

See also

The *Customizing list views* recipe in this chapter.

Setting SharePoint list item validation with PowerShell

As we've learned from the recipe *Creating lists of custom structure*, you can create a list of a desired structure and deploy it to multiple sites in your SharePoint solution.

Since lists and libraries are containers of data in SharePoint, business users often require a mechanism to ensure that the correct metadata is associated to list items. In past versions of SharePoint, business users could define whether the metadata field is required to be filled in or not. With SharePoint 2010, you can define custom validation formulas which allow for more granular list item validation.

In this recipe, we'll learn how you can enforce business rules on list items by using list item validation formulas.

The benefit of performing this type of customization using a PowerShell script is that it gives you the ability to apply one or more rules across entire SharePoint farm when required to do so.

Getting ready

You are already familiar working with lists using PowerShell, as discussed in this chapter. For this recipe, we'll be using PowerGUI to author our script, which means you will need to be logged in with an administrator's role on the target Virtual Machine.

How to do it...

1. Click **Start | All Programs | PowerGUI | PowerGUI Script Editor**.

2. In the main script editing window of PowerGUI add the following script:

```
# Defining script variables

$SiteUrl = "http://intranet.contoso.com"
$ListTitle = "Custom List"
$ListDescription = "Custom List"

# Loading Microsoft.SharePoint.PowerShell
$snapin = Get-PSSnapin | Where-Object {$_.Name -eq 'Microsoft.
SharePoint.Powershell'}
if ($snapin -eq $null) {
Write-Host "Loading SharePoint Powershell Snapin"
Add-PSSnapin "Microsoft.SharePoint.Powershell"
}

$SPSite = Get-SPSite | Where-Object {$_.Url -eq $SiteUrl}
  if($SPSite -ne $null)
  {
    # Creating an instance of a custom list
    $RootWeb = $SPSite.RootWeb
    $NewListTemplate = $RootWeb.ListTemplates["Custom List"]
  $NewListInstance = $RootWeb.Lists.Add($ListTitle,
$ListDescription, $NewListTemplate)

  # Display list on quick launch
  $SPList = $RootWeb.Lists[$NewListInstance]
  $SPList.OnQuickLaunch = $true
  $SPList.Update()

  # Add few other fields to the list
  $ListFields = $SPList.Fields;
    $TextField = $ListFields.Add("TextField", [Microsoft.
SharePoint.SPFieldType]::Text, $false)
  $TextFieldInstance = $ListFields.GetField($TextField)
  $SPList.Update()
```

```
# Adding validation on the list
$SPList.ValidationFormula = "=IF(TextField=Title,FALSE,TRUE)"
$SPList.ValidationMessage = "The TextField and Title should not
be the same"

# Adding validation on the field
$TitleField = $ListFields["Title"];
$TitleField.ValidationFormula = '=IF(FIND("Contract",Title),
TRUE, FALSE)'
$TitleField.ValidationMessage = "The Title must contain a
contract number"
$TitleField.PushChangesToLists = $true
$TitleField.Update()
$SPList.Update()

# Add new fields to a default view
$ListView = $SPList.DefaultView;
  $ListViewFields = $ListView.ViewFields;
  $ListViewFields.Add($TextFieldInstance)
  $ListView.Update()

Write-Host "Validation added to list" $ListTitle "at" $RootWeb.
Url
  }
```

3. Click **File | Save** to save the script to your development machine's desktop. Set the filename of the script to `SetListItemValidation.ps1`.

4. Open the PowerShell console window and call `SetListItemValidation.ps1` using the following command:

   PS C:\ Users\Administrator\Desktop> .\ SetListItemValidation.ps1

5. As a result, your PowerShell script will create a list with results as shown in the following screenshot:

```
Administrator: Windows PowerShell
PS C:\Users\Administrator\Desktop> .\SetListItemValidation.ps1
WARNING: More results were found in Get-SPSite but were not returned.
all possible results.
Validation added to list Custom List at http://intranet.contoso.com
-----------------------------------------------------------------------
PS C:\Users\Administrator\Desktop> _
```

6. Now, in your browser, let's switch to our SharePoint test site: `http://intranet.contoso.com/`

7. On the **Quick launch** menu of your site, under the **Lists** section locate the list titled **Custom List**.

8. Open the list and select an option to add a new item.

9. For the **Title** field, enter a text value of **wrong value** and click **Save** to see the result as shown in the following screenshot:

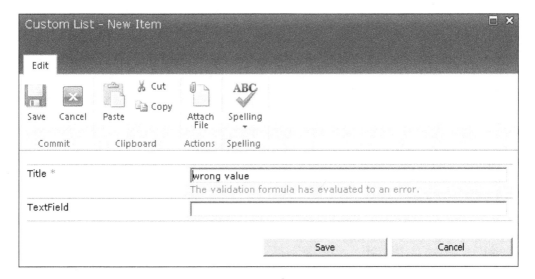

10. Now correct the value of the **Title** field to be **Contract #44** and click **Save** to see the item saved into the list.

11. Next, while in the list view, click the **List** tab in the ribbon and select **Settings | List Settings.**

12. From the settings page, click **Validation Settings** under **General Settings** to see the validation rules as shown in the following screenshot:

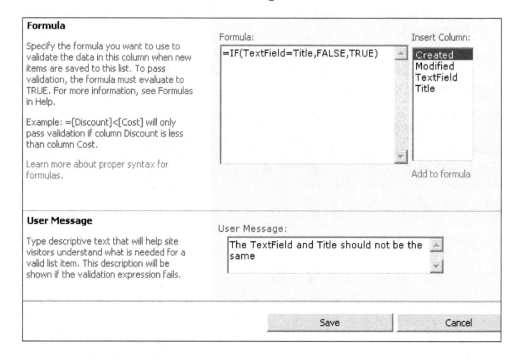

How it works...

As in previous recipes, we started by defining the script variables. In this recipe, we defined the site URL: `http://intranet.contoso.com`, as well as the title and description of the custom list we've created.

Next, we created a new list and added it to the quick launch menu of our site. By default, custom lists are provisioned with an out-of-the-box **Title** field, so we added another text field for our demonstration purposes:

```
$ListFields.Add("TextField", [Microsoft.SharePoint.SPFieldType]::Text,
$false)
```

Once added, we assign a validation formula to the list:

```
$SPList.ValidationFormula = "=IF(TextField=Title,FALSE,TRUE)"
```

This formula returns the value of TRUE and allows us to save an item only if the newly provisioned **TextField** and the **Title** fields have different values. Otherwise, the following message will be displayed:

```
$SPList.ValidationMessage = "The TextField and Title should not be the
same"
```

 You may have noticed how we added the new field first before the validation formula was declared for it. If you applied the list validation formula first, which uses columns that have not been created yet, you would get an error in your script informing you that referenced columns do not exist.

Next, we assigned the validation formula to the individual field that was added earlier:

```
$TitleField.ValidationFormula = '=IF(FIND("Contract",Title), TRUE,
FALSE)'
```

Here, the item is allowed to be saved when the word contract is found in the **Title** field. Otherwise, the error message is returned as defined in the following line of code:

```
$TitleField.ValidationMessage = "The Title must contain a contract
number"
```

To ensure the field changes are saved in the list, we set the property responsible for pushing field changes to true as shown in the following line of code:

```
$TitleField.PushChangesToLists = $true
```

Once we're all set with the validation definition, the field and the list are both updated.

There's more...

In this recipe, the goal was to demonstrate how you can assign validation on the entire list when a new item was inserted, or an existing item was edited. Also, we looked at how you can assign a validation formula on the individual list column.

In the case of assigning a validation rule to the individual column, only that column value can be referenced in the formula and no other columns can be used. Typically, an individual list column formula is used to validate the specific column in the list.

The list validation formula can be a bit more complex and allows you to define rules applying to more than one column. Here, you can specify values expected of other columns in relation to each other.

In both cases, unless all of the validation rules are satisfied, the item will not be added or edited.

Validation formulas have robust syntax which can be used to satisfy a variety of business scenarios. For more information on the syntax of validation formula, search for *Calculated Field Formulas* on *MSDN*.

Setting list item security

SharePoint lists represent a securable object to which you can apply desired permissions. Items in your SharePoint lists can also have their distinct set of permissions. This allows you to limit the level of access individuals on the site will have when accessing lists and items in them.

In organizations restructuring their SharePoint site, quite often there is an immediate need to assign a new set of permissions to a multitude of items within the site. Using PowerShell, you can not only speed up the process, but also have a reference point in case you are required to make an adjustment or are rolling back your changes.

Getting ready

You are already familiar working with lists using PowerShell. For this recipe, we will use PowerGUI to author the script, which means you will need to be logged in with an administrator's role on the target Virtual Machine.

How to do it...

1. Click **Start | All Programs | PowerGUI | PowerGUI Script Editor**.

2. In the main script editing window of PowerGUI, add the following script:

```
# Defining script variables
$SiteUrl = "http://intranet.contoso.com"

# Loading Microsoft.SharePoint.PowerShell
$snapin = Get-PSSnapin | Where-Object {$_.Name -eq 'Microsoft.
SharePoint.Powershell'}
if ($snapin -eq $null) {
Write-Host "Loading SharePoint Powershell Snapin"
Add-PSSnapin "Microsoft.SharePoint.Powershell"
}

$SPSite = Get-SPSite | Where-Object {$_.Url -eq $SiteUrl}
  if($SPSite -ne $null)
  {
    # Creating an instance of a custom list
    $RootWeb = $SPSite.RootWeb
    $NewListTemplate = $RootWeb.ListTemplates["Custom List"]
```

```
$NewListInstance = $RootWeb.Lists.Add("Custom List", "Custom
List", $NewListTemplate)
$SPList = $RootWeb.Lists[$NewListInstance]
$SPList.OnQuickLaunch = $true
$SPList.Update()

# Define unique permissions
$SPList.BreakRoleInheritance($false)

# Allow only approvers to have approve access on the list
$RoleAssignment = [Microsoft.SharePoint.SPRoleAssignment]($RootW
eb.SiteGroups["Approvers"])
$ApproveRoleDefinition = $RootWeb.RoleDefinitions | Where-Object
{$_.Name -eq "Approve"}
$RoleAssignment.RoleDefinitionBindings.Add($ApproveRoleDefinitio
n)
$SPList.RoleAssignments.Add($RoleAssignment)
$SPList.Update()

# Add a new list item
$SPListItem = $SPList.Items.Add()
$SPListItem["Title"] = "New Item Title"
$SPListItem.Update()

# Add unique permission to the list item
$SPListItem.BreakRoleInheritance($false)
$ReadRoleDefinition = $RootWeb.RoleDefinitions | Where-Object
{$_.Name -eq "Read"}
$ItemRoleAssignment = [Microsoft.SharePoint.SPRoleAssignment]($R
ootWeb.SiteGroups["Approvers"])
$ItemRoleAssignment.RoleDefinitionBindings.
Add($ReadRoleDefinition)
$SPListItem.RoleAssignments.Add($ItemRoleAssignment)
$SPListItem.Update()

Write-Host "Custom permissions added to list" $ListTitle "at"
$RootWeb.Url
}
```

3. Click **File | Save** to save the script to your development machine's desktop. Set the filename of the script to SetListSecurity.ps1.

4. Open the PowerShell console window and call SetListSecurity.ps1 using the following command:

```
PS C:\Users\Administrator\Desktop> .\ SetListSecurity.ps1
```

5. As a result, your PowerShell script will execute and return results as shown in the following screenshot:

6. Now, in your browser, let's switch to our SharePoint test site: `http://intranet.contoso.com/`.

7. On the **Quick launch** menu of your site, under the **Lists** section, locate the list titled **Custom List**.

8. Open the list and select the **List** tab in the ribbon.

9. Select **List Permissions** from the **Settings** group in the ribbon to see the list of assigned groups and roles similar to what is shown in the following screenshot:

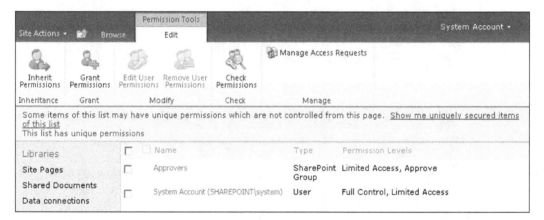

10. Take note of the **Approvers** group being the only group allowed access to the list.

11. Next, navigate to the **Custom List** default view and select the only existing item in the list.

12. While the item is selected, pick the **Item Permissions** option from the **Manage** group in the ribbon.

13. Observe how the **Approvers** group is the only group allowed access to the item. However, the role given to the **Approvers** group is **Read** and not **Approve**, as shown in the following screenshot:

How it works...

Let's take a look at exactly what happens in the script of this recipe. We start by defining the script variables. In this recipe, we define the site URL: `http://intranet.contoso.com`.

Next, we create a new list and add it to the **quick launch** menu of our site. By default, custom lists are provisioned with an out-of-the-box **Title** field.

Also, by default, newly created lists inherit their permissions from the parent, which is the root site in our case. In our script, we break the default permission inheritance in order to define our own:

```
$SPList.BreakRoleInheritance($false)
```

The `$false` parameter in the preceding code specifies that when a permission inheritance is broken, the parent groups and users are not to be automatically transferred over.

In some cases, you would want to transfer over the existing groups and users. This means that only users and groups at the time of breaking the inheritance would be transferred over. If at some point in the future we have new users or groups added to the site, those will not propagate to lists in which permission inheritance has been broken.

Next, we create a new role assignment which defines a group further assigned to access our list:

```
$RoleAssignment = [Microsoft.SharePoint.SPRoleAssignment]($RootWeb.
SiteGroups["Approvers"])
```

Group membership alone will not guarantee the level of access its members are going to have. Even though the group we're adding is called `Approvers`, the only way users in the group will be given the right to approve items is by having an **Approve** role assigned to the group for our list as shown in the following code:

```
$ApproveRoleDefinition = $RootWeb.RoleDefinitions | Where-Object
{$_.Name -eq "Approve"}.
```

After associating our new role to the group, we set it to be the first group allowed to access the list:

```
$SPList.RoleAssignments.Add($RoleAssignment)
```

Next, to demonstrate how we can assign unique permissions to the list item, we create a new list item. Similar to the list, we break the security inheritance on the item as shown in the following line of code:

```
$SPListItem.BreakRoleInheritance($false)
```

This time, we retrieve the `Read` role defined on the site:

```
$ReadRoleDefinition = $RootWeb.RoleDefinitions | Where-Object {$_.Name
-eq "Read"}
```

The `Read` role retrieved in the preceding line of code is assigned to the same `Approvers` group used before:

```
$ItemRoleAssignment = [Microsoft.SharePoint.SPRoleAssignment]($RootWeb
.SiteGroups["Approvers"])
```

Just as in the example with the list, we assign the new role and our group association to the permissions of the item:

```
$SPListItem.RoleAssignments.Add($ItemRoleAssignment)
```

This guarantees unique permissions for the item despite different sets of permissions defined in the list. The same security group, `Approvers`, has more limited access on the list item, despite having more permissive access on the list level.

There's more

In this recipe, the goal was to demonstrate how you can assign custom permissions to a new or existing SharePoint list. Also, we looked at how you can assign unique permissions and roles to an individual item in the list.

As we saw in this recipe, the SharePoint security group we used (the `Approvers` group) has a defined role on the site giving it certain privileges on the site level. When the `Approvers` group is added to the list item, we give it a completely different set of roles. In our case the, only role is to read an item and nothing else.

This demonstrates a powerful principle where you can define unique permissions on the list item using the same security group on the site but with a different set of roles.

Setting list relationships

Just as in its past versions, SharePoint 2010 allows you to create lists which contain lookup columns in other lists. This way, business users can define a new list item and populate its metadata based on fields from an existing list. In SharePoint 2010, business users can take advantage of new features allowing them to enforce referential integrity on the list items.

When attempting to delete a list item, if any items in other lists use this item to look up their values, the original item deletion can be prevented or the related item could automatically be deleted.

If you require setting up referential integrity in your organization's lists, you can speed up the provisioning process significantly using PowerShell.

Getting ready

You are already familiar working with lists using PowerShell. For this recipe, we are using PowerGUI to author the script, which means it is necessary for you to be logged in with an administrator's role on the target Virtual Machine.

How to do it...

1. Click **Start | All Programs | PowerGUI | PowerGUI Script Editor**.
2. In the main script editing window of PowerGUI, add the following script:

```
# Defining script variables

$SiteUrl = "http://intranet.contoso.com"
$ProductsListTitle = "Products"
$ProductLineListTitle = "Product Lines"

# Loading Microsoft.SharePoint.PowerShell
$snapin = Get-PSSnapin | Where-Object {$_.Name -eq 'Microsoft.
SharePoint.Powershell'}
if ($snapin -eq $null) {
Write-Host "Loading SharePoint Powershell Snapin"
Add-PSSnapin "Microsoft.SharePoint.Powershell"
}

$SPSite = Get-SPSite | Where-Object {$_.Url -eq $SiteUrl}
   if($SPSite -ne $null)
```

```powershell
{
Write-Host "Creating a products list"
  $RootWeb = $SPSite.RootWeb
    $NewListTemplate = $RootWeb.ListTemplates["Custom List"]
  $NewProductsListInstance = $RootWeb.Lists.
Add($ProductsListTitle, $ProductsListTitle, $NewListTemplate)
  $SPProductList = $RootWeb.Lists[$NewProductsListInstance]
  $SPProductList.OnQuickLaunch = $true
  $SPProductList.Update()

  Write-Host "Creating a product line list"
  $NewProductLinesListInstance = $RootWeb.Lists.
Add($ProductLineListTitle, $ProductLineListTitle,
$NewListTemplate)
 $SPProductLineList = $RootWeb.Lists[$NewProductLinesListInstance]
  $SPProductLineList.OnQuickLaunch = $true
  $SPProductLineList.Update()

 Write-Host "Add a product line reference"
  $ListFields = $SPProductList.Fields
    $LookupField = $ListFields.AddLookup("Product Line",
$NewProductLinesListInstance, $false)
  $LookupFieldInstance = $ListFields.GetField($LookupField)
  $LookupFieldInstance.RelationshipDeleteBehavior = [Microsoft.
SharePoint.SPRelationshipDeleteBehavior]::Cascade
  $LookupFieldInstance.Indexed = $true
  $LookupFieldInstance.PushChangesToLists = $true
  $LookupFieldInstance.Update()
  $SPProductList.Update()

  Write-Host "Add new field to a default view"
  $ListView = $SPProductList.DefaultView
    $ListViewFields = $ListView.ViewFields
    $ListViewFields.Add($LookupFieldInstance)
    $ListView.Update()

  Write-Host "Add new product line"
  $SPListItemProductLine = $SPProductLineList.Items.Add()
  $SPListItemProductLine["Title"] = "New Product Line 1"
  $SPListItemProductLine.Update()

  Write-Host "Add new products"
  $SPListItem = $SPProductList.Items.Add()
  $SPListItem["Title"] = "New Product 1"
  $SPListItem["Product Line"] = $SPListItemProductLine
```

```
$SPListItem.Update()
$SPListItem = $SPProductList.Items.Add()
$SPListItem["Title"] = "New Product 2"
$SPListItem["Product Line"] = $SPListItemProductLine
$SPListItem.Update()

Write-Host "Created list " $ProductsListTitle "related to "
$ProductLineListTitle "at" $RootWeb.Url
  }
```

3. Click **File** | **Save** to save the script to your development machine's desktop. Set the filename of the script to `CreateRelatedList.ps1`.

4. Open the PowerShell console window and call `CreateRelatedList.ps1` using the following command:

   PS C:\Users\Administrator\Desktop> .\ CreateRelatedList.ps1

5. As a result, your PowerShell script will set two related lists as shown in the following screenshot:

6. Now, in your browser, let's switch to our SharePoint test site: `http://intranet.contoso.com/`.

7. On the **Quick launch** menu of your site, locate the list titled **Products** under the **Lists** section.

8. Open the list and select the **List** tab in the ribbon.

9. Select **List Settings** from the **Settings** group in the ribbon.

10. From the list of **Columns**, click the **Product Line** column as shown in the following screenshot:

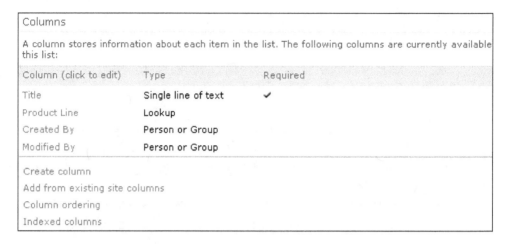

11. Take note of the new relationship behavior defined in the **Relationship** section of the column setting as shown in the following screenshot:

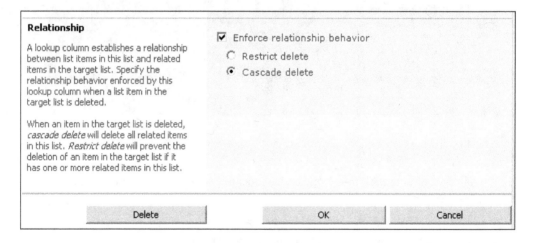

12. Navigate back to the default view of the **Product Lines** list and select the only item available in the list.

13. Delete the item.

14. Switch back to the **Products** list and ensure that all of the items associated with the product line item have also been deleted.

How it works...

We started by defining the script variables. In this recipe, we defined the site URL where our new list is going to be created: `http://intranet.contoso.com`.

Next, we created the **Products** list and the **Product lines** list. Once our lists are created, we add a new field to the **Product** list called **Product line**:

```
$LookupField = $ListFields.AddLookup("Product Line",
$NewProductLinesListInstance, $false)
```

This field holds a reference from each product to related product line. This is where we also establish a referential behavior for our newly created field:

```
$LookupFieldInstance.RelationshipDeleteBehavior = [Microsoft.
SharePoint.SPRelationshipDeleteBehavior]::Cascade
```

This is the field that is going to monitor the related items in the dependent list, and trigger a relationship behavior, which is an action we have specified. The referential action in our case is `Cascade` meaning all of the dependent items are deleted as soon as the parent item is deleted.

 If you would rather warn the user that they cannot delete items which have existing references, you can choose the `Restrict` option instead of `Cascade`.

To speed up the performance of the referential lookup, the columns which have referential rules defined on them are required to be indexed. This is achieved by setting the `Indexed` property of the column to `true`:

```
$LookupFieldInstance.Indexed = $true
```

The field changes are saved in the list and the field is then added to the default view.

Next, the test items are added to both **Products** and **Product lines** lists:

```
$SPListItemProductLine = $SPProductLineList.Items.Add()
$SPListItem = $SPProductList.Items.Add()
```

In the case of adding a new product, we also assign the associated product line to it:

```
$SPListItem["Product Line"] = $SPListItemProductLine
```

There's more...

In this recipe, we created a referential integrity rule between the **Product** and the **Product line** list. Every time the **Product** list item had a **Product line** assigned to it, the relationship has been established. When a **Product line** has been deleted, the associated **Product** has also been deleted.

This may not be the desired behavior since you may want to warn users that they are potentially deleting an item with a significant connection to other items. In this case, you would set the referential behavior to restrict the delete action.

As you're testing the creation of your lists, you're likely to want to delete the list in order to re-create it with a new set of properties. One rule to remember is that before deleting the list which has a referential integrity defined on its column, you are required to remove the rule first. If the rule is in place and you attempt to delete the list, you will receive an error in your script or SharePoint user interface.

Customizing list views

SharePoint list views are the core mechanism through which site users will interact with the data stored in lists and libraries. As you may know, SharePoint list views allow for many customizations related to how the data is displayed, filtered, and what some of the editing capabilities are available with it.

The most common requests coming from business users related to functionality of lists actually involves changes to list views.

In this recipe, we'll take a look at exactly what's involved in modifying a list view. We'll see how you can filter and order list items using a custom query, add fields displayed in a view, and change list view rendering parameters.

You will be able to increase the efficiency and consistency of how you deploy your list view changes on the site.

Getting ready

In this recipe, you are already familiar working with lists using PowerShell. For this recipe, we are using PowerGUI to author the script, which means it's necessary for you to be logged in with an administrator's role on the target Virtual Machine.

How to do it...

1. Click **Start | All Programs | PowerGUI | PowerGUI Script Editor**.

2. In the main script editing window of PowerGUI, add the following script:

```
# Defining script variables

$SiteUrl = "http://intranet.contoso.com"
$ListTitle = "Announcements List"

# Loading Microsoft.SharePoint.PowerShell
$snapin = Get-PSSnapin | Where-Object {$_.Name -eq 'Microsoft.
SharePoint.Powershell'}
if ($snapin -eq $null) {
Write-Host "Loading SharePoint Powershell Snapin"
Add-PSSnapin "Microsoft.SharePoint.Powershell"
}

$SPSite = Get-SPSite | Where-Object {$_.Url -eq $SiteUrl}
  if($SPSite -ne $null)
  {
    Write-Host "Creating a new instance of an announcement list"
    $RootWeb = $SPSite.RootWeb
    $NewListTemplate = $RootWeb.ListTemplates["Announcements"]
    $NewListInstance = $RootWeb.Lists.Add($ListTitle, $ListTitle,
$NewListTemplate)
    $SPList = $RootWeb.Lists[$NewListInstance]
    $SPList.OnQuickLaunch = $true
    $SPList.Update()

    Write-Host "Modifying announcements list default view"
    $ListView = $SPList.DefaultView;
    $ListFields = $SPList.Fields;
      $ListViewFields = $ListView.ViewFields;
      $ListViewFields.Add($ListFields["Body"]);
    $ListViewFields.Add($ListFields["Expires"]);
    $ListView.Query = "<OrderBy><FieldRef Name='Created'
Ascending='FALSE' /></OrderBy><Where><Gt><FieldRef Name='Expires'/
><Value Type='DateTime'><Today /></Value></Gt></Where>"
    $ListView.RowLimit = 5
    $ListView.InlineEdit = $true
    $SPList.Update()

    Write-Host "Adding few test announcements"
    $SPListItem = $SPList.Items.Add()
```

```
$SPListItem["Title"] = "New Announcement 1"
$SPListItem["Body"] = "This is a test announcement 1"
$SPListItem["Expires"] = [System.DateTime]::Now
$SPListItem.Update()

$SPListItem = $SPList.Items.Add()
$SPListItem["Title"] = "New Announcement 2"
$SPListItem["Body"] = "This is a test announcement 2"
$SPListItem["Expires"] = [System.DateTime]::Parse("1/1/2012")
$SPListItem.Update()

Write-Host "Created list" $ListTitle "of template"
$NewListTemplate.Name "at" $RootWeb.Url
    }
```

3. Click **File | Save** to save the script to your development machine's desktop. Set the filename of the script to `CreateListView.ps1`.

4. Open the PowerShell console window and call `CreateListView.ps1` using the following command:

   PS C:\Users\Administrator\Desktop> .\ CreateListView.ps1

5. As a result, your PowerShell script will execute with results as shown in the following screenshot:

6. Now, in your browser, let's switch to our SharePoint test site : `http://intranet.contoso.com/`.

7. On the **Quick launch** menu of your site, under the **Lists** section locate the list titled **Announcements List**.

8. Open the list and select the **List** tab in the ribbon.

9. Select **Modify View** from the **Manage Views** group in the ribbon.

10. From the list of **Views**, click the **All items** view.

11. Ensure the **Sort** and **Filter** sections of the view and their values are as shown in the following screenshot:

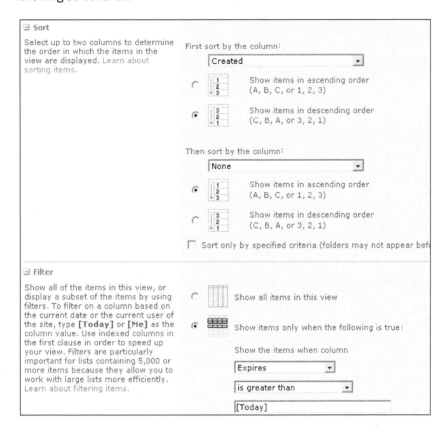

12. Similarly, ensure that the **Inline Editing** option for the list is now set to **enabled**.

13. Switch back to the list view and take note of the fact that only one item is displayed in the view despite adding two items. This is an example of how our view filters out the item based on the defined **Expiry** date column.

How it works...

In this recipe, we customized a view for our newly created **announcements** list. The view has been assigned some of the filtering options to show only the selected set of items. Also, this recipe demonstrates some of the view parameter changes to enhance view usability.

We start by defining the script variables. In this recipe, we define the site URL: `http://intranet.contoso.com` where our new list is going to be created. We also specify the title and the description of our announcements list.

Next, we create the **announcements** list and add it to the **quick launch**. Once created, the list is assigned a default list view. We get an instance of this view by executing the following command:

```
$ListView = $SPList.DefaultView;
```

Next, we get a hold of the collection of fields used in the view:

```
$ListFields = $SPList.Fields;
$ListViewFields = $ListView.ViewFields;
```

Once we have the object representing a list view field collection, we add a **Body** and an **Expires** field to the collection:

```
$ListViewFields.Add($ListFields["Body"]);
$ListViewFields.Add($ListFields["Expires"]);
```

Only the fields added to the view participate in view-related tasks such as item filtering. In other words, you cannot filter items based on the field that has not been explicitly added to the view, even if that field is already available in the list.

In our recipe, we define the list item filtering query:

```
$ListView.Query = "<OrderBy><FieldRef Name='Created' Ascending='FALSE'
/></OrderBy><Where><Gt><FieldRef Name='Expires'/><Value
Type='DateTime'><Today /></Value></Gt></Where>"
```

The query is a **Collaborative Application Markup Language (CAML)** query specifying the order of the items in the list within the `<OrderBy/>` tag. The query also defines the item filtering clause whereby any item must have the `Expires` field value greater than today's date in order to be displayed in the list view.

Next, we define some of the general list parameters, such as enabling in-line editing. In-line editing will add a user interface to the list view, allowing users to edit the item within a view without bringing up the **item edit** form.

The last parameter change we made to the view was setting the `RowLimit` value. This property value specifies how many items are going to be displayed for a given view. The default page view item limit is 30 items.

We conclude by adding a few test items to the list which demonstrates how our view can filter out items based on the query, as well as allow in-line editing for list items.

This recipe demonstrates how complex tasks involved with list view adjustments and changes can be automated across an entire farm using PowerShell.

Managing the use of content types in lists

The **Content Type** feature in SharePoint allows you to define a specific type of content and associated metadata fields, and make this content type available to a variety of lists and libraries. Since all of the rules were defined in an associated content type, users will not need to define those rules again for each list which uses the content type.

This powerful concept makes content types incredibly popular in many organizations.

As your site goes through its life cycle, your business users will ask you to modify the content type or add a new one and associate it to a variety of lists. When using the SharePoint 2010 user interface, the provisioning process could take a very long time. Let's see how much more efficiently this task can be accomplished with PowerShell.

Getting ready

You are already familiar working with lists using PowerShell. For this recipe, we are using PowerGUI to author the script, which means you need to be logged in with an administrator's role on the target Virtual Machine.

How to do it...

1. Click **Start | All Programs | PowerGUI | PowerGUI Script Editor**.

2. Add the following script in the main script editing window of PowerGUI:

    ```
    # Defining script variables

    $SiteUrl = "http://intranet.contoso.com"
    $ListTitle = "Announcements List"

    # Loading Microsoft.SharePoint.PowerShell
    $snapin = Get-PSSnapin | Where-Object {$_.Name -eq 'Microsoft.
    SharePoint.Powershell'}
    if ($snapin -eq $null) {
    Write-Host "Loading SharePoint Powershell Snapin"
    Add-PSSnapin "Microsoft.SharePoint.Powershell"
    }

    $SPSite = Get-SPSite | Where-Object {$_.Url -eq $SiteUrl}
      if($SPSite -ne $null)
      {
        Write-Host "Creating a new instance of an announcement list"
        $RootWeb = $SPSite.RootWeb
        $NewListTemplate = $RootWeb.ListTemplates["Announcements"]
    ```

```
    $NewListInstance = $RootWeb.Lists.Add($ListTitle, $ListTitle,
$NewListTemplate)
    $SPList = $RootWeb.Lists[$NewListInstance]
    $SPList.OnQuickLaunch = $true
    $SPList.Update()

    Write-Host "Creating a new content type based on Event content
type"
    $EventContentType = $RootWeb.AvailableContentTypes["Event"]
    $ContentType =  New-Object Microsoft.SharePoint.SPContentType
-ArgumentList @($EventContentType, $RootWeb.ContentTypes,
"EventCT")
    $CT = $RootWeb.ContentTypes.Add($ContentType)
    $NewCT = $RootWeb.ContentTypes[$ContentType.Id]
    $NewCTFields = $RootWeb.Fields
    $CTField = $NewCTFields.Add("CTField", [Microsoft.SharePoint.
SPFieldType]::Boolean, $false)
    $CTFieldObject = $NewCTFields.GetField($CTField)
    $NewCT.FieldLinks.Add($CTFieldObject)
    $NewCT.Update()

    Write-Host "Associating content type to a list"
    $SPList.ContentTypes.Add($NewCT)
    $SPList.ContentTypesEnabled = $true
    $SPList.Update()

    Write-Host "Associated " $EventContentType.Name "to" $SPList.
Title "at" $RootWeb.Url
    }
```

3. Click **File** | **Save** to save the script to your development machine's desktop. Set the filename of the script to `AssociateContentTypesToList.ps1`.

4. Open the PowerShell console window and call `AssociateContentTypesToList.ps1` using the following command:

    ```
    PS C:\Users\Administrator\Desktop> .\ AssociateContentTypesToList.
    ps1
    ```

5. As a result, your PowerShell script will create a content type with output results similar to the following screenshot:

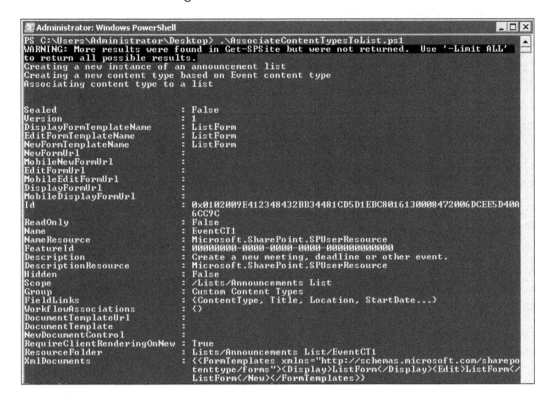

6. Now, in your browser, let's switch to our SharePoint test site: `http://intranet.contoso.com/`.

7. On the **Quick launch** menu of your site, under the **Lists** section, locate the list titled **Announcements List**.

8. Open the list and select the **List** tab in the ribbon.

9. Select **List Settings** from the **Settings** group in the ribbon.

10. From the list of the **General Settings** group, click the **Advanced Settings** link and ensure that the **Allow management of content types** option is set to **Yes**, as shown in the following screenshot:

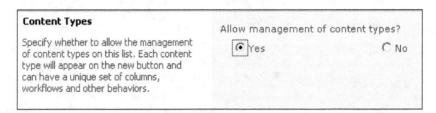

11. Switch back to the list settings and ensure that both the **Announcements** and our custom **EventCT** associated with the list are listed in the **Content Types** section as shown in the following screenshot:

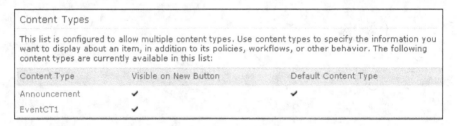

12. Switch back to the default view of the list and click the **Items** tab from the ribbon.

13. Select the **New** option and ensure you can select two of the available content types for our list, as shown in the following screenshot. Before our custom content type association this list was designated just for announcements.

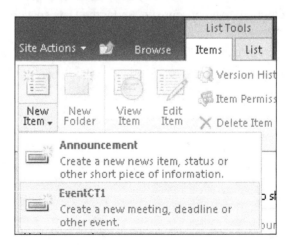

How it works...

Since content types define the rules and metadata associated with your business content, routing changes and updates to the content types are inevitable over time and across the entire SharePoint farm.

This recipe demonstrated how a task commonly known to be time consuming and mainly performed only during SharePoint solution deployment, can be automated and run anytime a content type update is required.

Script variables are defined first as in most of our scripts. In this recipe, we define the site URL where our new list is going to be created: `http://intranet.contoso.com`. We also specify the title and the description of our list, which is an **announcements list**.

Next, we create the **announcements** list instance and add it to the **Quick launch** menu.

Each content type inherits from a chosen parent content type. SharePoint 2010 has a variety of content types available to choose from which serve the purpose of the base type to be derived from. In our recipe, we use the **Event** content type and create a new instance of it called **EventCT**:

```
$EventContentType = $RootWeb.AvailableContentTypes["Event"]
$ContentType = New-Object Microsoft.SharePoint.SPContentType -
ArgumentList @($EventContentType, $RootWeb.ContentTypes, "EventCT")
```

In the preceding code, when a new content type object is created, we specify parameters such as:

- ▶ Content type parent
- ▶ The collection of content types
- ▶ The title of out content type

When ready, we add the content type to the collection of available content types on the site.

The copy of the content type we created is no different than its parent, which does not help anyone yet. Usually, content types have different fields which represent a different type of business content. Those fields have a variety of types just as SharePoint list fields do. To demonstrate how a new field can be added to the content type we added a new field called `CTFIeld`:

```
$CTField = $NewCTFields.Add("CTField", [Microsoft.SharePoint.
SPFieldType]::Boolean, $false)
```

This is how a new field, also known as a site column, is associated or linked to the content type:

```
$NewCT.FieldLinks.Add($CTFieldObject)
```

Once available on the site, a content type can be associated with lists and libraries on the site. Without being associated to the list, a content type cannot be used since no instances of it can be created.

We associate a content type to our **announcements list** the following way:

```
$SPList.ContentTypes.Add($NewCT)
```

As you have seen in this recipe, once associated, the items representing our new content type can be created. In our recipe, this means that the **announcements** list can now hold our custom events and announcements at the same time.

4
Managing External Data in SharePoint and Business Connectivity Services using PowerShell

In this chapter, we will cover:

- ▸ Importing a custom BCS model to SharePoint
- ▸ Exporting a SharePoint BCS model and schema
- ▸ Creating instances of external lists with PowerShell
- ▸ Managing permissions on an external list
- ▸ Throttling items returned with external lists

Introduction

The ability to access external business data into the familiar portal environment is one of the key features of SharePoint 2010. Business Connectivity Services (**BCS**) allows developers and administrators to define how SharePoint connects to external entities and create instances of lists which are used to interact with the external data.

When users require access to business data from external systems you can use PowerShell to import the BCS model. This approach simplifies the required setup involved in manual configuration across multiple environments.

Alternatively, when troubleshooting an existing environment with existing BCS connections established, creating a replica of that environment is crucial to be able to reproduce issues reported by users. In this chapter, we'll take a look at how you can export an already defined BCS model to be used in your sandbox environment.

When exposing external data to business users, you will require to create instances of external lists which will be used by your users. In this chapter, we'll take a look at how you can create an external list connecting to your BCS data using PowerShell. We'll also take a look at how you can manage permissions on already created external list. Automating this set of tasks using PowerShell will demonstrate a significant advantage when deploying a new or existing solution to the target environment.

As your users work with external business data, they will use many of SharePoint's tools to pull and update external data. Heavy usage may result in spikes in performance of the external system which can sometimes affect the functionality of your external application. We'll take a look at how you can throttle the usage of the data coming from an external system.

Importing a custom BCS model to SharePoint

Business users in many organizations use their company's SharePoint site for collaboration. Users also like to access data from other external business applications within their collaboration environment. For example, you may be asked to allow users to access business performance data from custom a CRM system. This may sound like a complex task, but with BCS you can create a connection to external data in no time.

In this recipe, we'll learn exactly what's involved in exporting a BCS model, and then create a PowerShell script which provisions a custom BCS model into your site. Once the model is provisioned, in the *Creating instances of external lists with PowerShell* recipe in this chapter, we'll see how you can provision a list which consumes our external data.

At the end of this recipe, you will be all set with the script allowing you to import custom SharePoint BCS models.

Getting ready

Assuming you have already set up your virtual development environment as described in *Chapter 1, PowerShell Scripting Methods and Creating Custom Commands*, we'll get right into authoring our script. We'll use PowerGUI to author the script, so ensure you're logged in with an administrator's permissions on the target Virtual Machine. We'll assume you have a SharePoint Designer client application installed on your target environment which we'll use to export our BCS model.

How to do it...

Let's take a look at how you can import a custom BCS model into SharePoint using the following sequence:

1. Click **Start** | **All Programs** | **SharePoint** | **Microsoft SharePoint Designer 2010**.

2. Click the **Open Site** button and provide our test site URL: `http://intranet.contoso.com`.

3. From the **Site Objects** menu on the left of the SharePoint Designer window, select **External Content Types** as shown in the following screenshot:

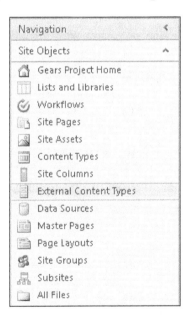

4. Select the **Supplier Info** model in the main window of the application and click the **Manage | Export BDC Model** button of the ribbon as shown in the following screenshot:

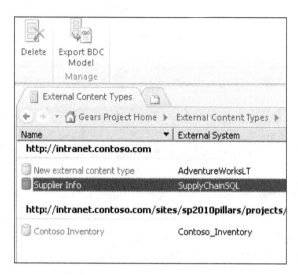

5. Provide the model filename as `model1` and chose to save the file to your desktop.

6. Locate the `model1.bdcm` file on your desktop, right-click the file and select **Open with | Notepad**.

7. Search for the following declaration in the `model1.bdcm` file opened in **Notepad**:

```
<Entity Namespace="http://intranet.contoso.com" Version="1.0.0.0"
EstimatedInstanceCount="10000" Name="Supplier Info" DefaultDisplay
Name="Supplier Info">
```

8. Rename the value of the property called `Name` and the `DefaultDisplayName` property from `Supplier Info` to `Test Model` and save the file.

9. Click **Start | All Programs | PowerGUI | PowerGUI Script Editor**.

10. In the main script editing window of PowerGUI, add the following script:

```
# Defining script variables

$SiteUrl = "http://intranet.contoso.com"

# Loading Microsoft.SharePoint.PowerShell
$snapin = Get-PSSnapin | Where-Object {$_.Name -eq 'Microsoft.
SharePoint.Powershell'}
if ($snapin -eq $null) {
Write-Host "Loading SharePoint Powershell Snapin"
Add-PSSnapin "Microsoft.SharePoint.Powershell"
}
```

```
$SPSite = Get-SPSite | Where-Object {$_.Url -eq $SiteUrl}
  if($SPSite -ne $null)
  {

  Write-Host "Connecting to DBC"
  $bdc = Get-SPBusinessDataCatalogMetadataObject -BdcObjectType
"Catalog" -ServiceContext $SiteUrl

  Write-Host "Importing ..."
  Import-SPBusinessDataCatalogModel -Identity $bdc -Path ".\
model1.bdcm" -force -ModelsIncluded -PropertiesIncluded -
PermissionsIncluded -Verbose -ErrorAction Stop -ErrorVariable $err

  Write-Host "Imported BDC Model"
  }
```

11. Click **File** | **Save** to save the script to your development machine's desktop. Set the filename of the script to `ImportBCSModel.ps1`.

12. Open the PowerShell console window and call `ImportBCSModel.ps1` using the following command:

    PS C:\Users\Administrator\Desktop> .\ ImportBCSModel.ps1

13. As a result, your PowerShell script will create a site structure as shown in the following screenshot:

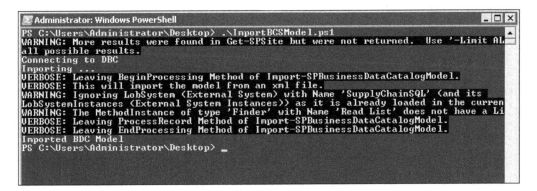

14. Let's now switch back to our SharePoint Designer application.

15. Press the **Refresh** button at the top of the SharePoint Designer application window.

16. Take note of the newly created BCS model called **Test Model** as defined in our DBCM file as shown in the following screenshot:

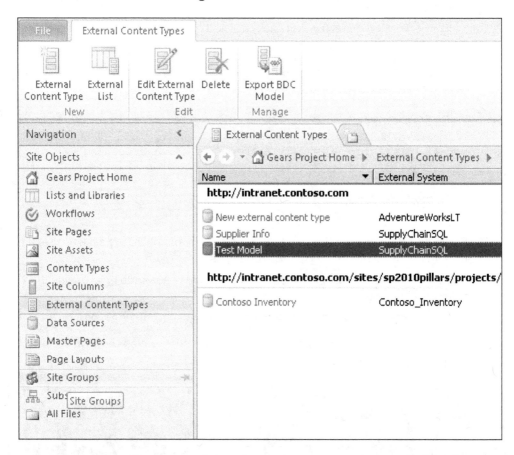

How it works...

First, we defined the script variables used. In this recipe, the variables only include a site URL.

Once a PowerShell snap-in has been loaded, we connect to the root site of our SharePoint site collection to ensure that the site exists.

Next, we use the `Get-SPBusinessDataCatalogMetadataObject` command to get a hold of the BCS Metadata Store metadata object.

The `BdcObjectType` parameter specifies the type of the metadata object to return. The type, which is `Catalog` in our case, must be one of the following: `Catalog`, `Model`, `LobSystem`, `LobSystemInstance`, or `Entity`.

The `ServiceContext` specifies the service context of the BCS Metadata Store metadata object, which in our case is `http://intranet.contoso.com`. The rest of the parameters are optional.

Next, we execute the `Import-SPBusinessDataCatalogModel` which imports the model into SharePoint. The `Identity` parameter will supply the BCS Metadata Store metadata object to import to. The `Path` specifies the path and name where the model is defined. In our case, the model file is `model1.bdcm`.

We also use the following optional parameters:

- ▶ `Force` instructs the command-let to overwrite the BCS Model if the file exists.

- ▶ `ModelsIncluded` specifies that models are included in the imported BCS Model file. A model contains the base XML metadata for a system.

- ▶ `PermissionsIncluded` specifies that permissions from the BCS Model are imported.

- ▶ `PropertiesIncluded` indicates that properties from the BCS Model are imported.

The last set of optional parameters specifies that the import transaction should stop if the import fails and any associated error messages related to the condition should be stored in the error variable:

```
-Verbose -ErrorAction Stop -ErrorVariable $err
```

This sequence ensures that the model is imported and you get verbose details about the import process as it progresses.

 To find out what's involved in removing a data model from the site, reference _MSDN_ with the keyword **Remove-SPBusinessDataCatalogModel**.

See also

The _Exporting SharePoint BCS model and schema_ and _Creating instances of external lists with PowerShell_ recipes in this chapter.

Exporting SharePoint BCS model and schema

As we've learned from the _Importing a custom BCS model to SharePoint_ recipe, you can import a SharePoint BCS schema into the farm to be consumed by a custom productivity application, out-of-the-box data, graph web parts, and so on.

When your solution is in production for some time and you need to troubleshoot a problem, the first item on the list is to synchronize your testing or development environment with the configuration in the production environment. External business connectivity models are no exception. In this recipe, you will see how this process can be radically simplified by using PowerShell.

The benefit of performing this type of operation using a PowerShell script gives you the ability to have a defined and traceable set of items to be exported from your environments. Additionally, by using the PowerShell approach, you will not be required to install any of the client applications, such as SharePoint Designer, on the server, which is a recommended strategy for any production server environment.

Getting ready

We'll assume you are already familiar with the concept of BCS in SharePoint and have looked at importing a BCS model into SharePoint, as discussed in the previous recipe. For this recipe, we'll use PowerGUI to author our script, which means you will need to be logged in with an administrator's role on the target Virtual Machine.

How to do it...

Let's take a look at how you can export the BCS model using the following sequence:

1. Click **Start | All Programs | Microsoft SharePoint 2010 Products | SharePoint 2010 Central Administration**.
2. Click **Application Management | Manage service applications**.
3. Click **Business Data Connectivity Service**, as shown in the following screenshot:

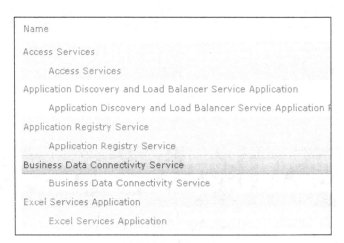

4. Ensure in your ribbon under **View** category, you have **BDC Models** selected from the drop-down as shown in the following screenshot:

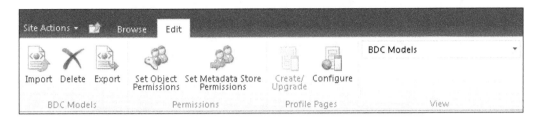

5. At the bottom of the page, you will see the list of the available BDC models. Take note of **model1** which we previously imported in *Importing a custom BCS model to SharePoint* recipe, as shown in the following screenshot:

Service Application Information

Name: Business Data Connectivity Service

Search [   ] 🔍

   BDC Model Name↑

☐ ContosoInventory

☐ model1

☐ SharePointDesigner-AdventureWorksLT2008-administrator-197ccaae-a159-4e14-85c8-9688b1b99c3e

☐ SharePointDesigner-AdventureWorksLT-administrator-48d7ede3-f335-4892-be46-5635af494f00

☐ SharePointDesigner-SupplyChainSQL-Administrator-00ef4ce3-6e27-40b0-92d5-fc55d6b6900c

6. Click **Start | All Programs | PowerGUI | PowerGUI Script Editor**.

In the main script editing window of PowerGUI add the following script:

```
# Defining script variables

$SiteUrl = "http://intranet.contoso.com"

# Loading Microsoft.SharePoint.PowerShell
$snapin = Get-PSSnapin | Where-Object {$_.Name -eq 'Microsoft.
SharePoint.Powershell'}
if ($snapin -eq $null) {
Write-Host "Loading SharePoint Powershell Snapin"
Add-PSSnapin "Microsoft.SharePoint.Powershell"
}
```

```
$SPSite = Get-SPSite | Where-Object {$_.Url -eq $SiteUrl}
  if($SPSite -ne $null)
  {

  Write-Host "Connecting to BDC"
  $model = Get-SPBusinessDataCatalogMetadataObject -BdcObjectType
"Model" -Name "model1" -ServiceContext $SiteUrl

  Write-Host "Exporting ..."
  Export-SPBusinessDataCatalogModel -Identity $model -
Path ".\model1.bdcm" -ModelsIncluded -PropertiesIncluded -
PermissionsIncluded -Verbose -ErrorAction Stop -ErrorVariable $err

  Write-Host "Exported BDC Model"
  }
```

7. Click **File | Save** to save the script to your development machine's desktop. Set the filename of the script to `ExportBCSModel.ps1`.

8. Open the PowerShell console window and call `ExportBCSModel.ps1` using the following command:

   PS C:\Users\Administrator\Desktop> .\ ExportBCSModel.ps1

9. As a result, your PowerShell script will create a list with results as shown in the following screenshot:

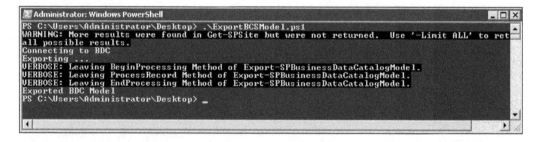

10. On your server desktop, you will now see the exported model file created with the filename as defined in the script: **model1.bdcm**.

How it works...

As in our previous recipe, we started by defining the script variables. In this recipe, we defined the site URL: `http://intranet.contoso.com`.

Once a PowerShell snap-in has been loaded, we connect to the root site of our SharePoint site collection to ensure that the site exists.

Next, we use the `Get-SPBusinessDataCatalogMetadataObject` command to get a hold of the BCS Metadata Store metadata object:

```
$model = Get-SPBusinessDataCatalogMetadataObject -BdcObjectType
"Model" -Name "model1" -ServiceContext $SiteUrl
```

The `BdcObjectType` parameter specifies the type of the metadata object to return. The type, which is `Model` in our case, must be one of the following: `Catalog`, `Model`, `LobSystem`, `LobSystemInstance`, or `Entity`.

We also need to specify the name of the model in the `Name` parameter. The name of the BDC model can be extracted from the **Central Administration** of your site as you've seen in the step sequence in the How to do it... section.

The `ServiceContext` specifies the service context of the BCS Metadata Store metadata object, which in our case is `http://intranet.contoso.com`. The rest of the parameters are optional.

Next, we execute `Export-SPBusinessDataCatalogModel` which exports the model into SharePoint. The `Identity` parameter will supply the BCS Metadata Store metadata object to import to. The `Path` specifies the path and name where the model will be created. In our case, the model file was `model1.bdcm`.

We also use the following optional parameters:

- ▸ `ModelsIncluded` specifies that models are included in the imported BCS Model file. A model contains the base XML metadata for a system.
- ▸ `PermissionsIncluded` specifies that permissions from the BCS Model are imported.
- ▸ `PropertiesIncluded` indicates that properties from the BCS Model are imported.

The last set of optional parameters specifies that the export transaction should stop if the import fails and any associated error messages related to the condition should be stored in the error variable:

```
-Verbose -ErrorAction Stop -ErrorVariable $err
```

This sequence ensures that the model is imported and you get verbose details about the import process as it progresses.

Creating instances of external lists with PowerShell

We've got the BCS model imported into our SharePoint 2010 environment as demonstrated in the *Importing a custom BCS model to SharePoint* recipe. However, the BCS model can only be used when users interact with the business data the model connects to. One of the most common containers of the business data is a SharePoint external list.

In this recipe, we'll see how you can automatically provision and configure an external list to connect to the BCS system, as well as how you can configure some of the parameters of the data retrieval from the BCS system.

The scenario described in this recipe will help you to provision consistently configured instances of SharePoint external lists when new external lists functionality are required to be added to an existing SharePoint solution. As opposed to provisioning external lists manually, or using a solution package, by using PowerShell, you will be able to provision external lists without causing environment down time.

Getting ready

In this recipe, we'll assume that you are already familiar working with lists using PowerShell, as discussed in *Chapter 3, Performing Advanced List and Content Operations in SharePoint using PowerShell*. For this recipe, we will use PowerGUI to author the script, which means you will need to be logged in with an administrator's role on the target Virtual Machine.

How to do it...

Let's take a look at the following sequence to see how you can use PowerShell to provision external lists into the site:

1. Click **Start | All Programs | PowerGUI | PowerGUI Script Editor**.

2. In the main script editing window of PowerGUI, add the following script:

```
# Defining script variables

$SiteUrl = "http://intranet.contoso.com"

# Loading Microsoft.SharePoint.PowerShell
$snapin = Get-PSSnapin | Where-Object {$_.Name -eq 'Microsoft.
SharePoint.Powershell'}
if ($snapin -eq $null) {
Write-Host "Loading SharePoint Powershell Snapin"
Add-PSSnapin "Microsoft.SharePoint.Powershell"
}
```

```
$SPSite = Get-SPSite | Where-Object {$_.Url -eq $SiteUrl}
  if($SPSite -ne $null)
  {
    $SPWeb = $SPSite.RootWeb

  Write-Host "Creating to BCS data source"
  $dataSource = New-Object Microsoft.SharePoint.SPListDataSource
  $dataSource.SetProperty("LobSystemInstance", "SupplyChainSQL")
  $dataSource.SetProperty("EntityNamespace", "http://intranet.
contoso.com")
  $dataSource.SetProperty("Entity", "Test Model")
  $datasource.SetProperty("SpecificFinder", "Read Item");

  Write-Host "Creating BCS list instance"
  $externalList = $SPWeb.Lists.Add("Test List Instance","","Lists/
Test List Instance",$dataSource)

  Write-Host "List created at:" $SPSite.Url
  }
```

3. Click **File | Save** to save the script to your development machine's desktop. Set the filename of the script to `ProvisionBCSListInstance.ps1`.

4. Open the PowerShell console window and call `ProvisionBCSListInstance.ps1` using the following command:

   PS C:\Users\Administrator\Desktop> .\ ProvisionBCSListInstance.ps1

5. As a result, your PowerShell script will execute and return results as shown in the following screenshot:

6. Now, in your browser, let's switch to our SharePoint test site : `http://intranet.contoso.com/`.

7. On the **quick launch** menu of your site, click **All Site Content**.

8. Under the **Lists** section, open **Test List Instance**.

9. You will be able to see the external data loaded into the list view similar to the one shown in the following screenshot:

ID	SupplierKey	Product	Location	Tier	Assembly Time(M)	MaxTime	Shipping ID
1	1	Shaft Stock	Toronto	3	4	8	1
2	2	Worm Gears	Denver	3	65	60	2
3	3	Bearings Bevel Assembly	Tuscon	3	16	20	3
4	4	Bevel Assembly	Cleveland	2	45	50	4
5	5	Worm	St. Louis	2	27	40	5

How it works...

Let's take a look at exactly what happens in the script of this recipe. We start by defining the script variables. In this recipe, we define the site URL: `http://intranet.contoso.com`.

Once the SharePoint snap-in is loaded, we create an instance of the BCS new SharePoint data source as follows:

```
$dataSource = New-Object Microsoft.SharePoint.SPListDataSource
```

The preceding command created the instance of the data source object which now needs the connection information to connect to our BCS data. The connection information is assigned in a series of properties. The `LobSystemInstance` property specifies an instance of the external entity. To retrieve the value of `LobSystemInstance` for your script, follow these steps:

1. Click **Start | All Programs | Microsoft SharePoint 2010 Products | SharePoint 2010 Central Administration**.
2. Click **Application Management | Manage service applications**.
3. Click **Business Data Connectivity Service** from the list of available service applications.
4. From the list of available BCS external content types, click the link representing a particular system you would like to connect to, in our example called **Test Model**.

After completing the preceding steps, you are provided with the details for the BCS entity as shown in the following screenshot:

External Content Type Information

Name :	Test Model
Display Name :	Test Model
Namespace :	http://intranet.contoso.com
Version :	1.0.0.0
External System :	SupplyChainSQL
BDC Model :	model1
Crawlable :	Yes
Default Action :	None

Fields (of default view)

Name↑	Type

The value of `LobSystemInstance` in the script can be extracted from the preceding user interface as **External System**.

The next property assigned to the data source is the `EntityNamespace`, which is a namespace allowing SharePoint to disambiguate external connections defined.

The value of `EntityNamespace` can be retrieved from the preceding Central Administration user interface as well.

Next, the `Entity` parameter is defined as follows:

```
$dataSource.SetProperty("Entity", "Test Model")
```

The `Entity` parameter value is defined as **Name** in the Central Administration user interface.

Finally, the `SpecificFinder` parameter in our script code:

```
$datasource.SetProperty("SpecificFinder", "Read Item")
```

This value is not in the default user interface of the SharePoint Central Administration. The `SpecificFinder` is responsible for retrieving individual item information from the external system. Although using SharePoint, you can also perform variety of other functions on your external data, being able to retrieve a single item is a minimum requirement to be able to create an external data connection.

By default, the `SpecificFinder` value is `Read Item` but can be named differently if your developers choose to name it differently.

Once we have assigned all of the required values for the external data source, we create an instance of our external list:

```
$externalList = $SPWeb.Lists.Add("Test List Instance","","Lists/Test
List Instance",$dataSource)
```

As you can see from the preceding code, the command which creates an instance of the external list is exactly the same as the one which creates an instance of a native SharePoint list. By specifying the data source in the Add parameter, SharePoint fills the underlying list object and related properties with values specific for interaction with external lists.

There's more

SharePoint external lists, although created using the same object as a native SharePoint list, have trimmed down functionality.

If you open an item from the external list instance, you will see that much of the functionality available in a native list is disabled right from the ribbon user interface, as shown in the following screenshot:

This difference between external and native SharePoint lists is important to understand from a PowerShell script authoring perspective. When interacting with external list properties, you must remember that some of those properties, although available on the list object, will have no bearing on the state of the object since they are not supported for external lists.

The following is an example of making the external list available on the **Quick launch**, where we assume you have an existing external list called **Test List Instance** available on the root of the site:

This command works and will make the external list available on the Quick launch.

Here is the output received from a command attempting to enable folder creation for external list:

```
PS C:\Users\Administrator\Desktop> $SPList.EnableFolderCreation

False

PS C:\Users\Administrator\Desktop> $SPList.EnableFolderCreation = $true

Exception setting "EnableFolderCreation": "Folders are not allowed for
this list templ

At line:1 char:9

+ $SPList. <<<< EnableFolderCreation = $true

    + CategoryInfo          : InvalidOperation: (:) [], RuntimeException

    + FullyQualifiedErrorId : PropertyAssignmentException
```

Similar output is received when you attempt to enable SharePoint **content types** on the list of an external list type:

```
PS C:\Users\Administrator\Desktop> $SPList.ContentTypesEnabled

False

PS C:\Users\Administrator\Desktop> $SPList.ContentTypesEnabled = $true

Exception setting "ContentTypesEnabled": "This list does not allow
content types"

At line:1 char:9

+ $SPList. <<<< ContentTypesEnabled = $true

    + CategoryInfo          : InvalidOperation: (:) [], RuntimeException

    + FullyQualifiedErrorId : PropertyAssignmentException
```

Managing permissions on an external list

In the previous recipe, the goal was to demonstrate how you can create an instance of an external list. This list would be accessible to a set of users defined on the BCS model. In this recipe, we'll take a look at how you can grant or revoke permissions to your external data for various users.

By using PowerShell to grant or revoke permissions in your environment, you will quickly be able to provision and configure appropriate access to the newly deployed external BCS model or adjust any changes to an existing system with an ability to trace back the settings.

Getting ready

In this recipe, we'll assume that you have already created an instance of an external list and are familiar with external list mode concepts, and that you have imported our test BCS model as discussed in this chapter. For this recipe, we are using PowerGUI to author the script, which means it is necessary for you to be logged in with an administrator's role on the target Virtual Machine.

How to do it...

Let's take a look at how you can manage permissions on external lists on your site:

1. Click **Start | All Programs | Microsoft SharePoint 2010 Products | SharePoint 2010 Central Administration**.

2. Click **Application Management | Manage service applications**.

3. Click **Business Data Connectivity Service** from the list of available service applications.

4. Ensure in your ribbon under **View** category, you have **BDC Models** selected from the drop-down as shown in the following screenshot:

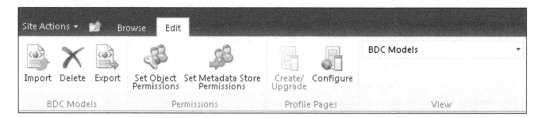

5. In the following screenshot, you will see the list of the available BDC models that access the context menu of the **model1** which we have previously imported in *Importing a custom BCS model to SharePoint* recipe, as shown in the following screenshot:

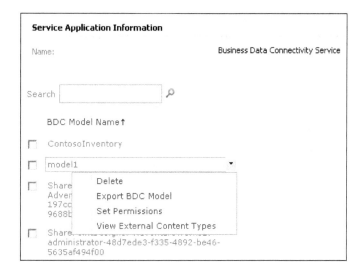

6. Select **Set Permissions** from the context menu.

7. From the following **Set Object Permissions** model window, take note that the only user who has access to **model1** is **Brad Sutton**. This user has **Edit**, **Execute**, **Selectable In Clients**, and **Set Permissions** access on the model, as shown in the following screenshot:

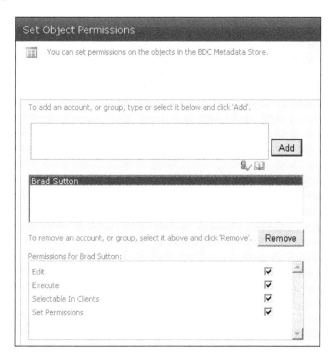

8. Close the **Set Object Permissions** by clicking **OK**.

9. Click **Start | All Programs | PowerGUI | PowerGUI Script Editor**.

10. In the main script editing window of PowerGUI, add the following script:

```
# Defining script variables

$SiteUrl = "http://intranet.contoso.com"

# Loading Microsoft.SharePoint.PowerShell
$snapin = Get-PSSnapin | Where-Object {$_.Name -eq 'Microsoft.
SharePoint.Powershell'}
if ($snapin -eq $null) {
Write-Host "Loading SharePoint Powershell Snapin"
Add-PSSnapin "Microsoft.SharePoint.Powershell"
}

$SPSite = Get-SPSite | Where-Object {$_.Url -eq $SiteUrl}
  if($SPSite -ne $null)
  {
    $SPWeb = $SPSite.RootWeb

  Write-Host "Create claims from user names"
    $userClaim1 = New-SPClaimsPrincipal -Identity "contoso\
administrator"  -IdentityType 1
    $userClaim2 = New-SPClaimsPrincipal -Identity "contoso\adamb"  -
IdentityType 1
    $userClaim3 = New-SPClaimsPrincipal -Identity "contoso\brads"  -
IdentityType 1

  Write-Host "Connecting to BCS model"
    $model = Get-SPBusinessDataCatalogMetadataObject -BdcObjectType
"Model" -ServiceContext http://intranet.contoso.com -Name "model1"

  Write-Host "Granting access to users"
    Grant-SPBusinessDataCatalogMetadataObject -Identity $model -
Principal $userClaim1 -Right Execute
    Grant-SPBusinessDataCatalogMetadataObject -Identity $model -
Principal $userClaim2 -Right Edit

  Write-Host "Revoking access to user"
    Revoke-SPBusinessDataCatalogMetadataObject -Identity $model -
Principal $userClaim3 -Right Execute

  Write-Host "Permissions assigned for BCS model"
  }
```

11. Click **File | Save** to save the script to your development machine's desktop. Set the filename of the script to `SetBCSSecurity.ps1`.

12. Open the PowerShell console window and call `SetBCSSecurity.ps1` using the following command:

PS C:\Users\Administrator\Desktop> .\ SetBCSSecurity.ps1

13. As a result, your PowerShell script will set two related lists as shown in the following screenshot:

14. Now, switch back to **SharePoint Central Administration** area where we accessed the BCS **Set Object Permissions** model window in previous steps.

15. Access the **Set Permissions** context menu option for the **model1** as we did before.

16. Ensure that we now have additional users with various permission access set on the **model1**, as shown in the following screenshot:

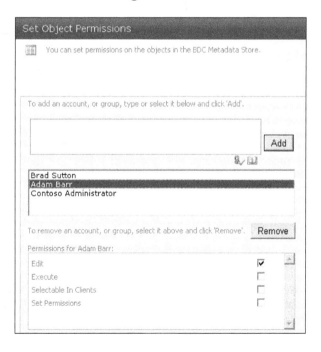

How it works...

We started by defining the script variables. In this recipe, we define the site URL where our new list is going to be created: `http://intranet.contoso.com`.

After SharePoint snap-in has loaded, we created claims for several user accounts we used in our script.

 The reason we created claims rather than pass Windows user identities is that the following permission management command only accepts user claims. This way, an administrator can assign users from various identity providers to use the external system.

Here is how the claim was created based on the Windows account from administrator user:

```
$userClaim1 = New-SPClaimsPrincipal -Identity "contoso\administrator"
-IdentityType 1
```

Here, the `Identity` parameter specifies the user account name. The `IdentityType` is a value representing an enumeration denoting the format of the identity. Our value of `1` specifies that the `IdentityType` is a `Name`.

 For other types of identity values, search MSDN with a keyword **IdentityType**.

Next, we connected to the model for which we would like to manage the permissions. In our case, this is the same model we imported in the *Importing a custom BCS model to SharePoint* recipe, as shown in the following line of code:

```
$model = Get-SPBusinessDataCatalogMetadataObject -BdcObjectType
"Model" -ServiceContext http://intranet.contoso.com -Name "model1"
```

The `BdcObjectType` parameter specifies the type of the object, in our case it's a `Model`. The types of objects include: `Catalog`, `Model`, `LobSystem`, `LobSystemInstance`, or `Entity`.

Finally, we called `Grant-SPBusinessDataCatalogMetadataObject` to grant access for a specific claim to the model object, as shown in the following code:

```
Grant-SPBusinessDataCatalogMetadataObject -Identity $model -Principal
$userClaim1 -Right Execute
```

Here, the `Identity` parameter passes the model which we granted access to. The `Principal` is the claim object we created earlier. The `Right` parameter determines the type of rights our user is given. Options include: `All`, `Execute`, `Edit`, `SetPermissions`, or `SelectableInClients`.

The `Revoke-SPBusinessDataCatalogMetadataObject` command works in the same way as its `Grant` counterpart with exactly the same set of parameters. However, in this case, the identified claim loses right defined in the `Right` parameter.

 Check out some of the additional options available for the `Revoke-SPBusinessDataCatalogMetadataObject` and `Grant-SPBusinessDataCatalogMetadataObject` commands by searching MSDN with the keyword `Grant-SPBusinessDataCatalogMetadataObject`.

Throttling items returned with external lists

There are many out-of-the-box tools in SharePoint to work with list data, and external lists are no exception. In fact, since SharePoint 2010, external lists share common implementation logic with native SharePoint lists, developers can easily support external data in their custom components. However, there is another side to the popularity of external lists. There are spikes in performance of the external system which can sometimes affect the functionality of external applications. In some other cases, you have a powerful data backend environment capable of supporting many requests from users allowing more users to access bigger data sets.

In this recipe, we'll take a look at how you can throttle the usage of the data coming from an external system.

The advantage of performing this configuration using a PowerShell is the ability to transfer your settings between environments as your application goes through its lifecycle.

Getting ready

In this recipe, we'll assume you are already familiar working with external lists using PowerShell, as discussed in this chapter. For this recipe, we'll use PowerGUI to author the script, which means it's necessary for you to be logged in with an administrator's role on the target Virtual Machine.

How to do it...

Let's see what's involved in setting up throttling on items returned in external list:

1. In your browser, switch to our SharePoint test site: `http://intranet.contoso.com/`.

2. On the **Quick launch** menu of your site, under the **Lists** section, locate the list titled **Test List Instance**. This list was created in *Creating instances of external lists with PowerShell recipe*.

3. Take note of the items in a list being displayed, as shown in the following screenshot:

ID	SupplierKey	Product	Location	Tier	Assembly Time(M)	MaxTime	Shipping ID
1	1	Shaft Stock	Toronto	3	4	8	1
2	2	Worm Gears	Denver	3	65	60	2
3	3	Bearings Bevel Assembly	Tuscon	3	16	20	3
4	4	Bevel Assembly	Cleveland	2	45	50	4
5	5	Worm Assembly	St. Louis	2	27	40	5
6	6	Gasket	Lexington	2	2	5	6

4. Click **Start | All Programs | PowerGUI | PowerGUI Script Editor**.

5. In the main script editing window of PowerGUI, add the following script:

```
# Loading Microsoft.SharePoint.PowerShell
$snapin = Get-PSSnapin | Where-Object {$_.Name -eq 'Microsoft.
SharePoint.Powershell'}
if ($snapin -eq $null) {
Write-Host "Loading SharePoint Powershell Snapin"
Add-PSSnapin "Microsoft.SharePoint.Powershell"
}

Write-Host "Connecting to BCS proxy"

$bcsProxy = Get-SPServiceApplicationProxy | where {$_.GetType().
FullName -eq ('Microsoft.SharePoint.BusinessData.SharedService.' +
'BdcServiceApplicationProxy')}

Write-Host "Creating maximum items rule"
$dbRule = Get-SPBusinessDataCatalogThrottleConfig -Scope Database
-ThrottleType Items -ServiceApplicationProxy $bcsProxy
Write-Host "Creating connection timeout rule"
$timeoutRule = Get-SPBusinessDataCatalogThrottleConfig -Scope
Database -ThrottleType Timeout -ServiceApplicationProxy $bcsProxy

Write-Host "Setting rule variables"
Set-SPBusinessDataCatalogThrottleConfig -Identity $dbRule -Maximum
30 -Default 30
Set-SPBusinessDataCatalogThrottleConfig -Identity $timeoutRule -
Maximum 10 -Default 10

Write-Host "Rules set on " + $bcsProxy.DisplayName
```

6. Click **File | Save** to save the script to your development machine's desktop. Set the filename of the script to `ThrottlingBCS.ps1`.

7. Open the PowerShell console window and call `ThrottlingBCS.ps1` using the following command:

PS C:\Users\Administrator\Desktop> .\ ThrottlingBCS.ps1

8. As a result, your PowerShell script will execute with results as shown in the following screenshot:

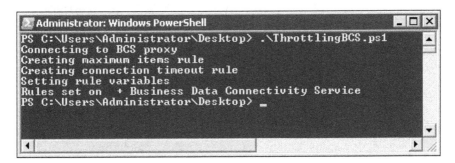

9. Now, in your browser, let's switch to our SharePoint test site: `http://intranet.contoso.com/`.

10. On the **Quick launch** menu of your site, under the **Lists** section, locate the list titled **Test List Instance** and take note of the message returned in a list view, as shown in the following screenshot:

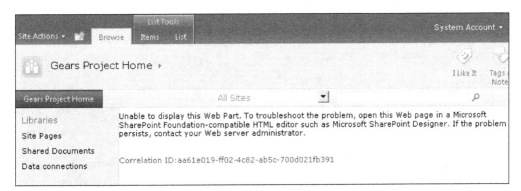

How it works...

In this recipe, we have set our custom throttling on the number of items which are returned from an SQL database to a SharePoint external list.

We start by loading SharePoint snap-in:

```
Add-PSSnapin "Microsoft.SharePoint.Powershell"
```

Next, we connect to the BCS connection proxy using the following command:

```
$bcsProxy = Get-SPServiceApplicationProxy | where {$_.GetType().
FullName -eq ('Microsoft.SharePoint.BusinessData.SharedService.' +
'BdcServiceApplicationProxy')}
```

The `Get-SPServiceApplicationProxy` returns an instance of the specified service application proxy. This means we need to specify the BCS proxy we're interested in. We identify the proxy by the type: `Microsoft.SharePoint.BusinessData.SharedService`.

In some cases, you might have more than one connection proxy. In that case, you could use a name of the proxy to identify the one you're interested in. To find out the name of the proxy:

1. Click **Start | All Programs | Microsoft SharePoint 2010 Products | SharePoint 2010 Central Administration**.
2. Click **Application Management | Manage service applications**.
3. Locate the Business Connectivity Services proxy with the name you have previously defined. This name will be the name of your BCS connection proxy.

Alternatively, you can execute the following command from the PowerShell window to list all of the Service Application proxies and their type:

```
PS C:\Users\Administrator> Get-SPServiceApplicationProxy | Select
DisplayName, TypeName
```

As the result, you will receive output similar to the following screenshot:

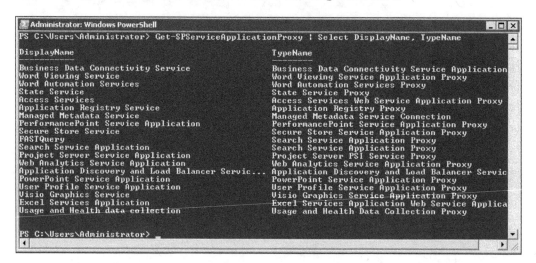

The preceding result shows the type of the Service Application, and its respective name, which helps identify the Service Applications you're looking for.

Next, we created a rule which restricts the number of items returned from BCS service application:

```
$dbRule = Get-SPBusinessDataCatalogThrottleConfig -Scope Database -
ThrottleType Items -ServiceApplicationProxy $bcsProxy
```

The `Get-SPBusinessDataCatalogThrottleConfig` command supports a variety of throttling configurations specified by its parameters. The `Scope` parameter specifies the scope of the configuration and includes the following acceptable values: `Wcf`, `WebService`, `Database`, `Global`, or `Custom`. The `ServiceApplicationProxy` specifies the proxy we have established in a previous command. `ThrottleType` defines the type of throttle, in our case, number of items. Other acceptable values for this parameter include: `None`, `Items`, `Size`, `Connections`, or `Timeout`.

Other parameters are optional. In our example, we limit the number of items returned from the BCS proxy connecting to the database.

Next, we created another rule specifying the acceptable timeout on the connection to the BCS proxy:

```
$timeoutRule = Get-SPBusinessDataCatalogThrottleConfig -Scope Database -
ThrottleType Timeout -ServiceApplicationProxy $bcsProxy
```

Parameters in this example are the same with a different timeout value for the `ThrottleType`.

Finally, the `Set-SPBusinessDataCatalogThrottleConfig` command will specify the throttling configuration on the rule we defined before. This command accepts the same set of parameters regardless of the rule. The `Default` parameter specifies the default setting for the throttle configuration. The `Identity` parameter specifies the rule we created in a previous command. The `Maximum` parameter specifies the maximum value for the defined configuration rule.

In our recipe example, the following command specifies a maximum of 30 items to be returned from the BCS connection from the database:

```
Set-SPBusinessDataCatalogThrottleConfig -Identity $dbRule -Maximum 30 -
Default 30
```

The setting can be set back by executing the same command with the new `Maximum` value.

A similar command was executed to throttle the timeout for the connection.

 It's important to understand the difference between the throttling configuration and configuration in a list view. The throttling configuration, in this recipe, will apply to any custom, out-of-the-box application, or command which interacts with the data through BCS, such as list view. For example, if you have created an external list and specified that only return a few items based on the filter formula, your list view may still fail to load. In order to perform the filter, the list view would have still requested all of the list items. Since the list view goes through a BCS proxy to do its job, it would be restricted by the throttling configuration specified on the proxy.

5
Managing SharePoint 2010 Metadata and Social Features Using PowerShell

In this chapter, we will cover:

- ▶ Creating new user profiles
- ▶ Adding and configuring new profile properties
- ▶ Bulk provisioning data into user profile properties
- ▶ Creating, importing, and exporting managed metadata taxonomy terms
- ▶ Enabling social rating on lists and libraries
- ▶ Bulk tagging content and deleting tags in SharePoint

Introduction

User profiles in SharePoint 2010 allow for an entire new set of functionality. With user profiles, custom and out-of-the-box components can store user-specific information in a profile database along with other details about the user. System components can use user profile information to provide better and more personal experiences to users. In this chapter, we'll see how you can provision user profiles using PowerShell to prepopulate user information for your user profiles.

As you make a full use of SharePoint 2010 user profiles, you will see how extensible user profile functionality is and how you can take advantage of creating custom profile properties to store specific information about users in your system. In this chapter, we'll see how you can create your custom user profile properties and populate them with values.

Managed metadata is new feature in SharePoint 2010 allowing users to store centralized metadata terms. Since terms can be managed centrally and used anywhere on the site, this makes them a perfect candidate to hold enterprise-wide metadata. With PowerShell, you will be able to reliably configure metadata stored on all of your environments without incurring a significant downtime.

Among other social features in SharePoint 2010, users are now able to rate items in lists and libraries to help their peers find the most relevant content on the site. However, social rating feature needs to be enabled manually on each library. With PowerShell, we'll see exactly what's involved in enabling social rating automatically on libraries within your portal.

Finally, we'll take a look at how you can use PowerShell to perform bulk tagging of the content on the site. This capability will allow you to mark certain content on the site as expired or belonging to a particular category making it much easier for users to find in search results and in document libraries.

Creating new user profiles

Any custom and out-of-the-box feature in SharePoint 2010 is much more successful if it can provide more relevant and personal information to the user who is using it. For example, if I am logged in to the corporate intranet in an overseas company branch, I would like to see personalized, rather than generic information, shown to me in various parts of the site.

User profiles in SharePoint 2010 allow storing personalized of information about the user which can be retrieved by out-of-the-box and custom features. In this recipe, we'll take a look at how you can provision new user profiles on the site which are bound to existing Active Directory user accounts.

At the end of this recipe, you will be all set with the script allowing you to create multiple user profiles on your SharePoint 2010 system.

Getting ready

Assuming you have already set up your virtual development environment as described in *Chapter 1, PowerShell Scripting Methods and Creating Custom Commands*, we'll get right into authoring our script. We'll also assume your current environment is using Active Directory where you have a few existing user accounts we'll create user profiles for. Since we'll be using PowerGUI to author the script, ensure you're logged in with an administrator's permissions on the target Virtual Machine.

How to do it...

Let's take a look at how we can create new user profiles with the following sequence:

1. Click **Start** | **All Programs** | **Microsoft SharePoint 2010 Products** | **SharePoint 2010 Central Administration**.

2. Click **Application Management** | **Manage service applications**.

3. Click **User Profile Service Application**, as shown in the following screenshot:

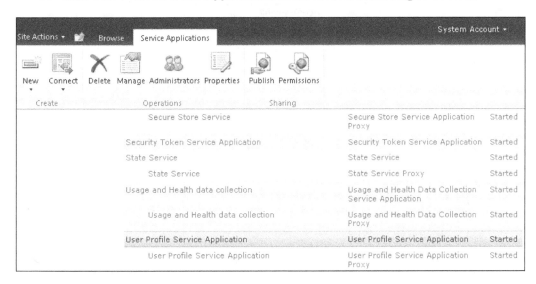

4. Select the **Manage User Profiles** link under the **People** category.

5. In the **Find profiles** textbox, enter a new or existing username provisioned in Active Directory of your server.

6. Click the **Find** button and ensure no profiles have been returned for the user, as shown in the following screenshot:

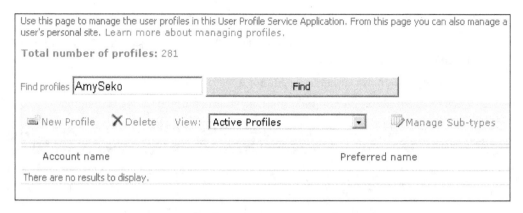

7. Click **Start | All Programs | PowerGUI | PowerGUI Script Editor**.

8. In the main script editing window of PowerGUI, add the following script:

```
# Defining script variables

$SiteUrl = "http://intranet.contoso.com"
$AccountName = "AmySeko"

# Loading Microsoft.SharePoint.PowerShell
$snapin = Get-PSSnapin | Where-Object {$_.Name -eq 'Microsoft.
SharePoint.Powershell'}
if ($snapin -eq $null) {
Write-Host "Loading SharePoint Powershell Snapin"
Add-PSSnapin "Microsoft.SharePoint.Powershell"
}

Write-Host "Loading user profile assemblies"
[System.Reflection.Assembly]::LoadWithPartialName("Microsoft.
Office.Server")
[System.Reflection.Assembly]::LoadWithPartialName("Microsoft.
Office.Server.UserProfiles")

$SPSite = Get-SPSite | Where-Object {$_.Url -eq $SiteUrl}
  if($SPSite -ne $null)
  {
    Write-Host "Loading current server context"
    $ServerContext = [Microsoft.Office.Server.ServerContext]::
GetContext($SPSite)
```

```
Write-Host "Creating user profile"
$ProfileManager = New-Object Microsoft.Office.Server.
UserProfiles.UserProfileManager($ServerContext);
$NewProfile = $ProfileManager.CreateUserProfile($AccountName,
$AccountName);

Write-Host "Saving profile changes"
$NewProfile.Commit();

Write-Host "User profile provisioned"
}
```

9. Click **File | Save** to save the script to your development machine's desktop. Set the filename of the script to CreateUserProfile.ps1.

10. Open the PowerShell console window and call CreateUserProfile.ps1 using the following command:

    PS C:\Users\Administrator\Desktop> .\ CreateUserProfile.ps1

11. As a result, your PowerShell script will create a site structure as shown in the following screenshot:

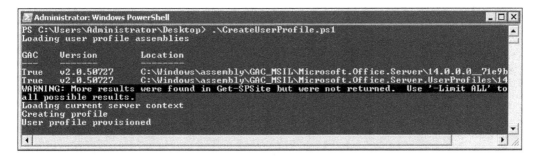

12. Let's now switch to our **Manage User Profiles** section for **User Profile Service Application**.

13. In the **Find profiles** textbox, enter the same username as in previous steps.

14. Click the **Find** button and ensure a new profile is returned for the user, as shown in the following screenshot:

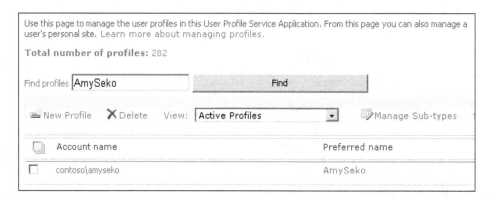

15. Access the context menu of the returned user profile and click **Edit My Profile** option. Take note of the profile properties as shown in the following screenshot:

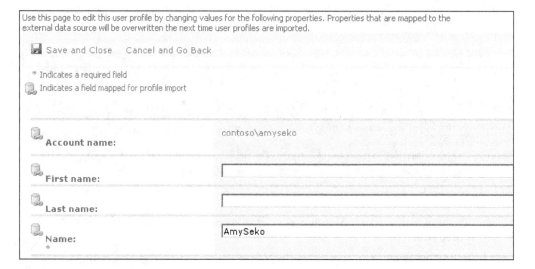

How it works...

First, we defined the script variables used. In this recipe, the variables include a site URL: `http://intranet.contoso.com` and a username of the Active Directory user we'll be creating a profile for, as `$AccountName`.

Once a PowerShell snap-in has been loaded, we load two libraries which facilitate functionality related to working with user profiles in SharePoint:

```
[System.Reflection.Assembly]::LoadWithPartialName("Microsoft.Office.
Server")
[System.Reflection.Assembly]::LoadWithPartialName("Microsoft.Office.
Server.UserProfiles")
```

Next, we connect to the root site of our SharePoint site collection. The root site collection object will be used to establish a link to our **User Profile Service Application**.

The following command will create an object representing a server context:

```
$ServerContext = [Microsoft.Office.Server.ServerContext]::
GetContext($SPSite)
```

The server context created will be used next to establish a link to a user profile manager. User profile manager represents a collection of user profile objects that are used to access user profile data.

```
$ProfileManager = New-Object Microsoft.Office.Server.UserProfiles.User
ProfileManager($ServerContext);
```

 As well noted in _MSDN_ reference on user profiles, the user profile manager object instance must be created before accessing or creating user profiles. Full access to everyone's user profile requires **Manage User Profiles** rights. Full access to one's own profile requires **Use Personal Features** rights. Everyone has read access to all profiles.

To create a new user profile, we call the `UserProfileManager` class' method:

```
$NewProfile = $ProfileManager.CreateUserProfile($AccountName,
$AccountName);
```

Here, the `CreateUserProfile` method has several variations. The variation used in this recipe accepts two parameters: the account name as the first parameter, and the preferred name which is viewable by other users in SharePoint.

The account must be created in Active Directory before a user profile can be created for it.

 To find out which other methods are available when working with user profiles, reference _MSDN_ with the keyword **UserProfileManager**.

Adding and configuring new profile properties

As we've learned from the previous recipe, you can create a SharePoint user profile which can be consumed by custom components and applications as well as out-of-the-box web parts.

When your developers see the power of using user profiles to store user-specific information for their applications, there is no doubt you will receive requests to extend user profile properties to facilitate additional user profile information.

Adding user profile properties manually can result in a disconnect between your staging and production environments and additional manual steps during disaster recovery. As an alternative, you may want to choose to provision profile properties using a custom SharePoint solution, which will require a deployment down time.

Let's take a look at what's involved in provisioning custom user profile properties with PowerShell which introduces little to no downtime.

Getting ready

In this recipe, we'll assume you are already familiar with the concept of user profile creation in SharePoint and have looked at provisioning a new user profile into SharePoint using PowerShell, as discussed in this chapter. For this recipe, we'll be using PowerGUI to author our script, which means you will need to be logged in with an administrator's role on the target Virtual Machine.

How to do it...

Let's take a look at how you can add new user profile properties using the following steps:

1. Click **Start | All Programs | Microsoft SharePoint 2010 Products | SharePoint 2010 Central Administration**.

2. Click **Application Management | Manage service applications**.

3. Click **User Profile Service Application**, as shown in the following screenshot:

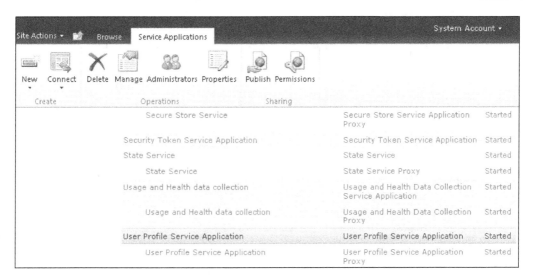

4. Select the **Manage User Properties** link under the **People** category.

5. Take note of the existing list of properties, as shown in the following screenshot:

Use this page to add, edit, organize, delete or map user profile properties. Profile properties can be mapped to Active Directory or LDAP compliant directory services. Profile properties can also be mapped to Application Entity Fields expo by Business Data Connectivity.

New Property   New Section   Manage Sub-types   Select a sub-type to filter the list

Property Name	Change Order	Property Type
> **Basic Information**	⌄	Section
Id	⌃ ⌄	unique identifier
SID	⌃ ⌄	binary
Active Directory Id	⌃ ⌄	binary
Account name	⌃ ⌄	Person
First name	⌃ ⌄	string (Single Value)
Phonetic First Name	⌃ ⌄	string (Single Value)
Last name	⌃ ⌄	string (Single Value)

6. Click **Start | All Programs | PowerGUI | PowerGUI Script Editor**.

7. In the main script editing window of PowerGUI, add the following script:

```
# Defining script variables

$SiteUrl = "http://intranet.contoso.com"
$BuildingNumberPropertyName = "BuildingNumber"

# Loading Microsoft.SharePoint.PowerShell
$snapin = Get-PSSnapin | Where-Object {$_.Name -eq 'Microsoft.
SharePoint.Powershell'}
if ($snapin -eq $null) {
Write-Host "Loading SharePoint Powershell Snapin"
Add-PSSnapin "Microsoft.SharePoint.Powershell"
}

Write-Host "Loading user profile assemblies"
[System.Reflection.Assembly]::LoadWithPartialName("Microsoft.
Office.Server")
[System.Reflection.Assembly]::LoadWithPartialName("Microsoft.
Office.Server.UserProfiles")

$SPSite = Get-SPSite | Where-Object {$_.Url -eq $SiteUrl}
  if($SPSite -ne $null)
  {
    Write-Host "Loading current server context"
    $ServerContext = [Microsoft.Office.Server.ServerContext]::
GetContext($SPSite)

  Write-Host "Creating user properties"
  $ProfileConfigManager = New-Object Microsoft.Office.Server.
UserProfiles.UserProfileConfigManager($ServerContext)
  $ProfileManager = New-Object Microsoft.Office.Server.
UserProfiles.UserProfileManager($ServerContext)
  $PropertyInstance = $ProfileManager.Properties.Create($false);

  Write-Host "Setting property rules"
  $PropertyInstance.Name = $BuildingNumberPropertyName
  $PropertyInstance.Type = "string"
  $PropertyInstance.Length = 50
    $PropertyInstance.DisplayName = $BuildingNumberPropertyName
    $PropertyInstance.Description = $BuildingNumberPropertyName
    $PropertyInstance.IsVisibleOnViewer = $true
    $PropertyInstance.IsSearchable = $true
```

```
Write-Host "Saving property changes"
    $PropertyInstance.Commit();

Write-Host "User property provisioned"
    }
```

8. Click **File** | **Save** to save the script to your development machine's desktop. Set the filename of the script to `CreateUserProperties.ps1`.

9. Open the PowerShell console window and call `CreateUserProperties.ps1` using the following command:

   PS C:\Users\Administrator\Desktop> .\ CreateUserProperties.ps1

10. As a result, your PowerShell script will create a list with results as shown in the following screenshot:

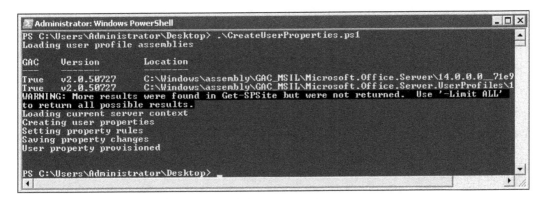

11. Now, switch back to the **Central Administration** window you had opened before, and open the **Manage User Properties** link under the **People** category.

12. Take note of the newly provisioned property under the **Custom Properties** category, as shown in the following screenshot:

> Delegation	∧ ∨	Section
> Newsfeed Settings	∧ ∨	Section
Interests	∧ ∨	string (Multi Value)
Email Notifications	∧ ∨	integer
> Custom Properties	∧	Section

13. Navigate back to the **User Profile Service Application** main page. This time, select the **Manage User Profiles** link under the **People** category.

14. In the **Find profiles** textbox, enter a new or existing username provisioned in Active Directory of your server.

15. Click on the **Find** button and take note of the newly provisioned property available under the active user profile:

Interests:	Share personal and business related interests. We will help you keep in touch with activities related to these interests through events in your newsfeed.
Email Notifications:	☑ Notify me when someone leaves a note on my profile. ☑ Notify me when someone adds me as a colleague. ☑ Send me suggestions for new colleagues and keywords. Select which e-mail notifications you want to receive.
BuildingNumber:	BuildingNumber
💾 Save and Close Cancel and Go Back	

How it works...

As in any previous recipe, we started by defining the script variables. In this recipe, we defined the site URL: `http://intranet.contoso.com` and the new property name.

Once a PowerShell snap-in has been loaded, we load SharePoint libraries facilitating work with user profiles:

```
[System.Reflection.Assembly]::LoadWithPartialName("Microsoft.Office.
Server")
[System.Reflection.Assembly]::LoadWithPartialName("Microsoft.Office.
Server.UserProfiles")
```

Next, we establish the current site context:

```
$ServerContext = [Microsoft.Office.Server.ServerContext]::
GetContext($SPSite)
```

Next, we create an instance of the User Profile Manager which stores collections of user properties and profiles as well as methods to work with properties and profiles. The profile manager connects to the current site context:

```
$ProfileManager = New-Object Microsoft.Office.Server.UserProfiles.User
ProfileManager($ServerContext)
```

Once connected to the profile manager, we access the `Properties` collection which has the `Create` method. The `Create` method will create a new property instance which can be assigned various rules and parameters. The method accepts one parameter specifying whether the property is a section. In our case, by passing `$false`, we create the property instance and not a section:

```
$PropertyInstance = $ProfileManager.Properties.Create($false);
```

Next, we assigned the value and rules to the property instance created earlier. Key properties here are: `Name`, `Type`, `Length`, `DisplayName`, `Description`, and `IsVisibleOnViewer`. The `IsVisibleOnViewer` property, although not mandatory, if not set, will not display the property in user profile property page and in the list of properties in Central Administration. This can be sometimes handy, since the property will still be available and able to store data but not displayed for anyone to modify or delete using SharePoint user interface.

To save all of the changes and rules of the newly created property instance we call a `Commit` method:

```
$PropertyInstance.Commit();
```

Now that the transaction is committed, the new property will show in the list of properties in Central Administration and available through the object model for developers to access.

See also

The *Creating new user profiles* recipe in this chapter.

Bulk provisioning data into user profile properties

We've got our user profiles created in the *Creating new user profiles* recipe. We've also provisioned additional properties into our SharePoint system in the previous recipe.

In this recipe, we'll see how you can automatically provision custom property values into our existing and custom properties. This approach will significantly speed up the rollout of any new values for the applications relying on custom properties.

As an example, if you would like to populate users interests list based on job title to help your users find colleagues easier, you can use PowerShell to make such a change in no time, without introducing a significant downtime to your production environment.

Getting ready

In this recipe, we'll assume you are already familiar with creating user profiles using PowerShell, as discussed in the *Creating new user profiles* recipe. We'll also assume you have created a few custom properties in your user profile system as discussed in the previous recipe. For this recipe, we'll use PowerGUI to author the script, which means you will need to be logged in with an administrator's role on the target Virtual Machine.

How to do it...

Let's see how we can provision user profile property values using the following sequence:

1. Click **Start | All Programs | PowerGUI | PowerGUI Script Editor**.
2. In the main script editing window of PowerGUI, add the following script:

```
# Defining script variables

$SiteUrl = "http://intranet.contoso.com"
$ProfileSearchTerm = "Human Resources"
$PropertyValue = "35"
$BuildingNumberPropertyName = "BuildingNumber"

# Loading Microsoft.SharePoint.PowerShell
$snapin = Get-PSSnapin | Where-Object {$_.Name -eq 'Microsoft.
SharePoint.Powershell'}
if ($snapin -eq $null) {
Write-Host "Loading SharePoint Powershell Snapin"
Add-PSSnapin "Microsoft.SharePoint.Powershell"
}

Write-Host "Loading user profile assemblies"
[System.Reflection.Assembly]::LoadWithPartialName("Microsoft.
Office.Server")
[System.Reflection.Assembly]::LoadWithPartialName("Microsoft.
Office.Server.UserProfiles")

$SPSite = Get-SPSite | Where-Object {$_.Url -eq $SiteUrl}
  if($SPSite -ne $null)
  {
    Write-Host "Loading current server context"
    $ServerContext = [Microsoft.Office.Server.ServerContext]::
GetContext($SPSite)

    Write-Host "Creating user profile"
    $ProfileManager = New-Object Microsoft.Office.Server.
```

```
UserProfiles.UserProfileManager($ServerContext)
    $Profiles = $ProfileManager.Search($ProfileSearchTerm)

    Write-Host "Profiles found:"
    $Profiles | Select DisplayName

    Write-Host "Editing profile and saving changes"
    $Profiles | ForEach-Object {$_.[$BuildingNumberPropertyName].
Add($PropertyValue); $_.Commit()}

    Write-Host "User profiles updated"
    }
```

3. Click **File | Save** to save the script to your development machine's desktop. Set the filename of the script to `ProvisioningProfileData.ps1`.

4. Open the PowerShell console window and call `ProvisioningProfileData.ps1` using the following command:

   PS C:\Users\Administrator\Desktop> .\ ProvisioningProfileData.ps1

5. As a result, your PowerShell script will execute and return results as shown in the following screenshot:

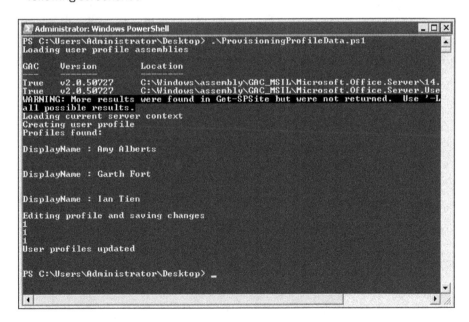

6. Click **Start | All Programs | Microsoft SharePoint 2010 Products | SharePoint 2010 Central Administration**.

7. Click **Application Management | Manage service applications**.

8. Click **User Profile Service Application**, as shown in the following screenshot:

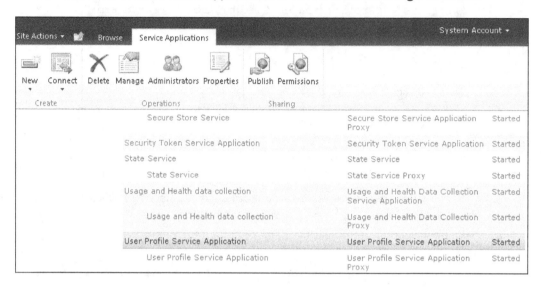

9. Select the **Manage User Profiles** link under the **People** category.

10. In the **Find profiles** textbox, enter a property value which is contained in some of the user profiles. In our case, we'll enter **Human Resources**, a value for the **Department** property.

11. Click the **Find** button and ensure no profiles have been returned for the user, as shown in the following screenshot:

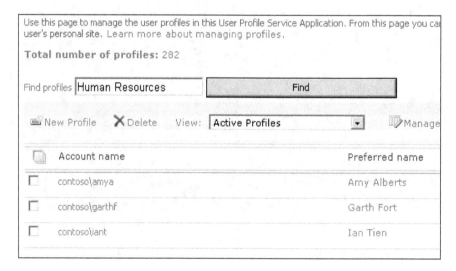

12. Access one of the user profiles by clicking the **Edit My Profile** option of the profile's context menu.

13. Scroll to the bottom of the user profile page to find the **BuildingNumber** property value set to **35** as specified in our script.

How it works...

Let's take a look at exactly what happens in the script of this recipe. We start by defining the script variables. In this recipe, we define the site URL: `http://intranet.contoso.com`.

`$ProfileSearchTerm` is used to store the search term we will be searching by in our user profiles. `$PropertyValue` will hold a value which will be assigned to our custom property. `$BuildingNumberPropertyName` will hold the value representing a custom property name we will be saving data into.

Once the SharePoint snap-in is loaded, we load additional assemblies facilitating the work with SharePoint user profiles, as follows:

```
[System.Reflection.Assembly]::LoadWithPartialName("Microsoft.Office.
Server")
[System.Reflection.Assembly]::LoadWithPartialName("Microsoft.Office.
Server.UserProfiles")
```

Next, we get a hold of the current server context:

```
ServerContext = [Microsoft.Office.Server.ServerContext]::
GetContext($SPSite)
```

Based on the specified server context, we connect to the user profile manager and create an instance of its object as follows:

```
ProfileManager = New-Object Microsoft.Office.Server.UserProfiles.UserP
rofileManager($ServerContext)
```

We can now search for a user profile with a specified search term. In our recipe, we searched for the name of the department. The search will search through all of the properties marked as **searchable** and return properties which contain the value searched:

```
Profiles = $ProfileManager.Search($ProfileSearchTerm)
```

Next, we display the list of the usernames that were found as a part of our query, as shown in the following code:

```
Profiles | Select DisplayName
```

Finally, we enumerate through each of the found user profiles and access the `BuildingNumber` property. Each item in the array of results is assigned our custom value using the following command:

```
$Profiles | ForEach-Object {$_[$BuildingNumberPropertyName].
Add($PropertyValue); $_.Commit()}
```

To verify that the property has been set for each user, access the profile for one of the users found in our search results, and validate that the profile property value for **BuildingNumber** is of the correct value by using the following steps:

1. Ensure you are logged into the **User Profile Service Application** home page.

2. Select the **Manage User Profiles** link under the **People** category.

3. In the **Find profiles** textbox, enter a property value which is contained in some of the user profiles. In our case, we'll enter **Human Resources**, a value for the **Department** property.

4. Click the **Find** button and ensure no profiles have been returned for the user.

5. Access one of the user profiles by clicking **Edit My Profile** option of the profile's context menu.

6. Scroll to the bottom of the user profile page to find the **BuildingNumber** property value set to **35**, as shown below:

Interests:	Fishing;
	Share personal and business related interests. We will help you keep in touch with activities related to these interests through events in your newsfeed.
Email Notifications:	☑ Notify me when someone leaves a note on my profile. ☑ Notify me when someone adds me as a colleague. ☑ Send me suggestions for new colleagues and keywords. Select which e-mail notifications you want to receive.
BuildingNumber:	35 BuildingNumber

Save and Close   Cancel and Go Back

See also

The *Creating new user profiles* and *Adding and configuring new profile properties* recipes in this chapter.

Creating, importing, and exporting managed metadata taxonomy terms

Managed metadata is a new feature in SharePoint 2010 which allows users to store centralized metadata terms. Terms in SharePoint can be managed centrally and used anywhere on the site allowing your users to hold enterprise-wide metadata.

Once in the system, managed metadata frequently needs to travel between staging, development, and production environments. With PowerShell, you will be able to reliably configure metadata stored on all of your environments without incurring a significant downtime.

Currently, there is no alternative out-of-the-box user interface allowing administrators to export metadata terms, which makes PowerShell a perfect candidate to perform such tasks automatically, without requiring significant development.

Getting ready

Assuming you have already set up your virtual development environment as described in *Chapter 1, PowerShell Scripting Methods and Creating Custom Commands*, we'll get right into authoring our script. Since we'll be using PowerGUI to author the script, ensure you're logged in with an administrator's permissions on the target Virtual Machine.

How to do it...

Let's see how you can manage metadata taxonomy terms using the following sequence of steps:

1. Click **Start | All Programs | Microsoft SharePoint 2010 Products | SharePoint 2010 Central Administration**.
2. Click **Application Management | Manage service applications**.
3. Click **Managed Metadata Service** from the list of available service applications.
4. Take note of the taxonomy tree and existing items in it, we will be adding an additional node to the tree.
5. Click **Start | All Programs | PowerGUI | PowerGUI Script Editor**.
6. In the main script editing window of PowerGUI, add the following script:

```
# Defining script variables

SiteUrl = "http://intranet.contoso.com"

# Loading Microsoft.SharePoint.PowerShell
snapin = Get-PSSnapin | Where-Object {$_.Name -eq 'Microsoft.
SharePoint.Powershell'}
```

```
if ($snapin -eq $null) {
Write-Host "Loading SharePoint Powershell Snapin"
Add-PSSnapin "Microsoft.SharePoint.Powershell"
}

Write-Host "Connecting to the term store and creating a new group"
$TaxonomySession=Get-SPTaxonomySession -Site $SiteUrl
$TermStore=$TaxonomySession.TermStores["Managed Metadata Service"]
$Group=$TermStore.CreateGroup("Branch Metadata")
$TermStore.CommitAll()

Write-Host "Creating a term set"
$TermSet=$Group.CreateTermSet("Branch Departments")
$TermStore.CommitAll()

Write-Host "Creating a term"
$MarketingTerm=$TermSet.CreateTerm("Marketing",1033)
$HRTerm=$TermSet.CreateTerm("HR",1033)
$DeliveryTerm=$TermSet.CreateTerm("Delivery",1033)
$TermStore.CommitAll()

Write-Host "Saving structure to file"
'"Term Set Name",
"Term Set Description",
"LCID","Available for Tagging",
"Term Description",
"Level 1 Term",
"Level 2 Term",
"Level 3 Term",
"Level 4 Term",
"Level 5 Term",
"Level 6 Term",
"Level 7 Term"' | out-file "BranchMetadata.csv" -Append
$Group.TermSets | ForEach-Object
{'"' + $_.Name + '",
"' + $_.Description + '",
"1033",
"' + $_.IsAvailableForTagging +
'",,,,,,,,';
$_.Terms | ForEach-Object
{',,"1033","TRUE",,"'
+ $_.Name +
'",,,,,,'}} | out-file "BranchMetadata.csv" -Append
```

7. Click **File | Save** to save the script to your development machine's desktop. Set the filename of the script to WorkingWithManagedMetadata.ps1.

8. Open the PowerShell console window and call WorkingWithManagedMetadata. ps1 using the following command:

    8PS C:\Users\Administrator\Desktop> .\ WorkingWithManagedMetadata. ps1

9. As a result, your PowerShell script will set two related lists as shown in the following screenshot:

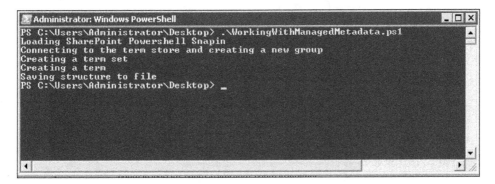

10. Now, switch back to **SharePoint Central Administration** area displaying the taxonomy tree and refresh the page.

11. Take note of additional tree branch added to the taxonomy tree called **Branch Metadata,** as shown in the following screenshot:

12. Switch to the **Desktop** of your server where our script has also created an exported version of the branch we have seen in the taxonomy tree. The exported filename is `BranchMetadata.csv`. It's a comma-separated file describing various part of the tree.

13. Now, in **SharePoint Central Administration** area displaying the taxonomy tree, ensure the top node called **Managed Metadata Service** is selected.

14. In the main area of the page, take note of the link to view the sample format used which we can import the items into the tree, seen below. This is the same format used in our PowerShell script to export our custom tree branch.

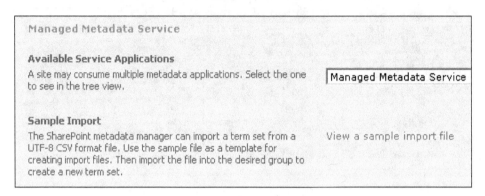

15. In the taxonomy tree, delete the **Branch Departments** node, as shown in the following screenshot:

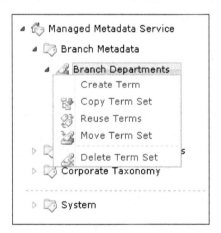

16. Now, click on **Branch Metadata** taxonomy group and select the **Import Term Set** option, as shown in the following screenshot:

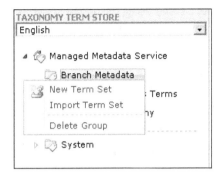

17. In the model window, specify the path to **BranchMetadata.csv** and click **OK** to start importing our term set into the **Branch Metadata** node.

How it works...

We started by defining the script variables. In this recipe, we define the site URL which will be used to establish the service application context: `http://intranet.contoso.com`.

After SharePoint snap-in has loaded, we connect to the taxonomy service application and create an object representing the taxonomy instance. The taxonomy session object was used to connect to the first node of the taxonomy tree of the **Term Store**, called **Managed Metadata Service**, using the following command:

`$TaxonomySession.TermStores["Managed Metadata Service"]`

Since taxonomy tree terms cannot just live off the preceding root element, we need to create a taxonomy group, called **Branch Metadata**, by using the following command:

`$Group=$TermStore.CreateGroup("Branch Metadata")`

The only parameter here is the name of the group.

Before any of the data is persisted in the taxonomy database, we need to call the `Commit` command as follows:

`$TermStore.CommitAll()`

Once we have the group created, we can go ahead and create a term set in that group. The term set will contain actual keywords. In our hierarchy, the term set is called **Branch Departments**, as shown in the following command:

`$TermSet=$Group.CreateTermSet("Branch Departments")`

Just as before, we commit changes to the database by calling the `Commit` command.

 You don't need to call the `Commit` command each time you create an element in the tree. Instead, you can create the entire structure and call one commit which commits the entire set to the database. It's really up to the level of granularity at which you would like to report errors in case creation of some nodes fail.

Next, we provisioned our nodes to the term set, in our case **Marketing**, **HR**, and **Delivery** keywords, as shown in the following command:

```
$MarketingTerm=$TermSet.CreateTerm("Marketing",1033)
```

The first parameter value is the name of the keyword. The second parameter, `1033`, is the language ID of the language we create a managed taxonomy term for. If you're using a site targeted for multiple languages and you stored your corporate taxonomy each with the individual language IDs, your custom and out-of-the-box functionality can retrieve the right keyword for the right language locale.

 For the list of locale IDs, search *MSDN* with the keyword **Locale ID**.

Now that the structure has been created, we export it to file. The file can then be imported into another system, if necessary. The target system needs to have a keyword group created, as the imported file can only be imported on a pre-created group.

 To see the details of the keyword file format, search *MSDN* with the keyword **Managed metadata input file format**.

In essence, the file that has been created will contain the header where the data is added. Once the header is added, we add all of the nodes representing the hierarchy. Also, additional configuration options available in the **Managed Metadata Service** home page in **Central Administration** are also available to be configured using the import file.

Since SharePoint provides a user interface to import the metadata tree export, you do not need to create custom script to import your files on the target system.

Enabling social ratings on lists and libraries

Among other new social features in SharePoint 2010, users are now able to rate items in lists and libraries to help their peers find the most relevant content on the site.

Unless your SharePoint portal is a brand new implementation, the social rating feature will need to be enabled manually on each library before users can work with it.

One alternative is for users to enable the feature manually. However, for this to happen, your users require higher-level access to the site. An alternative is for the administrator to enable the feature in multiple libraries of the SharePoint user interface, and PowerShell can help with that. Additionally, during a disaster recovery of your site, it will be much simpler and faster to restore this configuration rather than leaving it to be manually implemented.

Getting ready

Assuming you have already set up your virtual development environment as described in *Chapter 1, PowerShell Scripting Methods and Creating Custom Commands*, we'll get right into authoring our script. Since we'll be using PowerGUI to author the script, ensure you're logged in with an administrator's permissions on the target Virtual Machine.

How to do it...

Let's see how we can enable the rating functionality on lists and libraries using the following sequence:

1. In your browser, let's switch to our SharePoint test site: `http://intranet.contoso.com/`.

2. On the **Quick launch** menu of your site, under the **Libraries** section, locate **Shared Documents**. This document library was provisioned to the test site as a part of the virtual image and it will contain several of the demo files.

3. Take note of the SharePoint rating feature currently not available in a default view of any item as well as the properties window when you select to view properties of any file.

4. Click **Start | All Programs | PowerGUI | PowerGUI Script Editor**.

5. In the main script editing window of PowerGUI, add the following script:

```
# Defining script variables

$SiteUrl = "http://intranet.contoso.com"
$ListName = "Calendar"

# Loading Microsoft.SharePoint.PowerShell
```

```
$snapin = Get-PSSnapin | Where-Object {$_.Name -eq 'Microsoft.
SharePoint.Powershell'}
if ($snapin -eq $null) {
Write-Host "Loading SharePoint Powershell Snapin"
Add-PSSnapin "Microsoft.SharePoint.Powershell"
}

Write-Host "Loading user profile assemblies"

$SPSite = Get-SPSite | Where-Object {$_.Url -eq $SiteUrl}
  if($SPSite -ne $null)
  {
      $AverageRatingId =
[Guid]("5a14d1ab-1513-48c7-97b3-657a5ba6c742")
      $RatingCountId =
[Guid]("b1996002-9167-45e5-a4df-b2c41c6723c7")
      $list = $SPSite.RootWeb.Lists[$ListName]

    $AverageField = $list.ParentWeb.AvailableFields[$AverageRatingI
d]
      if ($list.Fields.ContainsField($AverageField.StaticName) -ne
$null)
      {
        $list.Fields.AddFieldAsXml($AverageField.SchemaXml, $true,
[Microsoft.SharePoint.SPAddFieldOptions]::AddFieldToDefaultView)
      }
    $RatingCountField = $list.ParentWeb.
AvailableFields[$RatingCountId]
    if ($list.Fields.ContainsField($RatingCountField.StaticName)
-ne $null)
    {
     $list.Fields.AddFieldAsXml($RatingCountField.SchemaXml, $true,
[Microsoft.SharePoint.SPAddFieldOptions]::AddFieldToDefaultView)
    }

    $list.Update();

  Write-Host "Rating enabled on the list"
  }
```

6. Click **File | Save** to save the script to your development machine's desktop. Set the file name of the script to EnableSocialRating.ps1.

7. Open the PowerShell console window and call `EnableSocialRating.ps1` using the following command:

```
PS C:\Users\Administrator\Desktop> .\ EnableSocialRating.ps1
```

8. As a result, your PowerShell script will execute with results as shown in the following screenshot:

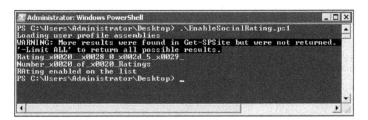

9. Now, again, in your browser, let's switch back to our SharePoint test site : `http://intranet.contoso.com/`.

10. On the **Quick launch** menu of your site, under the **Libraries** section, locate **Shared Documents**. This document library was provisioned to the test site as a part of the virtual image and it will contain several of the demo files.

11. Take note of the SharePoint rating feature available in a default view for the list, as shown in the following screenshot:

	Type	Name	Rating (0-5)	Number of Ratings
☐		Activity_Duration_Report_2011-05-05T214823	☆☆☆☆☆	
		Approval - SharePoint 2010	☆☆☆☆☆	
		Contoso's Most Resilient Gear	☆☆☆☆☆	
		Gears Sales History	☆☆☆☆☆	
		Longest-Lasting Gear	☆☆☆☆☆	
		M300 Product Information	☆☆☆☆☆	
		New Document for Sprockets	☆☆☆☆☆	
		New Product Archive	☆☆☆☆☆	
		New Product Archive	☆☆☆☆☆	
		Project budget workbook	☆☆☆☆☆	

✚ Add document

12. Additionally, the rating control and rating count field are available when item properties are viewed for an individual item, as shown in the following screenshot:

How it works...

As in most cases, we started our script with configuring the script variables, such as the site URL where our library is located, as well as the title of the library for which we need to enable SharePoint rating feature:

```
$SiteUrl = "http://intranet.contoso.com"
$ListName = "Shared Documents"
```

We then load the SharePoint snap-in and connect to the site:

```
Add-PSSnapin "Microsoft.SharePoint.Powershell"
```

Next, we create two variables which will hold the IDs of two columns representing an **Average Rating** and **Rating Count** respectively, for each item in the library:

```
$AverageRatingId = [Guid]("5a14d1ab-1513-48c7-97b3-657a5ba6c742")
$RatingCountId = [Guid]("b1996002-9167-45e5-a4df-b2c41c6723c7")
```

The IDs referenced are actually SharePoint columns which are already installed in SharePoint system instance. Those fields, when added to the list, drive the rating functionality for the library.

We connect to our document library:

```
$list = $SPSite.RootWeb.Lists[$ListName]
```

Next, we create actual field objects representing an **Average Rating** field, the objects are created using the following command below where we pass already known column IDs:

```
$AverageField = $list.ParentWeb.AvailableFields[$AverageRatingId]
```

Before adding those fields to the list, we need to ensure they are not already provisioned to the list. This is achieved by evaluating the following statement:

```
$list.Fields.ContainsField($AverageField.StaticName) -ne $null
```

If the field has not been added to the list, yet we add it using the following command:

```
$list.Fields.AddFieldAsXml($AverageField.SchemaXml, $true, [Microsoft.
SharePoint.SPAddFieldOptions]::AddFieldToDefaultView)
```

The `AddFieldAsXml` method creates a field based on the specified schema, which in our case is the schema of the field we have already gotten a hold of. The next parameter specifies if the field will be added to the default view of the list. This option, in most cases, is set to `true` because most users want to see the rating of items in the list as they look at the list. Otherwise, to see the rating for each item, your users would have had to call the item view or edit form. Finally, the last parameter specifies a list of options that can be applied when a new field is added to a list.

 For more information on the list of available options search *MSDN* with the keyword **SPAddFieldOptions**.

The same is done for the **Rating Count** field after which we update the entire list.

As a result, apart from seeing the rating columns added to the default view, you will also be able to see the rating setting enabled for the list, as shown in the following screenshot:

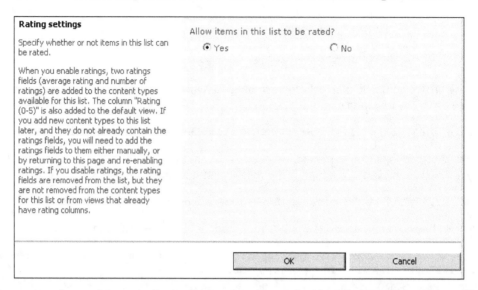

Bulk tagging content and deleting tags in SharePoint

SharePoint has a variety of features that allow users to find content fast. One of the new features in SharePoint 2010 is the ability to tag content which improves its visibility in search results and libraries.

When deciding to add this feature in an incremental upgrade scenario, you might want to pre-populate content on your site with the appropriate tags reflecting a type of content. For example, if you'd like to tag all of the content on the product site as the product name, you will improve the visibility and relevancy of search results returned to users who look for a product category.

In this recipe, we'll take a look at how you can use PowerShell to bulk tag your content based on the defined condition. This task will help you with the deployment of new tagging functionality without consuming significant amounts of time.

Getting ready

Assuming you have already set up your virtual development environment as described in *Chapter 1, PowerShell Scripting Methods and Creating Custom Commands*, we'll get right into authoring our script. We'll also assume you had a chance to learn about metadata taxonomy as described in *the Creating, importing, and exporting managed metadata taxonomy terms* recipe. We'll be using PowerGUI to author the script, so ensure you're logged in with administrator's permissions on the target Virtual Machine.

How to do it...

The following sequence demonstrates how SharePoint content can be tagged using PowerShell:

1. In your browser, let's switch to our SharePoint test site : `http://intranet.contoso.com/`.

2. On the **Quick launch** menu of your site, under the **Libraries** section, locate the library titled **Shared Documents**. This will already contain a set of demo documents to which you can add a few files.

3. Select one of the items and see the **Tags & Notes** ribbon button activate under **Tags and Notes** ribbon group, as shown in the following screenshot:

4. Click **Start | All Programs | PowerGUI | PowerGUI Script Editor**.

5. In the main script editing window of PowerGUI, add the following script:

```
# Defining script variables

$SiteUrl = "http://intranet.contoso.com"
$ListName = "Shared Documents"

# Loading Microsoft.SharePoint.PowerShell
$snapin = Get-PSSnapin | Where-Object {$_.Name -eq 'Microsoft.
SharePoint.Powershell'}
if ($snapin -eq $null) {
Write-Host "Loading SharePoint Powershell Snapin"
Add-PSSnapin "Microsoft.SharePoint.Powershell"
}

Write-Host "Loading user profile assemblies"
[System.Reflection.Assembly]::LoadWithPartialName("Microsoft.
Office.Server")
[System.Reflection.Assembly]::LoadWithPartialName("Microsoft.
Office.Server.UserProfiles")

$SPSite = Get-SPSite | Where-Object {$_.Url -eq $SiteUrl}
   if($SPSite -ne $null)
   {
     Write-Host "Loading current server context"
     $ServerContext = [Microsoft.SharePoint.SPServiceContext]::
GetContext($SPSite)

   Write-Host "Connecting to Social Tag Manager"
   $SocialTagManager = New-Object Microsoft.Office.Server.
SocialData.SocialTagManager($ServerContext)

   Write-Host "Retrieving a tag term from metadata store"
   $TaxonomySession=Get-SPTaxonomySession -Site $SiteUrl
   $TermStore=$TaxonomySession.TermStores["Managed Metadata
Service"]
   $TagTerm = $TermStore.Groups["Branch Metadata"].TermSets["Branch
Departments"].Terms["Marketing"]

   $RootWeb = $SPSite.RootWeb
   $SPList = $RootWeb.Lists[$ListName]
   foreach ($SPListItem in $SPList.Items)
     {
     $FileUrl = $RootWeb.Url +"/"+ $SPListItem.File.Url
```

```
        $Tagged = $SocialTagManager.AddTag($FileUrl, $TagTerm)
        Write-Host "Tagged:" $SPListItem.Name -foregroundcolor Green
    }

  Write-Host "Content tagging completed"
    }
```

6. Click **File | Save** to save the script to your development machine's desktop. Set the filename of the script to TagContent.ps1.

7. Open the PowerShell console window and call TagContent.ps1 using the following command:

   PS C:\Users\Administrator\Desktop> .\ TagContent.ps1

8. As a result, your PowerShell script will execute with results as shown in the following screenshot:

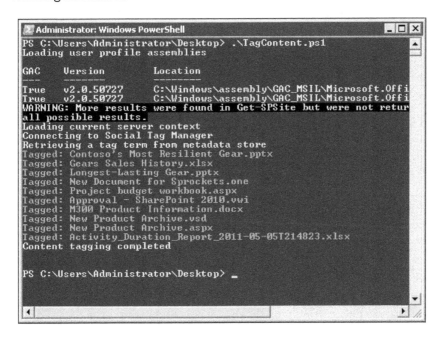

9. Now, in your browser, let's switch to our SharePoint test site : http://intranet. contoso.com/.

10. On the **Quick launch** menu of your site, open **Shared Documents** library, select one of the items and click **Tags & Notes** button on the ribbon, the window you'll see will look similar to the following one:

11. Go through a few other items in **Tags & Notes** and take note of each of those items in **Shared Documents** have a **Marketing** tag on them.

How it works...

In this recipe, we've looked at how you can tag content in a document library to improve the relevancy of that content in search results and other content features in SharePoint 2010.

We start by defining our variables used in the script, the URL of the site, and the title of the library where we tagged all of the items:

```
$SiteUrl = "http://intranet.contoso.com"
$ListName = "Shared Documents"
```

Once the SharePoint snap-in has been loaded to the environment, we reference two assemblies which participate in content tagging. Those assemblies are actually User Profile assemblies, and the following command will load them:

```
[System.Reflection.Assembly]::LoadWithPartialName("Microsoft.Office.
Server")
[System.Reflection.Assembly]::LoadWithPartialName("Microsoft.Office.
Server.UserProfiles")
```

Next, we connect to the URL of the site where our library is defined. To be able to use the social tagging features, we need to establish the **Server Context** to which we are going to connect, as shown in the following command:

```
$ServerContext = [Microsoft.SharePoint.SPServiceContext]::
GetContext($SPSite)
```

Next, we create an instance of the **Social Tag Manager**. This is the object instance which has access to all of the properties and functionality related to social tagging:

```
$SocialTagManager = New-Object Microsoft.Office.Server.SocialData.Soci
alTagManager($ServerContext)
```

Now that we have a **Social Tag Manager**, we need one last piece before we can actually start tagging content: a term to tag the content with.

 We've learned all about terms and how to provision them in the *Creating, importing, and exporting managed metadata taxonomy terms* recipe.

The term will represent the keyword which the content, such as a document in a library, will be tagged with. We connect to the term store, as shown in the following code:

```
$TaxonomySession=Get-SPTaxonomySession -Site $SiteUrl
```

We then get a hold of the root element in the term store:

```
$TermStore=$TaxonomySession.TermStores["Managed Metadata Service"]
```

Lastly, we get a hold of the actual term object in the term store, which is the same term we created in the *Creating, importing, and exporting managed metadata taxonomy terms* recipe:

```
$TagTerm = $TermStore.Groups["Branch Metadata"].TermSets["Branch
Departments"].Terms["Marketing"]
```

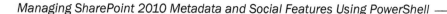
Now that we have all of the components required to tag the content, we connect to the document library on the root web of our site and loop through the item list. In your specific case, you would apply your own logic as to how you want to tag items and whether those items are on the same site or if you need to iterate through sites. The source code example for this chapter will give you general technical implementation.

Once the right content is found, we use the `AddTag` method of the **Social Tag Manager** object instance to tag the URL with the term we loaded before, as shown in the following command:

```
$Tagged = $SocialTagManager.AddTag($FileUrl, $TagTerm)
```

Finally, we display the message that the specified content has been tagged. Additional information is available in the resulting `Tagged` variable if you need it in your scenario.

See also

The *Creating, importing, and exporting managed metadata taxonomy terms* recipe in this chapter.

6
Managing SharePoint Search and FAST Search with PowerShell

In this chapter, we will cover:

- ▶ Configuring search query suggestions in your search center
- ▶ Configuring search best bets
- ▶ Configuring visual best bets
- ▶ Configuring search audience targeting
- ▶ Configuring search web parts with PowerShell

Introduction

SharePoint FAST Search is all about helping users in your organization get to relevant content fast. To facilitate this, SharePoint FAST Search comes with a variety of key features, many of which we will be discussing in detail in this chapter.

We'll start with the search suggestions feature which allows users to select the most common search suggestions while trying to refine their search query. In this chapter, we'll take a look at what's involved in configuring search suggestions and how to pre-populate the list of suggestions for your users when your new search has only just been launched.

Best bets allow users to visually separate regular search results from the results which the search engine considers to be exactly what the user is searching for. For example, your new employees may be looking for a collection of company policies and type respective keywords which search for the type of policy. In this chapter, we'll take a look at how you can configure search to direct your users to the source where they can find the most up-to-date and relevant set of policies, rather than let them come to the same source after performing a series of separate searches.

Similar to the best bets, **visual best bets** will help your users find the most relevant source of information they are looking for by using visual cues representing a best bet. We'll take a look at exactly what's involved in provisioning visual best bets to various environments in your site.

Your users may have various opinions about the performance of your search depending on their role and the patters in which they search for content. In the recipe of this chapter, we'll take a look at how you can target different types of content to different type of users by using the **audience targeting** feature of FAST Search for SharePoint.

Finally, all of the search configurations and features will come down to a user interface your users will work with while executing their search queries. In this chapter, we'll take a look at exactly what's involved in making changes to your search results pages to fit your organization's needs.

Configuring search query suggestions in your search center

Many popular Internet search engines allow you to see search queries many other users have searched for as you start typing your own query. This is a feature your users are already familiar with, so why not enable the same functionality for your organization's intranet search? In this recipe, we'll take a look at how you can configure search suggestions to populate new search queries based on what your users are searching for.

We'll also take a look at how you can pre-populate an initial list of search suggestions. This is particularly handy when you roll out a new search experience to an existing intranet and would like to populate the same search suggestions for users to get started with. Since there is no out-of-the-box SharePoint user interface allowing you to pre-populate your suggested queries at this time, it makes PowerShell a perfect candidate for the job.

Getting ready

We'll assume you are running your environment with SharePoint Search configured and working. This is the case for the environment you downloaded from the Microsoft Download Center as described in *Chapter 1, PowerShell Scripting Methods and Creating Custom Commands*. Let's get right into authoring our script PowerShell script using PowerGUI, so ensure you're logged in with an administrator's permissions on the target Virtual Machine.

How to do it...

Let's take a look at how you can configure search suggestions in our search center using the following sequence:

1. Navigate to the root of your SharePoint test site: `http://intranet.contoso.com`.

2. Click **Search** on the top navigation menu to be taken to the search site.

3. In the keyword textbox, type **software** and observe no search suggestions appearing as you type your keyword, as shown in the following screenshot:

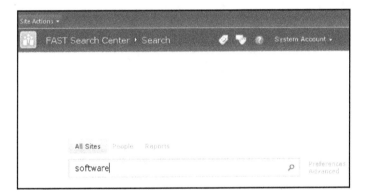

4. Click **Start** | **All Programs** | **PowerGUI** | **PowerGUI Script Editor**.

5. In the main script editing window of PowerGUI, add the following script:

```
# Defining script variables

$SearchApplication = "FastQuery"
$Keyword1 = "Software licences"
$Keyword2 = "Software usage policy"
$Keyword3 = "Software support"

# Loading Microsoft.SharePoint.PowerShell
$snapin = Get-PSSnapin | Where-Object {$_.Name -eq 'Microsoft.SharePoint.Powershell'}
```

```
if ($snapin -eq $null) {
Write-Host "Loading SharePoint Powershell Snapin"
Add-PSSnapin "Microsoft.SharePoint.Powershell"
}

Write-Host "Setting new keyword suggestions"
New-SPEnterpriseSearchLanguageResourcePhrase -Language en-us -Type
QuerySuggestionAlwaysSuggest -SearchApplication $SearchApplication
-Name $Keyword1
New-SPEnterpriseSearchLanguageResourcePhrase -Language en-us -Type
QuerySuggestionAlwaysSuggest -SearchApplication $SearchApplication
-Name $Keyword2
New-SPEnterpriseSearchLanguageResourcePhrase -Language en-us -Type
QuerySuggestionAlwaysSuggest -SearchApplication $SearchApplication
-Name $Keyword3

Write-Host "Existing keywords:"
$keywords = Get-SPEnterpriseSearchLanguageResourcePhrase -Language
en-us -Type QuerySuggestionAlwaysSuggest -SearchApplication
$SearchApplication
$keywords | Select Phrase

Write-Host "Pushing down query suggestions"
Get-SPTimerJob "Prepare query suggestions" | Start-SPTimerJob

$KeywordToDelete = $keywords | Where-Object {$_.Phrase -like
"*software lic*"}

Write-Host "Deleting keyword suggestion"
Remove-SPEnterpriseSearchLanguageResourcePhrase -Language
en-us -Type QuerySuggestionBlockList -SearchApplication
$SearchApplication -Identity $KeywordToDelete

Write-Host "Keyword suggestions configured"
```

6. Click **File | Save** to save the script to your development machine's desktop. Set the filename of the script to SetSearchSuggestions.ps1.

7. Open the PowerShell console window and call SetSearchSuggestions.ps1 using the following command:

   PS C:\Users\Administrator\Desktop> .\ SetSearchSuggestions.ps1

8. As a result, your PowerShell script will create a site structure as shown in the following screenshot:

9. Now, let's switch to our **SharePoint FAST Search Site:**
   http://intranet.contoso.com/search.

10. In the **Keyword** textbox, type **software** and take note of the search suggestions appearing as you type, as shown in the following screenshot:

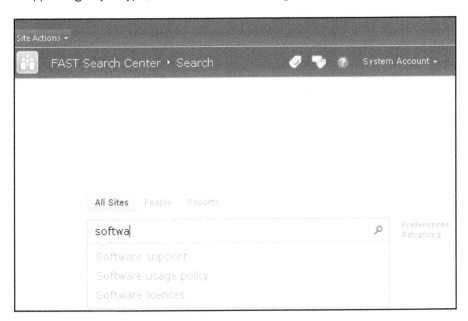

How it works...

First, we defined the script variables used. In this recipe, the variables include a Search application name, `Fast Query,` and three keywords we have added to the list of search suggestions, as three variables `$Keyword1`, `$Keyword2`, and `$Keyword3`.

Once a PowerShell snap-in has been loaded, we provision all of our search query suggestions to the site with the following command:

```
New-SPEnterpriseSearchLanguageResourcePhrase -Language en-us -Type
QuerySuggestionAlwaysSuggest -SearchApplication $SearchApplication -Name
$Keyword1
```

A few of the required parameters for `New-SPEnterpriseSearchLanguageResourcePhra se` include:

▶ `Name` is the actual term to be added to query suggestions.

▶ `Language` specifies the locale for which the keyword is added. This option makes is possible to add same keyword for various locales in a multilingual environment.

▶ `SearchApplication` is the search application to which the keywords are going to be mapped.

▶ `Type` is the parameter which actually specifies that the keyword we're adding is for the keyword suggestion list.

 For the list of other available options for the type parameter for the preceding command, search *MSDN* with the keyword: **New-SPEnterpriseSearchLanguageResourcePhrase**.

The remaining attributes are optional.

Next, we retrieved the list of existing keywords in our suggestion list collection using the following command:

```
Get-SPEnterpriseSearchLanguageResourcePhrase -Language en-us -Type
QuerySuggestionAlwaysSuggest -SearchApplication $SearchApplication
```

The parameter list of the `Get-SPEnterpriseSearchLanguageResourcePhrase` command includes all of the parameters you're familiar with from the CmdLet we used to insert keywords.

By default, when new queries are added to the list, the SharePoint 2010 timer job is responsible for updating those queries on the search sites that use them and runs on a predefined schedule. This means that if you want to see results right away, you will need to run a timer job to synchronize search queries on demand.

To run a timer job synchronizing the suggestion keywords on demand, we run the following command:

```
Get-SPTimerJob "Prepare query suggestions" | Start-SPTimerJob
```

Finally, to demonstrate how you can remove keywords from the suggested keyword list, we run the following command:

```
$KeywordToDelete = $keywords | Where-Object {$_.Phrase -like "*software lic*"}
```

Here, we enumerate all of the keywords registered in the system based on the specified search criteria. Once the keyword has been found, we execute the following command to remove the keyword from the list of suggested keywords:

```
Remove-SPEnterpriseSearchLanguageResourcePhrase -Language en-us -Type
QuerySuggestionBlockList -SearchApplication $SearchApplication -Identity
$KeywordToDelete
```

As before, the parameter list for this command is similar to `New-SPEnterpriseSearch LanguageResourcePhrase,` with the exception of the keyword we need to delete rather than add.

Configuring search best bets

SharePoint search best bets is a feature that has been available in earlier versions of SharePoint. Best bets are defined based on simple rules where the administrator can choose which search results should be returned based on the search query your users are searching for. Many organizations use best bets to clearly define an authoritative source for the most typical type of content users are searching for. If you define key audiences in your organization and the type of content they would most likely search for, you can point them to that content source using a best bet list. This feature can be used in conjunction with SharePoint search analytics to determine the most common types of search queries that are being performed by your users. This way, you're not starting from square one when defining your best bets.

As a result of this exercise, many organizations come up with an extensive list of best bets which can be cumbersome to add using the SharePoint user interface.

Let's take a look at what's involved in provisioning best bets using PowerShell, which can provision your best bets in a simple transaction with little to no downtime.

Getting ready

We'll assume you are running your environment with SharePoint Search configured and working. This is the case for the environment you downloaded from the Microsoft Download Center as described in *Chapter 1, PowerShell Scripting Methods and Creating Custom Commands*. Let's get right into authoring our script PowerShell script using PowerGUI, so ensure you're logged in with an administrator's permissions on the target Virtual Machine.

How to do it...

Using the following sequence, we'll provision best bet terms using our PowerShell script.

1. Click **Start** | **All Programs** | **PowerGUI** | **PowerGUI Script Editor**.

2. In the main script editing window of PowerGUI, add the following script:

```
# Defining script variables
[xml]$BestBetsFile = get-content BestBets.xml
$SiteUrl = "http://intranet.contoso.com"

# Loading Microsoft.SharePoint.PowerShell
$snapin = Get-PSSnapin | Where-Object {$_.Name -eq 'Microsoft.
SharePoint.Powershell'}
if ($snapin -eq $null) {
Write-Host "Loading SharePoint Powershell Snapin"
Add-PSSnapin "Microsoft.SharePoint.Powershell"
}

# Loading Microsoft.FASTSearch.PowerShell
$snapin = Get-PSSnapin | Where-Object {$_.Name -eq 'Microsoft.
FASTSearch.PowerShell'}
if ($snapin -eq $null) {
Write-Host "Loading FAST Search Powershell Snapin"
Add-PSSnapin "Microsoft.FASTSearch.PowerShell"
}

   Write-Host "Retrieving Search Settings Group"
   $FASTSearchSettingGroup = Get-FASTSearchSearchSettingGroup

   Write-Host "Provisioning Best Bets with:"
   $BestBets = $BestBetsFile.BestBets
     if($BestBets.BestBet.Length -gt 0)
     {
       foreach ($BestBet in $BestBets.BestBet)
       {
```

```
     Write-Host "Keyword:" $BestBet.Keyword
     $keyword = $FASTSearchSettingGroup.Keywords.
GetKeyword($BestBet.Keyword)
     if($keyword -eq $null)
       {
       $keyword = $FASTSearchSettingGroup.Keywords.
AddKeyword($BestBet.Keyword)
        $BestBetUrl = [Uri]($BestBet.Url)
        $bestBetInstance = $keyword.AddBestBet($BestBet.Title,
$BestBet.Description, $BestBetUrl)
       }
     Write-Host "Title:" $BestBet.Title
     Write-Host "Description:" $BestBet.Description
     Write-Host "Url:" $BestBet.Url
     Write-Host "---"
       }
     }
```

3. Click **File | Save** to save the script to your development machine's desktop. Set the filename of the script to `ProvisionBestBets.ps1`.

4. Click **File | New** in the PowerGUI user interface and add the following XML:

```xml
<?xml version="1.0" encoding="utf-8" ?>
<BestBets>
  <BestBet>
    <Keyword>legal</Keyword>
    <Title>Legal Department Home</Title>
    <Description>Legal Department Home</Description>
    <Url>http://legal.contoso.com</Url>
  </BestBet>
<BestBet>
    <Keyword>HR</Keyword>
    <Title>HR Department Home</Title>
    <Description>HR Department Home</Description>
    <Url>http://hrweb.contoso.com</Url>
  </BestBet>
<BestBet>
    <Keyword>finance</Keyword>
    <Title>Finance Department Home</Title>
    <Description>Finance Department Home</Description>
    <Url>http://finweb.contoso.com</Url>
  </BestBet>
</BestBets>
```

5. Click **File** | **Save** to save the XML file to your development machine's desktop. Set the filename of the file to `BestBets.xml`.

6. Open the PowerShell console window and call `ProvisionBestBets.ps1` using the following command:

   PS C:\Users\Administrator\Desktop> .\ ProvisionBestBets.ps1

7. As a result, your PowerShell script will create a list with results as shown in the following screenshot:

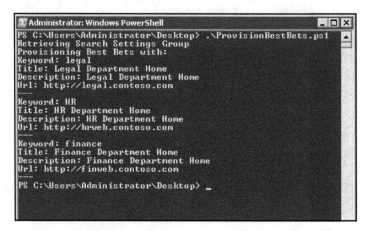

8. Now, let's switch to our **SharePoint FAST Search Site:** `http://intranet. contoso.com/search`.

9. In the keyword section, enter **hr** to get a result set similar to the one shown in the following screenshot:

How it works...

As in any of our previous recipes, we started by defining the script variables. In this recipe, we defined the filename in the same directory as our script, which will hold the information about our best bets:

```
[xml]$BestBetsFile = get-content BestBets.xml
```

Once a PowerShell snap-in has been loaded, we retrieve FAST for SharePoint Search Setting group using the following command:

$FASTSearchSettingGroup = Get-FASTSearchSearchSettingGroup

Now that our XML structure representing best bets has been loaded into memory, we can traverse the XML and build best bets based on the information given to us. First, we retrieve the root element of the XML file:

```
$BestBets = $BestBetsFile.BestBets
```

Next, for each best bet definition, we extract the details to provision the keyword:

```
foreach ($BestBet in $BestBets.BestBet) { ... }
```

First, we verified if the keyword has been already created, which might be true:

```
$keyword = $FASTSearchSettingGroup.Keywords.GetKeyword($BestBet.
Keyword)
```

The only parameter here is the keyword name. If the keyword does not exist, we create it as shown in the following code:

```
$keyword = $FASTSearchSettingGroup.Keywords.AddKeyword($BestBet.
Keyword)
```

Having the keyword created, we can now provision a best bet using the following command:

**$bestBetInstance = $keyword.AddBestBet($BestBet.Title, $BestBet.
Description, $BestBetUrl)**

In the preceding code, we accept parameters such as the title of the best bet, the description which is going to be displayed to the user along with the title, and finally, the best bet URL, which is the target link of the best bet location.

By creating a best bet for the keyword, your users will be able to see an authoritative result above all of the other results where which best matches the user's search term.

SharePoint 2010 has a user interface where you can see the list of keywords and their best bets, here is how to find those:

1. While at the root of your SharePoint site: `http://intranet.contoso.com`, click **Site Actions** | **Site Settings**.
2. From **Site Collection Administration** group, click **FAST Search keywords**.

You will be able to see the collection of keywords and access their associated best bets, if any, using a context menu, as shown in the following screenshot:

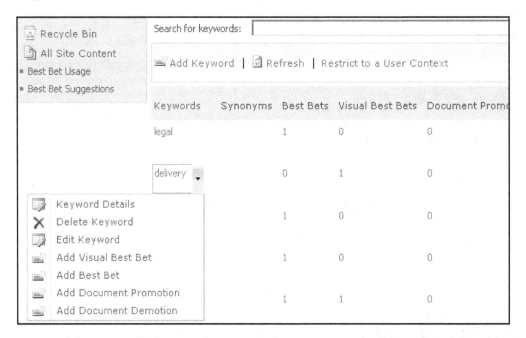

Configuring visual best bets

Just as we have seen in the previous recipe, you can create a visual best bet to give your users a visual cue for more visual types of best bets.

A use case for using visual best bets would be a SharePoint site where users search for product keywords, and rather than receiving a textual best bet, they receive a visual version of a best bet to help them identify whether they have gotten the right search best bet.

Just as in the scenario with textual best bets, in your organization you might face a challenge with too many best bets needed to be added fast either initially or an on-going basis.

Let's take a look at how you can speed up the process of provisioning new visual best bets using PowerShell.

Getting ready

We'll assume you are running your environment with SharePoint Search configured and working. This is the case for the environment you downloaded from the Microsoft Download Center as described in *Chapter 1, PowerShell Scripting Methods and Creating Custom PowerShell Commands*.

We'll also assume you have tried working with textual best bets as previously described in this chapter. Let's get right into authoring our script PowerShell script using PowerGUI, so ensure you're logged in with an administrator's permissions on the target Virtual Machine.

How to do it...

The following steps will cover almost all of the configurations on a SharePoint best bet:

1. Click **Start | All Programs | PowerGUI | PowerGUI Script Editor**.

2. In the main script editing window of PowerGUI, add the following script:

```
# Defining script variables
[xml]$BestBetsFile = get-content VisualBestBets.xml


# Loading Microsoft.SharePoint.PowerShell
$snapin = Get-PSSnapin | Where-Object {$_.Name -eq 'Microsoft.
SharePoint.Powershell'}
if ($snapin -eq $null) {
Write-Host "Loading SharePoint Powershell Snapin"
Add-PSSnapin "Microsoft.SharePoint.Powershell"
}


# Loading Microsoft.FASTSearch.PowerShell
$snapin = Get-PSSnapin | Where-Object {$_.Name -eq 'Microsoft.
FASTSearch.PowerShell'}
if ($snapin -eq $null) {
Write-Host "Loading FAST Search Powershell Snapin"
Add-PSSnapin "Microsoft.FASTSearch.PowerShell"
}

  Write-Host "Retrieving Search Settings Group"
  $FASTSearchSettingGroup = Get-FASTSearchSearchSettingGroup

 Write-Host "Provisioning Best Bets with:"
 $BestBets = $BestBetsFile.BestBets
 foreach ($BestBet in $BestBets.BestBet)
 {
 Write-Host "Keyword:" $BestBet.Keyword
```

```
$keyword = $FASTSearchSettingGroup.Keywords.GetKeyword($BestBet.
Keyword)
if($keyword -eq $null)
{
   $keyword = $FASTSearchSettingGroup.Keywords.
AddKeyword($BestBet.Keyword)
}
$BestBetUrl = [Uri]($BestBet.Url)
$VisualBestBet = $keyword.AddFeaturedContent($BestBet.Title)
$VisualBestBet.Uri = $BestBetUrl
Write-Host "Title:" $BestBet.Title
Write-Host "Url:" $BestBet.Url
Write-Host "---"
}
```

3. Click **File | Save** to save the script to your development machine's desktop. Set the filename of the script to `ProvisionVisualBestBets.ps1`.

4. Click **File | New** in the PowerGUI user interface and add the following XML:

```xml
<?xml version="1.0" encoding="utf-8" ?>
<BestBets>
  <BestBet>
    <Keyword>delivery</Keyword>
    <Title>Delivery Department Home</Title> <Url>http://intranet.
contoso.com/_layouts/images/homepageSamplePhoto.jpg</Url>
  </BestBet>
</BestBets>
```

5. Click **File | Save** to save the XML file to your development machine's desktop. Set the filename of the file to `VisualBestBets.xml`.

6. Open the PowerShell console window and call `ProvisionVisualBestBets.ps1` using the following command:

   PS C:\Users\Administrator\Desktop> .\ ProvisionVisualBestBets.ps1

7. As a result, your PowerShell script will execute and return results as shown in the following screenshot:

8. Now, let's switch to our **SharePoint FAST Search Site**: `http://intranet.contoso.com/search`.

9. In the keyword section, enter **Delivery** to get the result set similar to the one in the following screenshot:

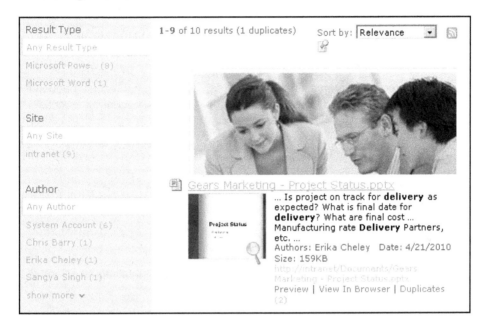

How it works...

We started by defining the script variables. In this recipe, we defined the filename in the same directory as our script. This XML file will hold the information about our best bets:

```
[xml]$BestBetsFile = get-content VisualBestBets.xml
```

We then load PowerShell SharePoint snap-in as well as specific snap-in facilitating work with FAST Search. We used the following commands to load both snap-ins:

```
Add-PSSnapin "Microsoft.SharePoint.Powershell"
Add-PSSnapin "Microsoft.FASTSearch.PowerShell"
```

Now that our snap-ins are loaded, we can call the command which will load the FAST settings into an instance of an object that we'll be interacting with further. We used the following command to load FAST Search settings group:

```
$FASTSearchSettingGroup = Get-FASTSearchSearchSettingGroup
```

An optional parameter for this command accepts the specific group ID you would like to load. In our case, we accepted the default version of the command with no parameters.

We continue with getting a hold of the elements in our XML file to process them:

```
$BestBets = $BestBetsFile.BestBets
```

Next, for each best bet definition, we extract the details to provision the keyword:

```
foreach ($BestBet in $BestBets.BestBet) { ... }
```

First, we verified if the keyword has already been created. This scenario could happen if we have an existing keyword and would like to add the visual best bet only. In our case, we provisioned the keyword if it hasn't been created yet:

```
$keyword = $FASTSearchSettingGroup.Keywords.GetKeyword($BestBet.
Keyword)
```

The only preceding parameter is the keyword name. The following command created a keyword which has not been created yet:

```
$keyword = $FASTSearchSettingGroup.Keywords.AddKeyword($BestBet.
Keyword)
```

Having the keyword created, we can now provision a visual best bet using the following command:

$VisualBestBet = $keyword.AddFeaturedContent($BestBet.Title)

In the preceding line, we accept parameters such as the title of the visual best bet and URL. The URL in this case represents a path to an image which all users have access to. The following command binds a URL to a visual best bet:

$VisualBestBet.Uri = $BestBetUrl

In addition to verifying the functionality by searching for the keyword on the FAST Search site, you can use SharePoint administrative user interface using the following steps:

1. While at the root of your SharePoint site: `http://intranet.contoso.com`, click **Site Actions | Site Settings**.

2. From the **Site Collection Administration** group, click **FAST Search keywords**.

3. You will be able to see the collection of keywords and access their associated visual best bets, if any, by clicking the **Keyword Details** context menu option, as shown in the following screenshot:

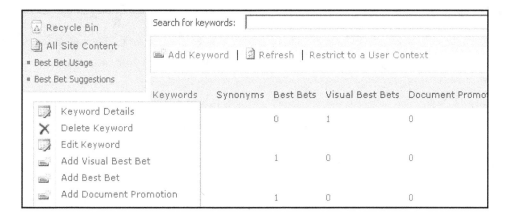

This is where you can also change or delete the visual best bet information, as shown in the following screenshot:

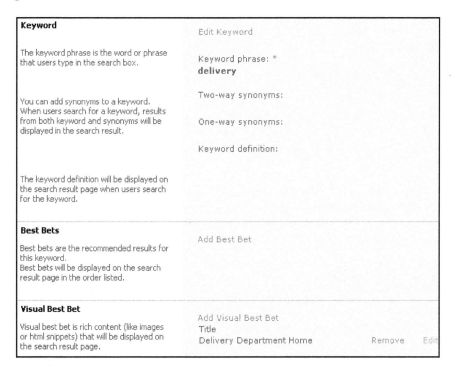

See also

The *Configuring search best bets* recipe in this chapter.

Configuring search audience targeting

When it comes to search, some users may be very pleased with how fast they can find relevant content, while some may have much more difficulty.

In FAST Search for SharePoint, you have the ability to construct an audience profile and target search results to different groups of audiences depending on who they are.

In the *Bulk provisioning data into user profile properties* recipe in *Chapter 5, Managing SharePoint 2010 Metadata and Social Features using PowerShell*, we looked at how you can use out-of-the-box and create custom user profile properties containing various information about the user. In this recipe, we will take a look at how you can construct a custom profile which will use user profile properties to make up an audience. Using this audience, we can then target different content than other audiences will receive.

Currently, there is no alternative out-of-the-box SharePoint user interface which allows administrators to create search audience profiles based on user profile properties. This makes PowerShell a perfect candidate to perform such tasks automatically without requiring significant development.

Getting ready

We'll assume you are running your environment with SharePoint Search configured and working. This is the case for the environment you downloaded from the Microsoft Download Center as described in *Chapter 1, PowerShell Scripting Methods and Creating Custom Commands*.

We'll also assume you are familiar with SharePoint user profile properties as described in *Chapter 5, Managing SharePoint 2010 Metadata and Social Features using PowerShell*. Let's get right into authoring our script PowerShell script using PowerGUI, so ensure you're logged in with an administrator's permissions on the target Virtual Machine.

How to do it...

The following sequence demonstrates what's involved in targeting your search results to a particular audience by leveraging FAST Search features:

1. Click **Start | All Programs | PowerGUI | PowerGUI Script Editor**.

2. In the main script editing window of PowerGUI, add the following script:

```
# Defining script variables
$SiteUrl = "http://intranet.contoso.com"
$DeliveryContext = "Delivery"

# Loading Microsoft.SharePoint.PowerShell
```

```powershell
$snapin = Get-PSSnapin | Where-Object {$_.Name -eq 'Microsoft.
SharePoint.Powershell'}
if ($snapin -eq $null) {
Write-Host "Loading SharePoint Powershell Snapin"
Add-PSSnapin "Microsoft.SharePoint.Powershell"
}

# Loading Microsoft.FASTSearch.PowerShell
$snapin = Get-PSSnapin | Where-Object {$_.Name -eq 'Microsoft.
FASTSearch.PowerShell'}
if ($snapin -eq $null) {
Write-Host "Loading FAST Search Powershell Snapin"
Add-PSSnapin "Microsoft.FASTSearch.PowerShell"
}
  Write-Host "Retrieving existing context properties"
  $contextProps = Get-SPEnterpriseSearchExtendedQueryProperty
-SearchApplication "FASTQuery" -Identity
"FASTSearchContextProperties"

  Write-Host "Existing content properties"
  Write-Host $contextProps.Value

  Write-Host "Setting context properties"
  Set-SPEnterpriseSearchExtendedQueryProperty -SearchApplication
"FASTQuery" -Identity "FASTSearchContextProperties" -Value
"Department"

  $searchSettingGroup = Get-FASTSearchSearchSettingGroup

  Write-Host "Creating a new context"
  $context = $searchSettingGroup.Contexts.AddContext($DeliveryCont
ext)

  Write-Host "Retrieving keyword"
  $keyword = $searchSettingGroup.Keywords.GetKeyword("delivery")
  $visualBestBet = $keyword.FeaturedContent.GetFeaturedContent("De
livery Department Home")

  Write-Host "Adding context to a keyword"
  $visualBestBet.Contexts.AddContext($DeliveryContext)

  Write-Host "Context properties updated"
```

3. Click **File | Save** to save the script to your development machine's desktop. Set the filename of the script to `CreateUserContext.ps1`.

4. Open the PowerShell console window and call `CreateUserContext.ps1` using the following command:

   PS C:\Users\Administrator\Desktop> .\ CreateUserContext.ps1

5. As a result, your PowerShell script will set two related lists as shown in the following screenshot:

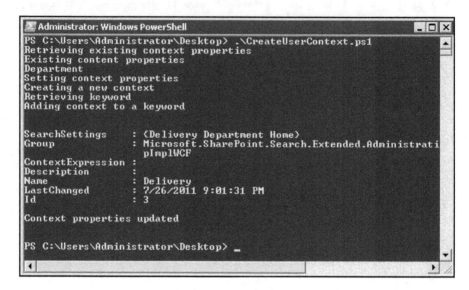

6. Now, switch back to the root of your SharePoint site: `http://intranet.contoso.com`, click **Site Actions | Site Settings**.

7. From the **Site Collection Administration** group, click **FAST Search keywords**.

8. From the preceding page, you will be able to see the collection of keywords. Select the **delivery** keyword and click the **Keyword Details** context menu option.

9. Under the **Visual Best Bets** category, select **Edit** for the only best bet defined, as shown in the following screenshot:

Visual Best Bet			
Visual best bet is rich content (like images or html snippets) that will be displayed on the search result page.	Add Visual Best Bet		
	Title		
	Delivery Department Home	Remove	Edit

10. Take note of the **User Context** category and the **Delivery** context added to the list, as shown in the following screenshot:

```
* Indicates a required field
Title                          Title: *
Enter a title for this visual  ┌─────────────────────────────────┐
best bet. The title will not be│Delivery Department Home         │
displayed on the search        └─────────────────────────────────┘
results page.

Visual Best Bet                URL: *
Enter a URL for the visual     ┌─────────────────────────────────────────────┐
best bet.                      │http://intranet.contoso.com/_layouts/images/homepageSamplePhc│
                               └─────────────────────────────────────────────┘

User Context                   User context:
Add one or more user           ┌──────────────────────────┐  ┌──────────────┐
contexts for which the         │Delivery                  │  │     Add      │
visual best bet should apply.  │                          │  └──────────────┘
Leave blank if the visual      │                          │  ┌──────────────┐
best bet applies for any       │                          │  │   Remove     │
user context.                  │                          │  └──────────────┘
                               │                          │
To create a new user           │                          │
context, go to the user        │                          │
context page.                  └──────────────────────────┘

Start and End Date             Start date (leave blank for immediate start):
In the start date box, type    ┌──────────────────────┐ ▦
the date that you want the     └──────────────────────┘
```

How it works...

We started by defining the script variables. In this recipe, we define the site name of the context that will be provisioned to the site:

```
$DeliveryContext = "Delivery"
```

Next, we load SharePoint and PowerShell snap-ins as follows:

```
Add-PSSnapin "Microsoft.SharePoint.Powershell"
Add-PSSnapin "Microsoft.FASTSearch.PowerShell"
```

Next, we call `Get-SPEnterpriseSearchExtendedQueryProperty` to access context properties of the FAST Search service application. The following command retrieves the context based on the parameters passed:

```
$contextProps = Get-SPEnterpriseSearchExtendedQueryProperty -
SearchApplication "FASTQuery" -Identity "FASTSearchContextProperties"
```

The list of current context properties is then displayed. Next, similar to reading the context properties, we are going to record new context properties which are going to make up our context. The following command will erase all of the existing context properties and record `Department` as the only property available to build context from:

```
Set-SPEnterpriseSearchExtendedQueryProperty -SearchApplication
"FASTQuery" -Identity "FASTSearchContextProperties" -Value "Department"
```

> There are many more user profile properties available to build context from. You can even provision your own custom properties and build context based on those properties. To learn all about provisioning your custom properties and using out-of-the-box user profile properties, please refer to *Chapter 5, Managing SharePoint 2010 Metadata and Social Features using Powershell*.

Now that the property has been added to the site, you can actually see it if you decide to manually build a user profile context using the following steps:

1. While at the root of your SharePoint site: `http://intranet.contoso.com`, click **Site Actions | Site Settings**.

2. From the **Site Collection Administration** group, click **FAST Search user context**.

3. Click **Add User Context**, where you are given an option to create a context with **Department** as one of the properties we have added, as shown in the following screenshot:

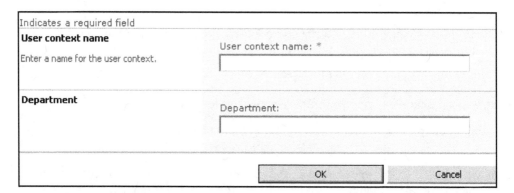

Next, in our script, we provision the new context using a script with the following command:

```
$context = $searchSettingGroup.Contexts.AddContext($DeliveryContext)
```

Now that the context is ready, we can assign it to one of the keywords we created in the *Configuring visual best bets* recipe. We get a hold of the keyword already provisioned on the site, called `delivery`, as shown in the following line of code:

```
$keyword = $searchSettingGroup.Keywords.GetKeyword("delivery")
```

We then extract the visual best bet from the keyword:

```
$visualBestBet = $keyword.FeaturedContent.GetFeaturedContent("Delivery
Department Home")
```

Having the keyword available, we add newly created context to the best bet, as follows:

```
$visualBestBet.Contexts.AddContext($DeliveryContext)
```

Using context for keywords, we can target the best bet to members of a particular department but not another. Every time the user searches with the keyword, their context is evaluated based on the profile properties for that user. If properties for the user match the context requested for the keyword, appropriate content will be displayed.

See also

The *Bulk provisioning data into user profile properties* recipe in *Chapter 5, Managing SharePoint 2010 Metadata and Social Features Using PowerShell* and the *Configuring Visual Best Bets* recipe in this chapter.

Configuring search web parts automatically with PowerShell

The effectiveness of configurations described earlier will be put to the test when your users navigate to the search page and execute their search query. At that moment, SharePoint will return a result page where your users find all of the features described so far.

SharePoint has a variety of out-of-the-box web parts allowing you to help users navigate through content on the search results page. In this recipe, we'll take a look at what's involved in configuring those web parts using PowerShell. The approach described here will allow you to have a scriptable set of changes that can be applied to any of your environments, rather than a lengthy list of manual configurations which might need to be restored during a disaster recovery.

Getting ready

We'll assume you are running an environment with SharePoint Search configured and working. This is the case for the environment you downloaded from the Microsoft Download Center as described in *Chapter 1, PowerShell Scripting Methods and Creating Custom Commands*.

We'll also assume that you are familiar with working with SharePoint pages and web parts as described in the Bulk provisioning data in to user profile properties recipe in *Chapter 5, Managing SharePoint 2010 Metadata and Social Features Using PowerShell*. Let's get right into authoring our script PowerShell script using PowerGUI, so ensure you're logged in with an administrator's permissions on the target Virtual Machine.

How to do it...

Let's see how we can configure search web parts on your site using PowerShell.

1. Navigate to the root of your SharePoint test site: `http://intranet.contoso.com`.

2. Click **Search** on the top navigation menu to be taken to the search site.

3. In the keyword textbox, type **test** and let SharePoint redirect you to the **FAST Search Center** page.

4. Click **Start | All Programs | PowerGUI | PowerGUI Script Editor**.

5. In the main script editing window of PowerGUI, add the following script:

```
# Defining script variables
$SiteUrl = "http://intranet.contoso.com"

# Loading Microsoft.SharePoint.PowerShell
$snapin = Get-PSSnapin | Where-Object {$_.Name -eq 'Microsoft.
SharePoint.Powershell'}
if ($snapin -eq $null) {
Write-Host "Loading SharePoint Powershell Snapin"
Add-PSSnapin "Microsoft.SharePoint.Powershell"
}

$SPSite = Get-SPSite | Where-Object {$_.Url -eq $SiteUrl}
  if($SPSite -ne $null)
  {
  Write-Host "Connecting to search site"
  $SearchWeb = $SPSite.OpenWeb("/search")
  $pubWeb = [Microsoft.SharePoint.Publishing.PublishingWeb]::Get
   PublishingWeb($SearchWeb)

  Write-Host "Retrieving the search results page"
  $resultsPage=$pubWeb.GetPublishingPages() | Where-Object {$_
.Name -eq "results.aspx"}
  $resultsPage.CheckOut()

  Write-Host "Adding a web part to search results page"
  $webPartManager=$SearchWeb.GetLimitedWebPartManager($resultsPage
.Url, [System.Web.UI.WebControls.WebParts.PersonalizationScope]::
```

```
Shared)
   $webPart=new-object  Microsoft.SharePoint.WebPartPages.
ContentEditorWebPart
   $webPart.ChromeType=[System.Web.UI.WebControls.WebParts.
PartChromeType]::TitleOnly
   $webPart.Title="Yaroslavs Content Editor Webpart"
   $webPartManager.AddWebPart($webPart, "Right", 0);

   Write-Host "Modifying properties of search box web part"
   $searchResults = $webPartManager.WebParts | Where-Object {$_
.Title -eq "Search Core Results"}
   $searchResults.ResultsPerPage = 25
   $webPartManager.SaveChanges($searchResults)

   Write-Host "Checking in and publishing changes"
   $resultsPage.CheckIn("Checked in Webpart")
   $resultsPage.listItem.File.Publish("Published Webpart")
   if ($resultsPage.listItem.ParentList.EnableModeration)
   {
       $modInformation = $resultsPage.listItem.ModerationInformation
       if($modInformation.Status -ne [Microsoft.SharePoint.
SPModerationStatusType]::Approved)
       {
           $resultsPage.ListItem.File.Approve("Approved Page")
       }
   }

   $SearchWeb.Dispose()
   }
$SPSite.Dispose()
```

6. Click **File | Save** to save the script to your development machine's desktop. Set the filename of the script to ConfigureSearchWebParts.ps1.

7. Open the PowerShell console window and call ConfigureSearchWebParts.ps1 using the following command:

PS C:\Users\Administrator\Desktop> .\ ConfigureSearchWebParts.ps1

8. As a result, your PowerShell script will execute with results as shown in the following screenshot:

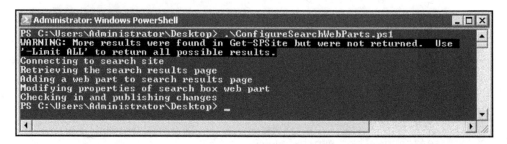

9. Again, in your browser, let's now switch back to our SharePoint FAST Search site: http://intranet.contoso.com/search.

10. In the keyword textbox, type **test** and let SharePoint perform the search again.

11. Take note of SharePoint returning more than 10 default results in the search result area and an instance of content editor web part on the right-hand side of the page, as seen in the following screenshot:

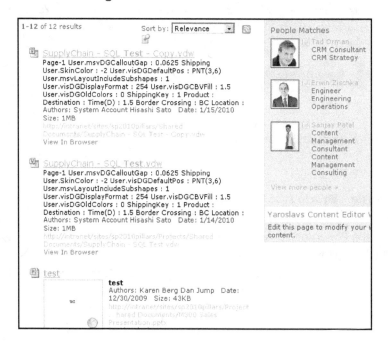

How it works...

We started our script with configuring the script variables such as the URL of our root site:

```
$SiteUrl = "http://intranet.contoso.com"
```

We then load the SharePoint snap-in and connect to the site:

```
Add-PSSnapin "Microsoft.SharePoint.Powershell"
```

Next, we connect to our root site and then establish the connection to our search center:

```
$SearchWeb = $SPSite.OpenWeb("/search")
```

Since FAST Search Center is an instance of the publishing site, we will create an instance of the publishing web object to be able to get a hold of the pages in the library as well as modify them:

```
$pubWeb = [Microsoft.SharePoint.Publishing.PublishingWeb]::GetPublishi
ngWeb($SearchWeb)
```

Next, we connect to the search result page in the pages library using the following command:

```
$resultsPage=$pubWeb.GetPublishingPages() | Where-Object {$_.Name -eq
"results.aspx"}
```

> In this example, we looked at modifying the search results page, however FAST Search Center has a variety of other pages it uses. To modify those pages, access the **Pages** library from within FAST Search Center where you will find the remaining pages and be able to view them.

Before making changes to the page, we need to check it out:

```
$resultsPage.CheckOut()
```

Web parts on the page interact with the user interface by using the controls on the page. When it comes to interacting with web part using PowerShell, we need to get a hold of the web part manager object, as follows:

```
$webPartManager=$SearchWeb.GetLimitedWebPartManager($resultsPage.Url,
[System.Web.UI.WebControls.WebParts.PersonalizationScope]::Shared)
```

In our example, we added the new content editor web part instance to the right-hand side of the search results page. This is achieved by creating a new object representing a content editor web part, as follows:

```
$webPart=new-object  Microsoft.SharePoint.WebPartPages.
ContentEditorWebPart
```

We then assign the chrome of the web part to actually display the title of the web part. Many web parts on the site do not have their chrome displayed, just the content, such as search box web part. To control the chrome state for your web part, we use the following command:

```
$webPart.ChromeType=[System.Web.UI.WebControls.WebParts.PartChromeType]::
TitleOnly
```

Finally, we add the title of the web part:

```
$webPart.Title="Yaroslavs Content Editor Webpart"
```

Now that we're happy with the properties we assigned to our web part, we can add it to the page's specific zone by using a web part manager command as follows:

```
$webPartManager.AddWebPart($webPart, "Right", 0);
```

Let's now take a look at how we can modify properties of the existing web part, the search results web part. First, we connect to the web part using web part manager and by specifying the title of the web part as a parameter:

```
$searchResults = $webPartManager.WebParts | Where-Object {$_.Title -eq
"Search Core Results"}
```

Next, we'll modify one of the web part's properties, the number of search results returned when a query is executed:

```
$searchResults.ResultsPerPage = 25
```

Since the web part is already on the page and we don't want to add it, we just need to save changes to the web part properties by running the following command on the web part manager:

```
$webPartManager.SaveChanges($searchResults)
```

When done with the web part configurations, we save the page changes by checking in first:

```
$resultsPage.CheckIn("Checked in Webpart")
```

Since FAST Search Center uses publishing infrastructure, we need to publish our changes before they are visible to all users. For that we use the following command:

```
$resultsPage.listItem.File.Publish("Published Webpart")
```

Since publishing page changes in some cases may have an approval enabled on the library requiring for the page to be approved before it's seen by everyone, we can run system approval by using the following command:

```
$resultsPage.ListItem.File.Approve("Approved Page")
```

Finally, we wrap the entire script execution by disposing the instance of the search web and the root site:

```
$SearchWeb.Dispose()
```

The approach here will allow you to make configuration changes on the existing or new environment without introducing a downtime to the environment.

7
Managing SharePoint Site Content in Bulk using PowerShell

In this chapter, we will cover the following topics:

- ▶ Creating basic and complex content types
- ▶ Creating and configuring document sets
- ▶ Creating and editing publishing pages with PowerShell
- ▶ Provisioning web parts in bulk on to SharePoint pages
- ▶ Configuring web parts in bulk with PowerShell
- ▶ Provisioning list rollups using PowerShell

Introduction

SharePoint **content types** are used to make it simpler for site managers to standardize what content and associated metadata gets uploaded to lists and libraries on the site. In this chapter, we'll take a look at how you can create various content types and assign them to be used in site containers.

As a subset of more complex content types, a **document set** will allow your users to store related items in libraries as a set of documents sharing common metadata. This approach will allow your users to run business processes on a batch of items in the document set as well as the whole set. In this chapter, we'll take a look at how you can define a document set to be used on your site.

Since users mostly interact with your SharePoint site through pages and views, the ability to modify SharePoint pages to accommodate business user requirements becomes an important part of site management. In this chapter, we'll take a look at how you can create and modify pages and content related to them. We will also take a look at how you can provision simple out-of-the-box web parts to your SharePoint publishing pages and configure their properties.

In this chapter, we will also take a look at how you can aggregate site content and display the roll up of that content anywhere else on the site. This approach will become very handy when enhancements and customizations are added to an existing site.

Creating basic and complex content types

SharePoint lists and libraries can store a variety of content on the site. SharePoint also has a user interface to customize what information you can collect from users to be attached as an item metadata.

In the scenario where the entire intranet or the department site within your organization requires a standard set of metadata to be collected with list and library items, content types are the easiest approach to implement the requirement.

With content types, you can define the type of business content your users will be interacting with. Once defined, you can also add a metadata field and any applicable validation to them just like we did for individual lists in *Chapter 3, Performing Advanced List and Content Operations in SharePoint using PowerShell*. Once defined, you can attach the newly created content type to the library or list of your choice so that newly uploaded or modified content can conform to the rules you defined on the site.

Getting ready

Considering you have already set up your virtual development environment as described in *Chapter 1, PowerShell Scripting Methods and Creating Custom PowerShell Commands*, we'll get right into authoring our script.

It's assumed you are familiar with how to interact with SharePoint lists and libraries using PowerShell as described in *Chapter 3, Performing Advanced List and Content Operations in SharePoint using PowerShell*.

In this recipe, we'll be using PowerGUI to author the script, which means you will be required to be logged in with an administrator's role on the target Virtual Machine.

How to do it...

Let's take a look at how we can provision site content types using PowerShell as follows:

1. Click **Start | All Programs | PowerGUI | PowerGUI Script Editor**.

2. In the main script editing window of PowerGUI, add the following script:

```
# Defining script variables
$SiteUrl = "http://intranet.contoso.com"
$ListName = "Shared Documents"

# Loading Microsoft.SharePoint.PowerShell
$snapin = Get-PSSnapin | Where-Object {$_.Name -eq 'Microsoft.
SharePoint.Powershell'}
if ($snapin -eq $null) {
Write-Host "Loading SharePoint Powershell Snapin"
Add-PSSnapin "Microsoft.SharePoint.Powershell"
}

$SPSite = Get-SPSite | Where-Object {$_.Url -eq $SiteUrl}
  if($SPSite -ne $null)
  {
    Write-Host "Connecting to the site" $SiteUrl ",list "
$ListName
  $RootWeb = $SPSite.RootWeb
  $SPList = $RootWeb.Lists[$ListName]

  Write-Host "Creating new content type from base type"
  $DocumentContentType = $RootWeb.AvailableContentTypes["Document"
]
    $ContentType =  New-Object Microsoft.SharePoint.SPContentType -
ArgumentList @($DocumentContentType, $RootWeb.ContentTypes, "Org
Document")

  Write-Host "Adding content type to site"
  $ct = $RootWeb.ContentTypes.Add($ContentType)

  Write-Host "Creating new fields"
  $OrgDocumentContentType = $RootWeb.ContentTypes[$ContentType.Id]
  $OrgFields = $RootWeb.Fields
  $choices = New-Object System.Collections.Specialized.
StringCollection
  $choices.Add("East")
  $choices.Add("West")
  $OrgDivision = $OrgFields.Add("Division", [Microsoft.SharePoint.
SPFieldType]::Choice, $false, $false, $choices)
```

```
$OrgBranch = $OrgFields.Add("Branch", [Microsoft.SharePoint.
SPFieldType]::Text, $false)

Write-Host "Adding fields to content type"
$OrgDivisionObject = $OrgFields.GetField($OrgDivision)
$OrgBranchObject = $OrgFields.GetField($OrgBranch)

$OrgDocumentContentType.FieldLinks.Add($OrgDivisionObject)
$OrgDocumentContentType.FieldLinks.Add($OrgBranchObject)
$OrgDocumentContentType.Update()

Write-Host "Associating content type to list" $ListName
$association = $SPList.ContentTypes.Add($OrgDocumentContentType)
$SPList.ContentTypesEnabled = $true
$SPList.Update()

Write-Host "Content type provisioning complete"
}
        $SPSite.Dispose()
```

3. Click **File | Save** to save the script to your development machine's desktop. Set the filename of the script to `CreateAssociateContentType.ps1`.

4. Open the PowerShell console window and call `CreateAssociateContentType.ps1` using the following command:

   PS C:\Users\Administrator\Desktop> .\ CreateAssociateContentType.ps1

5. As a result, your PowerShell script will create a site structure as shown in the following screenshot:

6. Now, from your browser, let's switch to our **SharePoint Intranet**: `http://intranet.contoso.com`.

7. From the home page's **Quick launch**, click the **Shared Documents** link.

8. On the ribbon, click the **Library** tab and select **Settings | Library Settings**.

9. Take note of the newly associated content type added to the **Content Types** area of the library settings, as shown in the following screenshot:

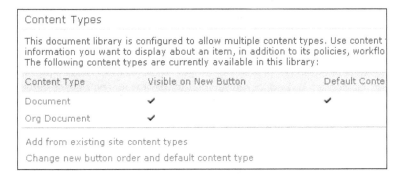

10. Navigate back to the **Shared Documents** library from the **Quick launch** menu on your site and select any of the existing documents in the library.

11. From the ribbons **Documents** tab, click **Manage | Edit Properties**.

12. Take note of how the item now has the **Content Type** option available, where you can pick newly provisioned **Org Document** content type.

13. Pick the **Org Document** content type and take note of the associated metadata showing up for the new content type, as shown in the following screenshot:

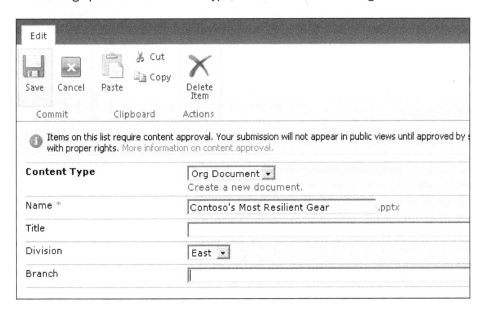

How it works...

First, we defined the script variables. In this recipe, the variables include a URL of the site where the content types are provisioned, `http://intranet.contoso.com`, and a document library to which the content type is associated:

```
$ListName = "Shared Documents"
```

Once a PowerShell snap-in has been loaded, we get a hold of the instance of the current site and its root web. Since we want our content type to inherit from the parent rather than just being defined from the scratch, we get a hold of the existing parent content type first, using the following command:

```
$DocumentContentType = $RootWeb.AvailableContentTypes["Document"]
```

Next, we created an instance of a new content type inheriting from our parent content type and provisioned it to the root site using the following command:

```
$ContentType = New-Object Microsoft.SharePoint.SPContentType -
ArgumentList @($DocumentContentType, $RootWeb.ContentTypes, "Org
Document")
```

Here, the new object takes the following parameters: the content type representing a parent, a web to which the new content type will be provisioned to, and the display name for the content type.

Once our content type object has been created, we add it to the list of existing content types on the site:

```
$ct = $RootWeb.ContentTypes.Add($ContentType)
```

Since most content types are unique by the fields they are using, we will add some business-specific fields to our content type. First, we get a hold of the collection of all of the available fields on the site:

```
$OrgFields = $RootWeb.Fields
```

Next, we create a string collection to hold the values for the choice field we are going to add to our content type:

```
$choices = New-Object System.Collections.Specialized.StringCollection
```

The field with list of choices was called `Division`, representing a company division. We provision the field to the site using the following command:

```
$OrgDivision = $OrgFields.Add("Division", [Microsoft.SharePoint.
SPFieldType]::Choice, $false, $false, $choices)
```

In the preceding command, the first parameter is the name of the field, followed by the type of the field, which in our case is choice field. We then specify whether the field will be a required field, followed by a parameter indicating whether the field name will be truncated to eight characters. The last parameter specifies the list of choices for the choice field.

Another field we add, representing a company branch, is simpler since it's a text field. We define the text field using the following command:

```
$OrgBranch = $OrgFields.Add("Branch", [Microsoft.SharePoint.
SPFieldType]::Text, $false)
```

We add both fields to the content type using the following commands:

```
$OrgDocumentContentType.FieldLinks.Add($OrgDivisionObject)
```

```
$OrgDocumentContentType.FieldLinks.Add($OrgBranchObject)
```

The last part is to associate the newly created content type to a library, in our case **Shared Documents**. We use the following command to associate the content type to the library:

```
$association = $SPList.ContentTypes.Add($OrgDocumentContentType)
```

To ensure the content types on the list are enabled, we set the `ContentTypesEnabled` property of the list to `$true`.

See also

The *Creating lists of custom structure* recipe in *Chapter 3, Performing Advanced List and Content Operations in SharePoint using PowerShell.*

Creating and configuring document sets

SharePoint document set is the new feature allowing users to group documents within their libraries in order to share common metadata value between the set of document. As an added benefit, with document sets, your users will be able to run out-of-the- box and custom workflows on the entire set and individual documents within a set.

The document set functionality in SharePoint is achieved using a concept of content types where you define your custom document set template in a form of the content type. Once your content type is defined, you can bind it to a set of desired libraries and let users work with the set.

Since document set configuration requires quite a few steps to make it available on the site, we can use PowerShell to script those configuration steps to help us quickly provision document sets to multiple environments. In the scenario where you have several document sets to be created and deployed, PowerShell will make it easier to get your site set up without incurring a significant downtime.

Getting ready

Considering you have already set up your virtual development environment as described in *Chapter 1, PowerShell Scripting Methods and Creating Custom Commands*, we'll get right into authoring our script.

We'll assume you are also familiar with the concept of content types and how you can use PowerShell to provision content types to your site as described in the previous recipe.

In this recipe, we'll be using PowerGUI to author the script, which means you will be required to be logged in with an administrator's role on the target Virtual Machine.

How to do it...

Let's see what's involved in creating documents sets with PowerShell:

1. Click **Start | All Programs | PowerGUI | PowerGUI Script Editor**.

2. In the main script editing window of PowerGUI, add the following script:

```
# Defining script variables
$SiteUrl = "http://intranet.contoso.com"
$ListName = "Shared Documents"


# Loading Microsoft.SharePoint.PowerShell
$snapin = Get-PSSnapin | Where-Object {$_.Name -eq 'Microsoft.
SharePoint.Powershell'}
if ($snapin -eq $null) {
Write-Host "Loading SharePoint Powershell Snapin"
Add-PSSnapin "Microsoft.SharePoint.Powershell"
}

Write-Host "Load document management library"
[System.Reflection.Assembly]::LoadWithPartialName("Microsoft.
Office.DocumentManagement")

$SPSite = Get-SPSite | Where-Object {$_.Url -eq $SiteUrl}
  if($SPSite -ne $null)
  {
    Write-Host "Connecting to the site" $SiteUrl ",list "
$ListName
  $RootWeb = $SPSite.RootWeb
  $SPList = $RootWeb.Lists[$ListName]

  Write-Host "Creating new document set content type"
  $DocumentSetContentType = $RootWeb.AvailableContentTypes
["Document Set"]
```

```
    $ContentType =  New-Object Microsoft.SharePoint.SPContentType
    -ArgumentList @($DocumentSetContentType, $RootWeb.ContentTypes,
    "Org Document Set")

    Write-Host "Adding content type to site"
    $ct = $RootWeb.ContentTypes.Add($ContentType)

    Write-Host "Configuring document set properties"
    $OrgDocumentSetContentType = $RootWeb.ContentTypes[$ContentType.
Id]
    $OrgFields = $RootWeb.Fields
    $choices = New-Object System.Collections.Specialized.
StringCollection
    $choices.Add("East")
    $choices.Add("West")
    $OrgDivision = $OrgFields.Add("Division", [Microsoft.SharePoint.
SPFieldType]::Choice, $false, $false, $choices)
    $OrgBranch = $OrgFields.Add("Branch", [Microsoft.SharePoint.
SPFieldType]::Text, $false)

    Write-Host "Adding fields to content type"
    $OrgDivisionObject = $OrgFields.GetField($OrgDivision)
    $OrgBranchObject = $OrgFields.GetField($OrgBranch)

    $OrgDocumentSetContentType.FieldLinks.Add($OrgDivisionObject)
    $OrgDocumentSetContentType.FieldLinks.Add($OrgBranchObject)
    $OrgDocumentSetContentType.Update()

    Write-Host "Associating document set content type to list"
$ListName
    $association = $SPList.ContentTypes.
Add($OrgDocumentSetContentType)
    $SPList.ContentTypesEnabled = $true
    $SPList.Update()

    Write-Host "Document set configuration complete"
    }
$SPSite.Dispose()
```

3. Click **File | Save** to save the script to your development machine's desktop. Set the filename of the script to `CreateDocumentSet.ps1`.

4. Open the PowerShell console window and call `CreateDocumentSet.ps1` using the following command:

   ```
   PS C:\Users\Administrator\Desktop> .\ CreateDocumentSet.ps1
   ```

5. As a result, your PowerShell script will create a list with results as shown in the following screenshot:

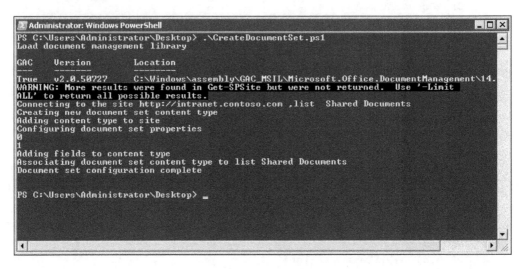

6. Now, from your browser, let's switch to our **SharePoint Intranet site**: http://intranet. contoso.com/

7. Click **Site Actions | Site Settings**.

8. Under **Galleries**, select **Site content types**.

9. Locate and click the **Org Document Set** link.

10. On the document sets settings page click **Configure Document Set**.

11. Under the **Welcome Page Columns** group, under the **Available columns** section, select both **Branch** and **Division** columns and choose **Add** to add them to the list of columns visible on the document set home page, as shown in the following screenshot:

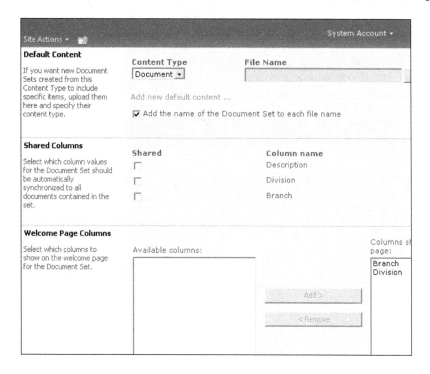

12. Click **OK** to save changes.

13. Click the **Shared Documents** library link from the **Quick launch** menu on your site.

14. From the ribbon, click the **Documents** tab, then click the **New Document | Org Document Set**, as shown in the following screenshot:

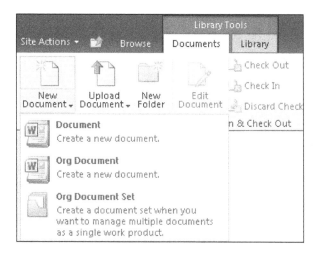

15. Provide the **Title** and other required metadata for the document set and click **OK** to create a new document set.

16. In the **Shared Documents** library, locate the newly created document set and open it. Take note of the entered metadata and other document set property values available on the home page of the set, as shown in the following screenshot:

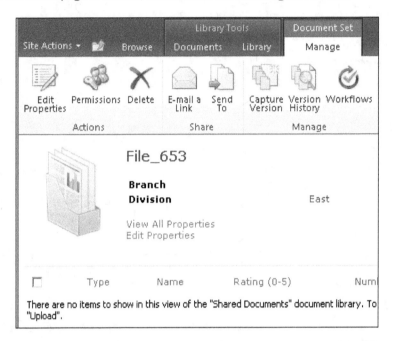

How it works...

Document sets represent complex content types, so their provisioning is similar to provisioning a content type.

We start by defining our script variables: a URL of the site where the document set is to be provisioned, `http://intranet.contoso.com`, and a document library to which the document set will be associated:

```
$ListName = "Shared Documents"
```

Once a PowerShell snap-in has been loaded, we get a hold of the instance of the current site and its root web. Our document set will inherit from SharePoint 2010 the base document set content type. First, we get a hold of the existing parent document set content type, using the following command:

```
$DocumentSetContentType = $RootWeb.AvailableContentTypes["Document Set"]
```

Next, we create an instance of a new document set content type inheriting from our parent using the following command:

```
$ContentType =  New-Object Microsoft.SharePoint.SPContentType -
ArgumentList @($DocumentSetContentType, $RootWeb.ContentTypes, "Org
Document Set")
```

Our new document set object takes the following parameters: parent document set content type, a web which will hold newly provisioned document set definition, and the display name of the document set.

Once our document set content type object has been created, we add it to the site:

```
$ct = $RootWeb.ContentTypes.Add($ContentType)
```

Just as in the previous recipe, we create the same set of fields which are used in our document set content type. In this case, the fields are going to be a company division and the branch.

We add both fields to the content type using the following commands:

```
$OrgDocumentSetContentType.FieldLinks.Add($OrgDivisionObject)
```

```
$OrgDocumentSetContentType.FieldLinks.Add($OrgBranchObject)
```

```
$OrgDocumentSetContentType.Update()
```

The last part is to associate the newly created content type to a **Shared Documents** library. We use the following command to associate our new document set content type to the library:

```
$association = $SPList.ContentTypes.Add($OrgDocumentSetContentType)
```

Lastly, we enable the content types on the library if they haven't already been enabled by setting the `ContentTypesEnabled` property of the library to `$true`.

See also

The *Creating basic and complex content types* recipe in this chapter.

Creating and editing publishing pages with PowerShell

Just about any SharePoint intranet and extranet site consists of a series of collaboration and publishing pages which your users interact with the site.

When it comes to maintaining content on the site, your organization may want to bulk change the content throughout the site, or migrate existing content to be hosted within SharePoint. As an example, you may be asked to pre-create a few hundred news article pages where your users can populate the content for them before the news release section of the site launches.

Whether you have been tasked with this assignment on an existing intranet or the new site, you can be sure that using PowerShell will minimize the impact on the environment downtime and you will have a reusable script to perform the deployment to multiple environments.

In this recipe, we will see how you can create a new SharePoint publishing page and edit its properties. We'll also take a look at how you can automatically approve the page and make it available for others to see.

Getting ready

Considering you have already set up your virtual development environment as described in *Chapter 1, PowerShell Scripting Methods and Creating Custom Commands*, we'll get right into authoring our script.

In this recipe, we'll be using PowerGUI to author the script, which means you will be required to be logged in with an administrator's role on the target Virtual Machine.

How to do it...

We'll take a look at how you can create publishing pages using PowerShell.

1. Click **Start | All Programs | PowerGUI | PowerGUI Script Editor**.

2. In the main script editing window of PowerGUI, add the following script:

```
# Defining script variables
$SiteUrl = "http://www.contoso.com"
$PressReleaseFileName = "PressRelease"

# Loading Microsoft.SharePoint.PowerShell
$snapin = Get-PSSnapin | Where-Object {$_.Name -eq 'Microsoft.
SharePoint.Powershell'}
if ($snapin -eq $null) {
Write-Host "Loading SharePoint Powershell Snapin"
Add-PSSnapin "Microsoft.SharePoint.Powershell"
}

$SPSite = Get-SPSite | Where-Object {$_.Url -eq $SiteUrl}
  if($SPSite -ne $null)
  {
  Write-Host "Connecting to root site site"
```

```
$PressReleaseWeb = $SPSite.OpenWeb("/PressReleases")
$pubWeb = [Microsoft.SharePoint.Publishing.PublishingWeb]::GetPu
blishingWeb($PressReleaseWeb)

Write-Host "Retrieving 'Blank Web Part page' page layout"
$pageLayout = $pubWeb.GetAvailablePageLayouts() | Where-Object
{$_.Title -eq "Blank Web Part page"}

Write-Host "Creating a new page"
$pageFileName = $PressReleaseFileName+".aspx"
$page = $pubWeb.GetPublishingPages().Add($pageFileName,
$pageLayout)

Write-Host "Setting new page metadata"
$page.Title = $PressReleaseFileName
$pageItem = $page.ListItem
$pageItem["Comments"]="New press release"
$pageItem["PublishingContactName"]="Brad"
$pageItem["PublishingContactEmail"]="brads@contoso.com"
$page.Update()

Write-Host "Retrieving and updating an existing page"
$existingPage=$pubWeb.GetPublishingPages() | Where-Object {$_.
Name -eq "default.aspx"}
$existingPage.CheckOut()
$existingPageItem = $existingPage.ListItem
$existingPageItem["Comments"]="Press release landing page"
$existingPage.Update()

Write-Host "Checking in and publishing changes"
$existingPage.CheckIn("Checked in by PowerShell script")
$existingPage.listItem.File.Publish("Published by PowerShell
script")
$page.CheckIn("Checked in by PowerShell script")
$page.listItem.File.Publish("Published by PowerShell script")
if ($existingPage.listItem.ParentList.EnableModeration)
{
    $modInformation = $existingPage.listItem.
ModerationInformation
    if($modInformation.Status -ne [Microsoft.SharePoint.SPModerat
ionStatusType]::Approved)
    {
        $existingPage.ListItem.File.Approve("Approved by
PowerShell script")
    }
```

```
        }
        if ($page.listItem.ParentList.EnableModeration)
        {
            $modInformation = $page.listItem.ModerationInformation
            if($modInformation.Status -ne [Microsoft.SharePoint.SPModerat
ionStatusType]::Approved)
            {
                $page.ListItem.File.Approve("Approved by PowerShell
script")
            }
        }
        $PressReleaseWeb.Dispose()
    }
$SPSite.Dispose()
```

3. Click **File** | **Save** to save the script to your development machine's desktop. Set the filename of the script to CreatingEditingPages.ps1.

4. Open the PowerShell console window and call CreatingEditingPages.ps1 using the following command:

   PS C:\Users\Administrator\Desktop> .\ CreatingEditingPages.ps1

5. As a result, your PowerShell script will execute and return results as shown in the following screenshot:

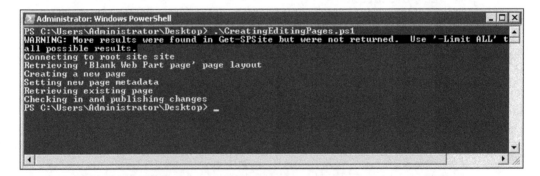

6. Now, let's switch to our **SharePoint Publishing Site**: http://www.contoso.com/

7. From the **Quick launch** of the site, click **Press Releases**.

8. Click **Site Actions** | **View All Site Content**.

9. Under the **Document Libraries** category, click the **Pages** library.

10. Take note of the newly created **PressRelease** page, as shown in the following screenshot:

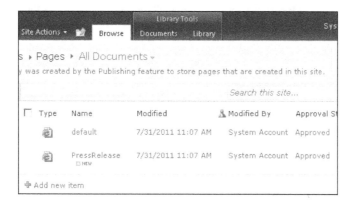

11. Access the content menu of the page and select **View Properties**.

12. Take note of a few of the new property values we have assigned in our script, as shown in the following screenshot:

How it works...

In this recipe, we defined the URL of the site as well as the newly provisioned page name as our script variables:

```
$SiteUrl = "http://www.contoso.com"
$PressReleaseFileName = "PressRelease"
```

Note that in this recipe, we're publishing a site collection with a different URL and not our collaboration site collection.

Next, we load PowerShell SharePoint snap-in and retrieve the current site collection object. The demonstration environment you have downloaded in *Chapter 1, PowerShell Scripting Methods and Creating Custom Commands*, contains the sub-site under the main site URL. The sub-site is used for demo press releases and we get a hold of it using the following command:

$PressReleaseWeb = $SPSite.OpenWeb("/PressReleases")

We then convert the press release web object to a publishing site object using the following command:

$pubWeb = [Microsoft.SharePoint.Publishing.PublishingWeb]::GetPublishingW eb($PressReleaseWeb)

Before we go ahead and create an instance of the page, we got a hold of the page layout which the page uses. The page layout will drive which web part zones are going to be displayed on the page. We get the `Blank Web Part page` page layout:

```
$pageLayout = $pubWeb.GetAvailablePageLayouts() | Where-Object {$_
.Title -eq "Blank Web Part page"}
```

Once our filename for the new page has been constructed, we can go ahead and create a new page object as shown in the following code:

```
$page = $pubWeb.GetPublishingPages().Add($pageFileName, $pageLayout)
```

Now that the page has been created, we can edit its properties. Have you noticed how we first got a hold of the `ListItem` object of the page before editing the properties? We do this since the page object doesn't have direct access to some of the properties of the page item. The page is just an item within the page library and in order to access its underlying object functionality we use the `ListItem` property and make updates to the underlying object directly as follows:

```
$pageItem["PublishingContactEmail"]="brads@contoso.com"
```

As a part of this recipe, we also retrieved the existing page in order to demonstrate how you can modify the existing page on the publishing site. We start by retrieving items in the page library with the filename. The page filename is `default.aspx`:

```
$existingPage=$pubWeb.GetPublishingPages() | Where-Object {$_.Name -eq
"default.aspx"}
```

We then check out the file and make changes to its properties just as in the example with the newly provisioned page. Once ready, we check in both pages using the following command:

`$page.CheckIn("Checked in by PowerShell script")`

Since publishing pages require to be published before displayed for everyone else, we publish the page using the following command:

`$page.listItem.File.Publish("Published by PowerShell script")`

Most publishing pages require items to be approved before published to the site. We first check whether the moderation is required for the library using the following command:

`$existingPage.listItem.ParentList.EnableModeration`

If the moderation is enabled on the library, we verify that the page has not been approved yet. If the page is pending approval, we approve the item by using the following command:

`$existingPage.ListItem.File.Approve("Approved by PowerShell script")`

Since we opened an instance of the **Press Release** web on the site, we close the object of both the web and the site to prevent memory leaks.

Provisioning web parts in bulk on to SharePoint pages

As we have seen in the previous recipe, pages contain web parts and other components which make up your SharePoint site.

Creating or editing existing pages alone wouldn't add much value if we weren't able to add new web parts to your pages.

In this recipe, we will take a look at how you can add an out-of-the-box web parts to one of the existing pages on the site. You can use the same mechanism to add the same web part to series of pages on the site.

As an alternative, you could navigate to each of the pages and perform the change using SharePoint user interface, or deploy a custom solution package which would make the appropriate change.

However, in both cases, you are either running the risk of user error while processing time consuming editing of multiple pages, or introducing a downtime while the solution package deploys.

Let's go ahead and see what's involved in provisioning SharePoint web parts using a PowerShell script.

This scenario will become particularly handy when a new functionality enclosed in a custom or out-of-the-box web part needs to be deployed to many pages within existing SharePoint site.

Getting ready

Considering you have already set up your virtual development environment as described in *Chapter 1, PowerShell Scripting Methods and Creating Custom Commands*, we'll get right into authoring our script.

We'll assume you are also familiar with editing SharePoint publishing pages as described in the previous recipe

In this recipe, we'll be using PowerGUI to author the script, which means you will be required to be logged in with an administrator's role on the target Virtual Machine.

How to do it...

Let's take a look at what's involved in provisioning web parts on to SharePoint pages using PowerShell:

1. Click **Start | All Programs | PowerGUI | PowerGUI Script Editor**.

2. In the main script editing window of PowerGUI, add the following script:

```
# Defining script variables
$SiteUrl = "http://www.contoso.com"
$PressReleaseFileName = "PressRelease.aspx"

# Loading Microsoft.SharePoint.PowerShell
$snapin = Get-PSSnapin | Where-Object {$_.Name -eq 'Microsoft.
SharePoint.Powershell'}
if ($snapin -eq $null) {
Write-Host "Loading SharePoint Powershell Snapin"
Add-PSSnapin "Microsoft.SharePoint.Powershell"
}

$SPSite = Get-SPSite | Where-Object {$_.Url -eq $SiteUrl}
  if($SPSite -ne $null)
  {
  Write-Host "Connecting to root site site"
```

```
$PressReleaseWeb = $SPSite.OpenWeb("/PressReleases")
$pubWeb = [Microsoft.SharePoint.Publishing.PublishingWeb]::GetPu
blishingWeb($PressReleaseWeb)


Write-Host "Retrieving a press release page"
$page=$pubWeb.GetPublishingPages() | Where-Object {$_.Name -eq
$PressReleaseFileName}


Write-Host "Adding an editor web part to a press release page"
$webPartManager=$PressReleaseWeb.GetLimitedWebPartManager($page.
Url, [System.Web.UI.WebControls.WebParts.
PersonalizationScope]::Shared)
$editorWebPart=new-object  Microsoft.SharePoint.WebPartPages.
ContentEditorWebPart
$editorWebPart.ChromeType=[System.Web.UI.WebControls.WebParts.
PartChromeType]::TitleOnly
$editorWebPart.Title="Press Release Information"
$webPartManager.AddWebPart($editorWebPart, "Right", 0);


Write-Host "Adding an image viewer web part to a press release
page"
$imageWebPart = new-object Microsoft.SharePoint.WebPartPages.
ImageWebPart
$imageWebPart.ChromeType=[System.Web.UI.WebControls.WebParts.
PartChromeType]::TitleOnly
$imageWebPart.Title="Press Release Info Image"
$webPartManager.AddWebPart($imageWebPart, "Footer", 0);


Write-Host "Checking in and publishing changes"
$page.CheckIn("Checked in by PowerShell script")
$page.listItem.File.Publish("Published by PowerShell script")


if ($page.listItem.ParentList.EnableModeration)
{
    $modInformation = $page.listItem.ModerationInformation
    if($modInformation.Status -ne [Microsoft.SharePoint.SPModerat
ionStatusType]::Approved)
    {
        $page.ListItem.File.Approve("Approved by PowerShell
script")
    }
}
 $PressReleaseWeb.Dispose()
}
$SPSite.Dispose()
```

3. Click **File | Save** to save the script to your development machine's desktop. Set the filename of the script to `ProvisioningWebParts.ps1`.

4. Open the PowerShell console window and call `ProvisioningWebParts.ps1` using the following command:

   PS C:\Users\Administrator\Desktop> .\ ProvisioningWebParts.ps1

5. As a result, your PowerShell script will set two related lists as shown in the following screenshot:

6. Now, let's switch to our **SharePoint Publishing Site**: http://www.contoso.com/

7. From the **Quick launch** of the site, click **Press Releases**.

8. Click **Site Actions | View All Site Content**.

9. Under the **Document Libraries** category, click the **Pages** library.

10. Click the **PressRelease** page to view it.

11. Take note of the two web parts provisioned to the page, **Press Release Info Image** and **Press Release Information**, as shown in the following screenshot:

How it works...

In this recipe, we defined the URL and the page where the web parts are going to be provisioned and the name of the page, as our script variables:

```
$SiteUrl = "http://www.contoso.com"
$PressReleaseFileName = "PressRelease.aspx"
```

Note that in this recipe, we're using publishing site collection with a different URL and not our collaboration site collection.

Next, we loaded PowerShell SharePoint snap-in and retrieved the current site collection object. The demonstration environment you have downloaded in *Chapter 1, PowerShell Scripting Methods and Creating Custom PowerShell Commands,* contains the sub-site under the main site URL. The sub-site is used for demo press releases and we get a hold of it using the following command:

$PressReleaseWeb = $SPSite.OpenWeb("/PressReleases")

We then convert the press release web object to a publishing site object using the following command:

$pubWeb = [Microsoft.SharePoint.Publishing.PublishingWeb]::GetPublishingWeb($PressReleaseWeb)

Next, we get a hold of the page which will have our new web parts provisioned using a command as follows:

$page=$pubWeb.GetPublishingPages() | Where-Object {$_.Name -eq $PressReleaseFileName}

Note that the page must be checked out before it's edited or any web parts managed on it.

Each SharePoint publishing page contains an instance of the web part manager object responsible for managing web parts on the page. We get hold of the web part manager using the following command:

$webPartManager=$PressReleaseWeb.GetLimitedWebPartManager($page.Url, [System.Web.UI.WebControls.WebParts.PersonalizationScope]::Shared)

In the preceding command, we pass in the URL of the page where we connect to the web part manager as well as the scope of the connection. By connecting to the Shared scope, we ensure that changes made to web part on the page will be visible to all users of the site.

Next, we create a new instance of the content editor web part object:

$editorWebPart=new-object Microsoft.SharePoint.WebPartPages. ContentEditorWebPart

We set some of the basic properties of the web part. More details on setting up properties will be dedicated in the next recipe. Once finished, we add the web part to the page:

```
$webPartManager.AddWebPart($editorWebPart, "Right", 0);
```

In a similar way, we also add an image viewer web part to the page using the following command:

```
$imageWebPart = new-object Microsoft.SharePoint.WebPartPages.ImageWebPart
```

In the preceding command, the image viewer web part is added to the footer of the page as you can see in the following command:

```
$webPartManager.AddWebPart($imageWebPart, "Footer", 0)
```

Finally, the page is checked in, published, and approved as described in details in the previous recipe

See also

The *Creating and editing publishing pages with PowerShell* recipe in this chapter.

Configuring web parts in bulk with PowerShell

When working with SharePoint pages and web parts on them, you may often find a need to modify web part properties for existing or new web parts throughout the site. For example, a new web part may be required to be deployed to many pages on the site and needs to be configured with the required parameters. In another scenario, your developers may have updated the functionality of the web part and now it consumes a new set of properties or expects different values for its properties. If the modified web part is used on multiple pages within your site, it may crash or not function properly until valid configuration values are provisioned on each page which uses it.

In this recipe, we'll take a look at how you can access the web part properties and make changes to the most common web part properties affecting the web part look and feel as well as some of the configuration parameters related to web part behavior.

Using this approach, you can make required customizations fast without introducing significant downtime in your environment. Let's take a look at what's involved in provisioning web part property changes using PowerShell.

Getting ready

Considering you have already set up your virtual development environment as described in *Chapter 1, PowerShell Scripting Methods and Creating Custom Commands*, we'll get right into authoring our script.

It's assumed you are also familiar with provisioning web parts to SharePoint publishing pages as described in the previous recipe.

In this recipe we'll be using PowerGUI to author the script, which means you will be required to be logged in with an administrator's role on the target Virtual Machine.

How to do it...

Let's take a look at what's involved in configuring web part properties on our SharePoint pages using PowerShell:

1. Click **Start | All Programs | PowerGUI | PowerGUI Script Editor**.

2. In the main script editing window of PowerGUI, add the following script:

```
# Defining script variables
$SiteUrl = "http://www.contoso.com"
$PressReleaseFileName = "PressRelease.aspx"


# Loading Microsoft.SharePoint.PowerShell
$snapin = Get-PSSnapin | Where-Object {$_.Name -eq 'Microsoft.
SharePoint.Powershell'}
if ($snapin -eq $null) {
Write-Host "Loading SharePoint Powershell Snapin"
Add-PSSnapin "Microsoft.SharePoint.Powershell"
}


$SPSite = Get-SPSite | Where-Object {$_.Url -eq $SiteUrl}
  if($SPSite -ne $null)
  {
  Write-Host "Connecting to root site site"
  $PressReleaseWeb = $SPSite.OpenWeb("/PressReleases")
  $pubWeb = [Microsoft.SharePoint.Publishing.PublishingWeb]::GetPu
blishingWeb($PressReleaseWeb)

  Write-Host "Retrieving a press release page"
  $page=$pubWeb.GetPublishingPages() | Where-Object {$_.Name -eq
$PressReleaseFileName}

  Write-Host "Configuring an editor web part on a press release
page"
```

```
$webPartManager=$PressReleaseWeb.GetLimitedWebPartManager($page.
Url, [System.Web.UI.WebControls.WebParts.
PersonalizationScope]::Shared)
    $editorWebPart = $webPartManager.WebParts | Where-Object {$_.
Title -eq "Press Release Information"}
    $xmlDoc = New-Object System.Xml.XmlDocument
    $xmlElement = $xmlDoc.CreateElement("ContentElement")
    $xmlElement.InnerText = "For press release information contact:
<strong>Brad Sutton</strong>"
    $editorWebPart.Content = $xmlElement
    $webPartManager.SaveChanges($editorWebPart)

    Write-Host "Configuring an image viewer web part on a press
release page"
    $imageWebPart = $webPartManager.WebParts | Where-Object {$_.
Title -eq "Press Release Info Image"}
    $imageWebPart.ImageLink = "http://www.contoso.com/
SiteCollectionImages/PR.gif"
    $imageWebPart.HorizontalAlignment = "Left"
    $imageWebPart.ZoneID = "Header"
    $webPartManager.SaveChanges($imageWebPart)

    Write-Host "Checking in and publishing changes"
    $page.CheckIn("Checked in by PowerShell script")
    $page.listItem.File.Publish("Published by PowerShell script")

    if ($page.listItem.ParentList.EnableModeration)
    {
        $modInformation = $page.listItem.ModerationInformation
        if($modInformation.Status -ne [Microsoft.SharePoint.SPModerat
ionStatusType]::Approved)
        {
            $page.ListItem.File.Approve("Approved by PowerShell
script")
        }
    }
    $PressReleaseWeb.Dispose()
    }
$SPSite.Dispose()
```

3. Click **File | Save** to save the script to your development machine's desktop. Set the filename of the script to `ConfiguringWebParts.ps1`.

4. Open the PowerShell console window and call `ConfiguringWebParts.ps1` using the following command:

   PS C:\Users\Administrator\Desktop> .\ ConfiguringWebParts.ps1

5. As a result, your PowerShell script will execute with results as shown in the following screenshot:

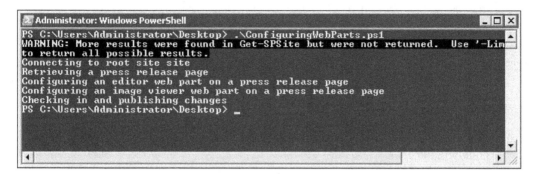

6. Now, let's switch to our **SharePoint Publishing Site**: http://www.contoso.com/

7. From the **Quick launch** of the site, click **Press Releases**.

8. Click **Site Actions | View All Site Content**.

9. Under the **Document Libraries** category, click the **Pages** library.

10. Click the **PressRelease** page to view it.

11. Take note of the two web parts earlier provisioned to the page with a new content in them as well as one of the web parts in the different zone, as shown in the following screenshot:

How it works...

We started by defining the URL and the page where existing web part properties are going to be changed and saved back to the page name specified:

```
$SiteUrl = "http://www.contoso.com"
$PressReleaseFileName = "PressRelease.aspx"
```

Just as before, in this recipe, we're publishing a site collection with a different URL and not our collaboration site collection.

We loaded PowerShell SharePoint snap-in and retrieved the current site collection object. The demonstration environment you have downloaded in *Chapter 1, PowerShell Scripting Methods and Creating Custom Commands*, contains the sub-site under the main site URL. The sub-site is used for demo press releases and we get a hold of it using the following command:

$PressReleaseWeb = $SPSite.OpenWeb("/PressReleases")

Next, we converted the press release web object to a publishing site object using the following command:

$pubWeb = [Microsoft.SharePoint.Publishing.PublishingWeb]::GetPublishingW eb($PressReleaseWeb)

Next, we get a hold of the page where our existing web parts are defined:

```
$page=$pubWeb.GetPublishingPages() | Where-Object {$_.Name -eq
$PressReleaseFileName}
```

In order to interact with our web parts, we established a connection to web part configuration manager:

```
$webPartManager=$PressReleaseWeb.GetLimitedWebPartManager($page.Url,
[System.Web.UI.WebControls.WebParts.PersonalizationScope]::Shared)
```

We can now connect to a desired web part using a variety of ways, in our case we enumerate all of the web parts on the page and select the one with the title Press Release Information, which happens to be our previously provisioned content editor web part:

```
$editorWebPart = $webPartManager.WebParts | Where-Object {$_.Title -eq
"Press Release Information"}
```

The content editor web part is one of the most common web parts used on SharePoint sites. The way the content editor web part stores content on the site is by using an XML element with the content defined as the element node. Therefore, in order to add content to a content editor web part, we create an XML node and add the content as one of the children on that node, as follows:

```
$xmlDoc = New-Object System.Xml.XmlDocument
$xmlElement = $xmlDoc.CreateElement("ContentElement")
```

```
$xmlElement.InnerText = "For press release information contact:
<strong>Brad Sutton</strong>"
$editorWebPart.Content = $xmlElement
```

To save changes to the page, we call the following command on the web part configuration manager:

$webPartManager.SaveChanges($editorWebPart)

Similar to the content editor web part, we get hold of the image viewer web part. This time, we pass the title of the image viewer web part `Press Release Info Image`:

```
$imageWebPart = $webPartManager.WebParts | Where-Object {$_.Title -eq
"Press Release Info Image"}
```

Naturally, the image viewer web part has a different set of properties, so we get a hold of each of the properties we need to change such as image link, horizontal alignment of the image, and zone ID. The `Zone ID`, in this case, is available for all of the SharePoint web parts and allows you to change the zone where the web part has been originally provisioned by specifying the zone keyword. The zone keyword is defined in the page layout, which is used by the current page.

Once ready, the web part properties are saved to the page using the following command:

$webPartManager.SaveChanges($imageWebPart)

Finally, the page is checked in, published, and approved as described in detail in the *Creating and editing publishing pages with PowerShell recipe*.

See also

The *Creating and editing publishing pages with PowerShell* and *Provisioning web parts in bulk on to SharePoint pages* recipes in this chapter

Provisioning list rollups using Powershell

Lists and libraries are used everywhere in SharePoint and content from various specific sites is often required to be rolled up on parent sites or a home page. For example, a company intranet may have a designated section for company news. Your business users may ask you to roll up company news to a home page so that everyone can see the latest company news or the latest company performance. Additionally, you may be asked to filter news items based on the category of the current news item.

Out-of-the-box SharePoint has a variety of tools you can use to roll up data. One of the tools we'll use here is **Content Query Web Part** which allows us to specify the data on the site we'd like to see and roll it up on the chosen page.

In this recipe, we'll take a look at what's involved with provisioning an instance of such a web part using PowerShell.

This approach will come in handy when you need to provision a series of roll ups for each instance of a page to roll up related items to this page based on the selected criteria.

Getting ready

Considering you have already set up your virtual development environment as described in *Chapter 1, PowerShell Scripting Methods and Creating Custom Commands*, we'll get right into authoring our script.

We'll assume you are also familiar with modifying out-of-the-box web part properties as described in the previous recipe.

In this recipe, we'll be using PowerGUI to author the script, which means you will be required to be logged in with an administrator's role on the target Virtual Machine.

How to do it...

Now we'll see how you can provision list rollups to pages on your intranet using PowerShell:

1. Click **Start | All Programs | PowerGUI | PowerGUI Script Editor**.

2. In the main script editing window of PowerGUI, add the following script:

```
# Defining script variables
$SiteUrl = "http://www.contoso.com"
$PressReleaseLanding = "default.aspx"

# Loading Microsoft.SharePoint.PowerShell
$snapin = Get-PSSnapin | Where-Object {$_.Name -eq 'Microsoft.
SharePoint.Powershell'}
if ($snapin -eq $null) {
Write-Host "Loading SharePoint Powershell Snapin"
Add-PSSnapin "Microsoft.SharePoint.Powershell"
}

$SPSite = Get-SPSite | Where-Object {$_.Url -eq $SiteUrl}
  if($SPSite -ne $null)
  {
  Write-Host "Connecting to root site site"
  $PressReleaseWeb = $SPSite.OpenWeb("/PressReleases")
  $pubWeb = [Microsoft.SharePoint.Publishing.PublishingWeb]::GetPu
blishingWeb($PressReleaseWeb)
```

```
Write-Host "Retrieving a press release page"
$page=$pubWeb.GetPublishingPages() | Where-Object {$_.Name -eq
$PressReleaseLanding}

Write-Host "Adding a list roll up to a press release page"
$webPartManager=$PressReleaseWeb.GetLimitedWebPartManager($page.
Url, [System.Web.UI.WebControls.WebParts.
PersonalizationScope]::Shared)
$queryWebPart = new-object Microsoft.SharePoint.Publishing.
WebControls.ContentByQueryWebPart
$queryWebPart.ChromeType=[System.Web.UI.WebControls.WebParts.
PartChromeType]::TitleOnly
$queryWebPart.WebUrl = "~sitecollection/PressReleases"
$queryWebPart.Title="Latest Press Releases"
$queryWebPart.FilterField1 = "{fa564e0f-0c70-4ab9-b863-
0177e6ddd247}"
$queryWebPart.FilterOperator1 = "Contains"
$queryWebPart.FilterDisplayValue1 = "press release"
$webPartManager.AddWebPart($queryWebPart, "Right", 1);

Write-Host "Checking in and publishing changes"
$page.CheckIn("Checked in by PowerShell script")
$page.listItem.File.Publish("Published by PowerShell script")

if ($page.listItem.ParentList.EnableModeration)
{
    $modInformation = $page.listItem.ModerationInformation
    if($modInformation.Status -ne [Microsoft.SharePoint.SPModerat
ionStatusType]::Approved)
    {
        $page.ListItem.File.Approve("Approved by PowerShell
script")
    }
}
 $PressReleaseWeb.Dispose()
}
$SPSite.Dispose()
```

3. Click **File | Save** to save the script to your development machine's desktop. Set the filename of the script to `ProvisionListRollup.ps1`.

4. Open the PowerShell console window and call `ProvisionListRollup.ps1` using the following command:

   PS C:\Users\Administrator\Desktop> .\ ProvisionListRollup.ps1

5. As a result, your PowerShell script will execute with results as shown in the following screenshot:

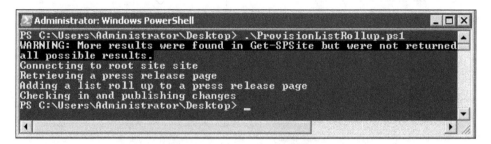

6. Next, let's switch to our **SharePoint Publishing Site**: http://www.contoso.com/

7. From the **Quick launch** of the site, click **Press Releases**.

8. Click **Site Actions | View All Site Content**.

9. Under the **Document Libraries** category, click the **Pages** library.

10. Select the **PressRelease** page and from the ribbon's **Documents** tab, click **Manage | Edit Properties**.

11. Ensure the value of the **Title** property includes **press release** since this is how our press releases are going to be rolled up, as shown in the following screenshot:

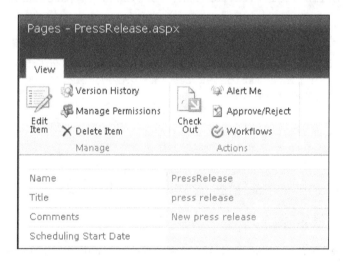

12. Click the **Press Releases** link from the **Quick launch** of the site and see the **Latest Press Releases** web part now rolling up our press release page.

How it works...

We started our script with configuring the script variables, such as site URL of our publishing site:

```
$SiteUrl = "http://www.contoso.com"
```

We also define the variable for the filename of the page which will have the rollup defined on it:

```
$PressReleaseLanding = "default.aspx".
```

We then load the SharePoint PowerShell snap-in:

```
Add-PSSnapin "Microsoft.SharePoint.Powershell"
```

From here, we connect to the press releases site where our rollup is going to be defined:

```
$PressReleaseWeb = $SPSite.OpenWeb("/PressReleases")
```

Since the press release site is a publishing site, we convert our existing site object to a publishing site object so we can take advantage of specific methods available for publishing sites:

```
$pubWeb = [Microsoft.SharePoint.Publishing.PublishingWeb]::GetPublishi
ngWeb($PressReleaseWeb)
```

We got a hold of the page that is going to have a rollup defined on it, which is a `default.aspx`, as shown in the following code:

```
$page=$pubWeb.GetPublishingPages() | Where-Object {$_.Name -eq
$PressReleaseLanding}
```

Note that you need to check out the page before we can make any changes on it.

We then connect to the shared view of the page by interfacing with the web part configuration manager as shown in the following code:

```
$webPartManager=$PressReleaseWeb.GetLimitedWebPartManager($page.Url,
[System.Web.UI.WebControls.WebParts.PersonalizationScope]::Shared)
```

To define our rollup, we are using **Content Query Web Part**, which is an out-of-the-box web part defined as follows:

```
$queryWebPart = new-object Microsoft.SharePoint.Publishing.
WebControls.ContentByQueryWebPart
```

Apart from some generic properties, such as a title and the chrome of the web part, we define the following:

Parameter	Description
WebUrl	The web from which the rolled up content will come from.
FilterField1	The field ID used to filter list items on. This property is optional and is only applicable when you require filtering on the content being rolled up. In our case, the field ID represents a Title field. Usually the ID will be given to you by the development team for fields which are custom.
FilterOperator1	An optional property which participates in a filtering operation and represents a filter operator. In this case, the value of Contains specifies value contained in the filter field.
FilterDisplayValue1	This property is used in a filtering operation and holds the value to which the field is to be compared to when filtering is performed.

When ready, we add a newly configured web part to a page:

```
$webPartManager.AddWebPart($queryWebPart, "Right", 1);
```

As you can see, **Content Query Web Part** contains a number of configuration properties which can facilitate effective content roll up. Using information in this recipe, you can apply mechanisms required to configure and provision this web part and its related properties. For more information on other parameters available in **Content Query Web Part**, search *MSDN* with the key word: **ContentByQueryWebPart Members**.

Finally, the page is checked in, published, and approved as described in detail in the recipe *Creating and editing publishing pages with PowerShell*.

See also

The *Provisioning web parts in bulk on to SharePoint pages* and *Configuring web parts in bulk with PowerShell* recipes in this chapter.

8
Managing Documents and Records in SharePoint with PowerShell

In this chapter, we will cover:

- ▸ Provisioning document and records center with PowerShell
- ▸ Configuring record routing
- ▸ Configuring a common record expiration policy
- ▸ Creating a custom expiration policy for the record
- ▸ Configuring a content hub for content types used in records center

Introduction

SharePoint record management features facilitate a variety of document management scenarios far beyond traditional records management. Using some of the features in the SharePoint 2010 record center site template, you can store documents and manage their retention and lifecycle based on a variety of metadata driven workflows. In this chapter, we'll take a look at how you can provision a record center site and configure some of its most popular features.

Since each record routed to a record center can be passed through a set of rules before directed to a final destination library, it's important to understand how you can create your own routing rules. In this chapter, we'll see how you can use PowerShell to quickly create the most common metadata-driven routing rules and without a significant downtime while deploying.

Once in the record center, each document is likely to go through the retention lifecycle. In this chapter, we'll see how you can create some of the most common retention rules and execute the most common retention actions based on those rules. This approach will allow your record center to have a long-term plan as to how the data inside the record repository is going to be disposed off when applicable. If a few of the most common retention scenarios don't apply to your particular case, you can always trigger custom retention actions as we do in the recipe of this chapter.

By using PowerShell for defining your rules, you will be able to reduce the time and manual errors associated within configuring the retention stages manually using the SharePoint user interface.

Finally, we'll take a look at one of the new features in SharePoint 2010, the **content hub** feature. This feature allows sites to share content type definitions across other sites. With this approach, you will be able to centrally define the metadata and the content types used on your site and easily propagate it to the rest of your sites. Using PowerShell, in this scenario, you will save downtime associated with configuring the content hub functionality using a solution package.

Provisioning documents and records center with PowerShell

Just as any other SharePoint site, record center functionality comes with a site template with a set of features which facilitate various document and record management scenarios. Typically, in an organization implementing record and document management features, the configuration involved with how records are stored is sensitive. After all, if important electronic records, which are trusted to reside in a safe record center environment, are lost, the organization may find itself vulnerable to regulations.

PowerShell provides an excellent solution allowing record center configuration to be scripted as a replicable and traceable set of commands to which you can always go back to. If your organization uses record routing rules based on metadata, as we'll see further, you can manage to create many of the rules quickly just by scripting them with PowerShell.

Let's take a look at what's involved in using PowerShell to script some of the main configurations involved in setting up a SharePoint record center.

Getting ready

Considering you have already set up your virtual development environment as described in *Chapter 1, PowerShell Scripting Methods and Creating Custom Commands*, you will already have access to a record center template with all of the features installed. In this recipe, we'll provision a new instance of a record center site based on the out-of-the-box template.

Since we'll be using PowerGUI in this recipe to author the script, you will require to be logged in with an administrator's role on the target Virtual Machine.

How to do it...

Let's take a look at how we create a record center site in SharePoint using PowerShell:

1. Click **Start | All Programs | PowerGUI | PowerGUI Script Editor**.

2. In the main script editing window of PowerGUI, add the following script:

```
# Defining script variables
$SiteUrl = "http://intranet.contoso.com"
$RecordCenterUrl = "recordscenter"

# Loading Microsoft.SharePoint.PowerShell
$snapin = Get-PSSnapin | Where-Object {$_.Name -eq 'Microsoft.
SharePoint.Powershell'}
if ($snapin -eq $null) {
Write-Host "Loading SharePoint Powershell Snapin"
Add-PSSnapin "Microsoft.SharePoint.Powershell"
}

$SPSite = Get-SPSite | Where-Object {$_.Url -eq $SiteUrl}
  if($SPSite -ne $null)
  {
    $RootWeb = $SPSite.RootWeb
  Write-Host "Provisioning records center"
   $RecordCenterWeb = New-SPWeb $SiteUrl/$RecordCenterUrl -Template
"OFFILE#1" -Addtotopnav -Useparenttopnav -Name "Record Center"

  Write-Host "Creating record library"
   $RecordLibraryTemplate = $RecordCenterWeb.ListTemplates | Where-
Object {$_.Name -eq "Record Library"}
   $RecordLibrary = $RecordCenterWeb.Lists.Add("New Records", "New
Records", $RecordLibraryTemplate);

  Write-Host "Records center provisioning complete"
  Write-Host "Configuring send-to connection"
```

```
$SendToHost = New-Object Microsoft.SharePoint.SPOfficialFileHost
$SendToHost.OfficialFileName = "My Record Center"
$SubmissionServiceUrl = $SiteUrl + "/" + $RecordCenterUrl + "/_
vti_bin/officialfile.asmx"
$SendToHost.OfficialFileUrl = $SubmissionServiceUrl
$SendToHost.ShowOnSendToMenu = $true
$SendToHost.Explanation = "Send a file to Records Center"
$SPSite.WebApplication.OfficialFileHosts.Add($SendToHost)
$SPSite.WebApplication.Update()

Write-Host "Send to configuration complete"
}
$SPSite.Dispose()
```

3. Click **File | Save** to save the script to your development machine's desktop. Set the filename of the script to `SetupRecordCenter.ps1`.

4. Open the PowerShell console window and call `SetupRecordCenter.ps1` using the following command:

    PS C:\Users\Administrator\Desktop> .\ SetupRecordCenter.ps1

5. As a result, your PowerShell script will create a site structure as shown in the following screenshot:

6. Now, from your browser, let's switch to our **SharePoint Intranet**: `http://intranet.contoso.com`.

7. From the home page's **main navigation**, click the **Record Center** link.

8. On the **Quick launch** menu, click the **All Site Content** link. On the resulting page, take note of the **New Records** library, as shown in the following screenshot:

9. Navigate back to the **SharePoint Intranet** site.

10. From the **Quick launch** menu on your site, click the **Shared Documents** library link.

11. Select any of the documents already provisioned into the library, and from the context menu of the item select **Send To | My Record Center**, as shown in the following screenshot:

12. Take note of how the item is now being moved to the drop off library of the newly created record center site with the resulting message as shown in the following screenshot:

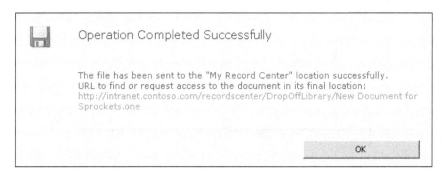

13. At this point, you can click the link provided in the window to navigate to the item which has now been sent to a record center.

How it works...

First, we defined the script variables. In this recipe, the variables include the URL of the intranet site and the URL of the records center site about to be provisioned:

```
$SiteUrl = "http://intranet.contoso.com"
$RecordCenterUrl = "recordscenter"
```

Once a PowerShell snap-in has been loaded, we get a hold of the instance of the current site and its root web. Provisioning of the record center site is no different from provisioning a SharePoint site of any other site template. The New-SPWeb command accepts the URL of the site and the template of our records center site as the main parameters as follows:

```
$RecordCenterWeb = New-SPWeb $SiteUrl/$RecordCenterUrl -Template
"OFFILE#1" -Addtotopnav -Useparenttopnav -Name "Record Center"
```

Next, we created an instance of a new record library so that incoming records can be routed to this library and not just dropped off in the default library. We start by enumerating available templates on the site and picking the record library template, as you can see in the following command:

```
$RecordCenterWeb.ListTemplates | Where-Object {$_.Name -eq "Record
Library"}
```

Next, we add the record library to the site by using the template just retrieved:

```
$RecordCenterWeb.Lists.Add("New Records", "New Records",
$RecordLibraryTemplate);
```

Now that the record center is created, we need to ensure that our users are able to send files to it from the **Intranet** site. SharePoint allows a connection inside the context menu of each item to be created, allowing user to pick an item and send it to the designated record center. You can have several connections defined representing several record centers where your users can drop off items to. SharePoint provides out-of-the-box configuration interface to add new item to the list of locations in the context menu. In this recipe, we provision the send-to locations using our script.

We start by creating an object which will represent a connection to a record center. This object will hold the URL, title, and other information which will help users identify where they send their files in the records center:

```
$SendToHost = New-Object Microsoft.SharePoint.SPOfficialFileHost
```

Once created, we give a name to our connection:

```
$SendToHost.OfficialFileName = "My Record Center"
```

Next, we define the web service which is going to handle the submission of items to a web service. SharePoint has an out-of-the-box web service which has all of the methods to facilitate submissions of new items to the records center. Next, we define the URL of the web service relative to the records center site we have provisioned above:

```
$SubmissionServiceUrl = $SiteUrl + "/" + $RecordCenterUrl + "/_vti_
bin/officialfile.asmx"

$SendToHost.OfficialFileUrl = $SubmissionServiceUrl
```

The next property will identify whether the connection will be displayed to users as an option in the context menu of the item on the **Intranet** site:

```
$SendToHost.ShowOnSendToMenu = $true
```

Finally, we capture the description of the connection for users to be able to identify where they send their items:

```
$SendToHost.Explanation = "Send a file to Records Center"
```

To ensure the connection is actually available for users to use, we need to add it to the collection of existing connections as follows:

```
$SPSite.WebApplication.OfficialFileHosts.Add($SendToHost)
```

We finalize the addition of our new connection by updating web application settings as shown in the following code:

```
$SPSite.WebApplication.Update()
```

See also

The *Provisioning site hierarchy automatically during solution deployment* recipe in *Chapter 2, Enterprise Content Deployment and Provisioning using PowerShell.*

Configuring record routing

Once created, your SharePoint record center site comes with variety of handy document management features. One of the most commonly used record management features is routing rules. By using routing rules, you can define which destination library your record will end up in based on the metadata of the incoming record or document. SharePoint comes with an out-of-the-box user interface which allows you to define record routing rules. However, in many cases, organizations have variety of routing rules which are used with different types of documents routed to different destinations based on the type of document. Some documents may need dedicated security permissions, others may need a special retention stages defined. In either case, if you need to define several dozen routing rules, PowerShell is your easiest rule provisioning option. Not only will you be able to script your configuration for a disaster-recovery scenario, but also the rule definition is easy when all you need to switch in your script is a couple of metadata values or the name of the destination library.

Let's take a look at what it takes to create a new record routing rule in SharePoint.

Getting ready

Considering you are using a virtual development environment as described in *Chapter 1, PowerShell Scripting Methods and Creating Custom Commands*, you already have a record center site instance provisioned and ready to use.

We'll assume you are also familiar with general record center concepts as described in this chapter.

In this recipe, we'll be using PowerGUI to author the script, which means you will be required to be logged in with an administrator's role on the target Virtual Machine.

How to do it...

Now that we have our record center in place, let's see how we can configure record routing using a PowerShell script.

1. Click **Start | All Programs | PowerGUI | PowerGUI Script Editor**.
2. In the main script editing window of PowerGUI, add the following script:

```
# Defining script variables
$SiteUrl = "http://intranet.contoso.com"
$RecordCenterUrl = "recordscenter"
```

```
# Loading Microsoft.SharePoint.PowerShell
$snapin = Get-PSSnapin | Where-Object {$_.Name -eq 'Microsoft.
SharePoint.Powershell'}
if ($snapin -eq $null) {
Write-Host "Loading SharePoint Powershell Snapin"
Add-PSSnapin "Microsoft.SharePoint.Powershell"
}

$SPSite = Get-SPSite | Where-Object {$_.Url -eq $SiteUrl}
  if($SPSite -ne $null)
  {
    Write-Host "Connecting to the Records Center at:"
$RecordCenterUrl
    $RecordsCenterWeb = $SPSite.OpenWeb($RecordCenterUrl)

  Write-Host "Creating record routing rule"
    $RoutingRules = $RecordsCenterWeb.Lists["Content Organizer
Rules"];
    $Rule = $RoutingRules.Items.Add()
    $Rule["RoutingRuleName"] = "New Library Rule"
    $Rule["Title"] = "New Library Rule"
    $Rule["RoutingEnabled"] = $true
    $Rule["RoutingPriority"] = 5
    $Rule["RoutingConditionProperties"] = "Title"
    $Rule["RoutingRuleExternal"] = $false
    $Rule["RoutingContentType"] = "Document"
    $Rule["RoutingTargetLibrary"] = "New Records"
    $Rule["RoutingTargetPath"] = "/recordscenter/New Records"
    $Rule["RoutingTargetPath"] = "/recordscenter/New Records"
    $Rule["RoutingConditions"] = '<Conditions><Condition
Column="fa564e0f-0c70-4ab9-b863-0177e6ddd247|Title|Title"
Operator="Contains" Value="document" /></Conditions>'
    $Rule.Update()

  Write-Host "Routing rules configuration complete"
    $RecordsCenterWeb.Dispose()
    }
  $SPSite.Dispose()
```

3. Click **File | Save** to save the script to your development machine's desktop. Set the filename of the script to `SetupRecordRouting.ps1`.

4. Open the PowerShell console window and call `SetupRecordRouting.ps1` using the following command:

   PS C:\Users\Administrator\Desktop> .\ SetupRecordRouting.ps1

5. As a result, your PowerShell script will execute with an output as shown in the following screenshot:

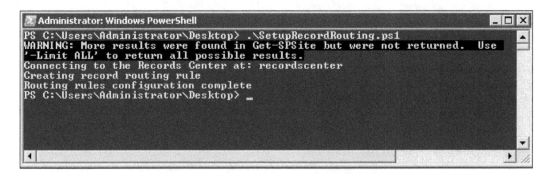

6. Now, from your browser, let's switch to our **SharePoint Intranet**: `http://intranet.contoso.com/`

7. From the home page's **Main navigation**, click the **Record Center** link.

8. Click **Site Action | Manage Records Center**.

9. Locate the section called **Setup Tasks and File Plan Creation** on the main page and click the link titled **Step 3: Create content organizer rules**.

10. In the **Content Organizer Rules** list, click on the newly created **New Library Rule**.

11. Select **Edit** from the routing rule model dialog and take note of the rule details as shown in the following screenshot:

Since some rules might be on hold and not used in the record routing, although defined, we enable the routing of our newly created rule by specifying the metadata as follows:

```
$Rule["RoutingEnabled"] = $true
```

The following routing priority will determine the priority of access to the web service as it's routing items in a busy record center. The valid property value here is 1 to 10:

```
$Rule["RoutingPriority"] = 5
```

Next, we capture the metadata fields which will be used in the rule engine to compare to values based on which item will be routed to the appropriate library:

```
$Rule["RoutingConditionProperties"] = "Title"
```

This value is followed by the parameter which determines whether the rule is going to route incoming items to external locations or not, in our case, it's `false`:

```
$Rule["RoutingRuleExternal"] = $false
```

Next, we specify the content type to which this rule applies:

```
$Rule["RoutingContentType"] = "Document"
```

The target library field is populated next, and will hold the value specifying the destination library for the record once it passes the rule conditions:

```
$Rule["RoutingTargetLibrary"] = "New Records"
```

If the preceding destination path includes folders, the following metadata field will capture the folder structure to where the record is going to be placed upon successfully passing the rule logic:

```
$Rule["RoutingTargetPath"] = "/recordscenter/New Records"
```

Finally, we define the routing conditions as a **CAML** rule. In this metadata field, we record the condition in the following format and specify the `Column`, `Operator`, and comparison `Value` using which the rule will need to execute:

```
$Rule["RoutingConditions"] = '<Conditions><Condition Column="fa564e0f-
0c70-4ab9-b863-0177e6ddd247|Title|Title" Operator="Contains"
Value="document" /></Conditions>'
```

The preceding line of code compares the value in the `Value` parameter to the `Column` parameter representing a column. The column here starts with the ID of the field followed by its internal and display name.

More info

To find out the ID and the internal name of your fields, navigate to the SharePoint root folder, as shown in the following screenshot, and open the `fields` library in the `Features` folder. The `fieldswss.xml` definition will contain most of the out-of-the-box fields and their respective information, as shown in the following screenshot:

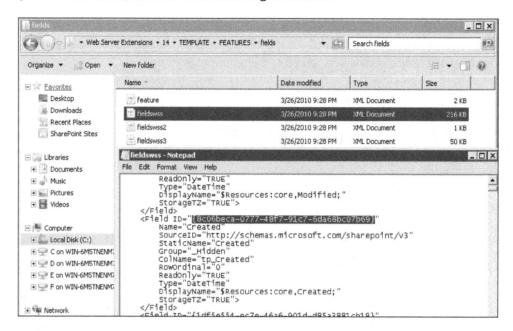

See also

The *Provisioning document and records center with PowerShell* recipe in this chapter.

Configuring a common record expiration policy

Record expiration policies are another handy feature in SharePoint which allow you to define what is going to happen with your document or record as it goes through its life cycle. Do you want to delete the record? Notify someone of document expiration? Launch a custom or out-of-the-box approval process before any action takes place? Those are all choices available to you when you choose to define expiration policy of the document or record container.

Record expiration policies are so common in document and record management scenarios, that many libraries in SharePoint typically have several policies defined on a library to capture variety of document types and scenarios.

With all of the policies defined in your libraries, it might be challenging to keep track of how various rules affect each other. Similarly, when you define a set of rules for the library, you may want to implement the same set for another library on one or more sites. Sounds complicated, it can be. Let's see how you can use PowerShell and how you can simplify the policy provisioning process for the library.

Getting ready

Considering you are using a virtual development environment as described in *Chapter 1, PowerShell Scripting Methods and Custom Commands*, you already have a record center site instance provisioned and ready to use.

We'll assume you are also familiar with general record center concepts as described in this chapter.

In this recipe, we'll be using PowerGUI to author the script, which means you will be required to be logged in with an administrator's role on the target Virtual Machine.

How to do it...

Let's see how expiration policy is configured for a record library using PowerShell.

1. Click **Start | All Programs | PowerGUI | PowerGUI Script Editor**.

2. In the main script editing window of PowerGUI, add the following script:

```
# Defining script variables
$SiteUrl = "http://intranet.contoso.com"
$RecordCenterUrl = "recordscenter"

# Loading Microsoft.SharePoint.PowerShell
$snapin = Get-PSSnapin | Where-Object {$_.Name -eq 'Microsoft.
SharePoint.Powershell'}
if ($snapin -eq $null) {
Write-Host "Loading SharePoint Powershell Snapin"
Add-PSSnapin "Microsoft.SharePoint.Powershell"
}

$SPSite = Get-SPSite | Where-Object {$_.Url -eq $SiteUrl}
   if($SPSite -ne $null)
   {
     Write-Host "Connecting to the Records Center at:"
$RecordCenterUrl
     $RecordsCenterWeb = $SPSite.OpenWeb($RecordCenterUrl)
```

```
Write-Host "Connecting to a record library"
$newRecords = $RecordsCenterWeb.Lists["New Records"];
Write-Host "Creating new record library policy"
$recordPolicy = [Microsoft.Office.RecordsManagement.
InformationPolicy.ListPolicySettings]($newRecords)
if ($recordPolicy.ListHasPolicy -eq 0)
{
  $recordPolicy.UseListPolicy = $true
  $recordPolicy.Update()
}
$contentType = $newRecords.ContentTypes["Document"]
[Microsoft.Office.RecordsManagement.InformationPolicy.Policy]::
CreatePolicy($contentType, $null)
$newPolicy = [Microsoft.Office.RecordsManagement.
InformationPolicy.Policy]::GetPolicy($contentType)
$newPolicy.Items.Add("Microsoft.Office.RecordsManagement.
PolicyFeatures.Expiration",
'<Schedules nextStageId="2" default="false"><Schedule
type="Default"><stages /></Schedule>'+
'<Schedule type="Record">'+
'<stages><data stageId="1">'+
'<formula id="Microsoft.Office.RecordsManagement.PolicyFeatures.
Expiration.Formula.BuiltIn">'+
'<number>1</number>'+
'<property>Created</property>'+
'<propertyId>8c06beca-0777-48f7-91c7-6da68bc07b69</propertyId>'+
'<period>days</period>'+
'</formula>'+
'<action type="action" id="Microsoft.Office.RecordsManagement.
PolicyFeatures.Expiration.Action.MoveToRecycleBin"/>'+
'</data></stages>'+
'</Schedule>'+
'</Schedules>')
$newPolicy.Update()
$newRecords.Update()

Write-Host "Routing rules configuration complete"
$RecordsCenterWeb.Dispose()
}
$SPSite.Dispose()
```

3. Click **File** | **Save** to save the script to your development machine's desktop. Set the filename of the script to `ProvisionRetentionPolicy.ps1`.

4. Open the PowerShell console window and call `ProvisionRetentionPolicy.ps1` using the following command:

   ```
   PS C:\Users\Administrator\Desktop> .\ ProvisionRetentionPolicy.ps1
   ```

5. As a result, your PowerShell script will execute and return results as shown in the following screenshot:

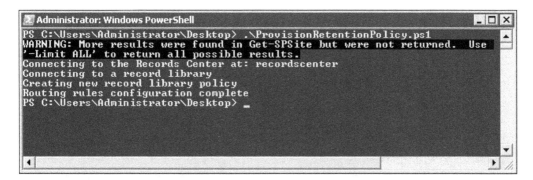

6. Now, from your browser, let's switch to our **SharePoint Intranet**: `http://intranet.contoso.com`

7. From the home page's **Main navigation**, click the **Record Center** link.

8. On the **Quick launch** menu, click the **All Site Content** link and from the resulting page click the **New Records** library.

9. From within the library, in the ribbon, click the **Library** tab, under the **Settings** group, click **Library Settings**.

10. From within the library settings, in the **Permissions and Management** category, click the **Information management policy settings** link.

11. Take note of the new policy assigned to the **Document** content type as shown in the following screenshot:

Content Type Policies

This table shows all the content types for this library, along with the policies and expiration schedules for each type. To modify the policy for a content type, click its name.

Content Type	Policy	Description	Retention Policy Defined
Document	Custom policy		Yes
Folder	None		No

*Note: Since this library is using library and folder retention, all documents will use those schedules. Content type retention policies are ignored.

12. Click the **Document** content type, and take note of the new policy provisioned for the content type under the **Retention** group, as shown in the following screenshot:

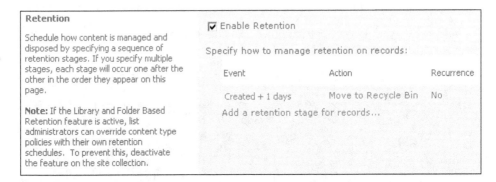

How it works...

First, we defined the script variables. In this recipe, the variables include the URL of the intranet site and the URL of the records center site we provisioned in this chapter:

```
$SiteUrl = "http://intranet.contoso.com"
$RecordCenterUrl = "recordscenter"
```

Once a PowerShell snap-in has been loaded, we get a hold of the instance of the current site and the record center created on it.

We access the record library we created in the preceding recipe:

```
$newRecords = $RecordsCenterWeb.Lists["New Records"];
```

Next, retrieve the policies setting on the library in order to turn on policy settings if they have not been turned on before for an existing library:

```
$recordPolicy = [Microsoft.Office.RecordsManagement.InformationPolicy.
ListPolicySettings]($newRecords)
```

Since each library may have multiple content types, we can have our retention policy defined per content type. This allows us to have multiple retention rules per library for a different content type, as shown in the following code:

```
$contentType = $newRecords.ContentTypes["Document"]
```

Here is how we create a new policy:

```
[Microsoft.Office.RecordsManagement.InformationPolicy.Policy]::CreateP
olicy($contentType, $null)
```

In the preceding code, the value of the content type will determine which content type the policy will be applied to. The actual policy is defined as shown in the following code:

```
$newPolicy.Items.Add("Microsoft.Office.RecordsManagement.
PolicyFeatures.Expiration",
  '<Schedules nextStageId="2" default="false"><Schedule
type="Default"><stages /></Schedule>'+
  '<Schedule type="Record">'+
  '<stages><data stageId="1">'+
  '<formula id="Microsoft.Office.RecordsManagement.PolicyFeatures.
Expiration.Formula.BuiltIn">'+
  '<number>1</number>'+
  '<property>Created</property>'+
  '<propertyId>8c06beca-0777-48f7-91c7-6da68bc07b69</propertyId>'+
  '<period>days</period>'+
  '</formula>'+
  '<action type="action" id="Microsoft.Office.RecordsManagement.
PolicyFeatures.Expiration.Action.MoveToRecycleBin"/>'+
  '</data></stages>'+
  '</Schedule>'+
  '</Schedules>')
```

Here, `<Schedule>` is defined for the policy, since each retention policy is activated by the value of the chosen date time column. The SharePoint timer job dedicated to monitoring retention in libraries will watch out for the policy definitions and items qualified for retention action. The schedule in our case is defined explicitly on the record, since we can have records and documents mixed together in SharePoint 2010.

The `<formula>` definition accepts the field title and ID as a parameter. This field information is also compared with the value of how many days from the defined column value it will take before the retention action takes place.

The `<action>` node defines the action to be triggered once the record policy conditions are satisfied. In our case, we move the item to a recycle bin, which is an out-of-the-box condition with implementation steps sealed in SharePoint as follows:

```
Microsoft.Office.RecordsManagement.PolicyFeatures.Expiration.Action.
MoveToRecycleBin
```

When done, we update both the policies and the record library with new changes:

```
$newPolicy.Update()
$newRecords.Update()
```

See also

The *Creating lists of custom structure and list items in them* recipe in *Chapter 3, Performing Advanced List and Content Operations in SharePoint using PowerShell*.

Creating a custom expiration policy for the record

In the previous recipe, you've become familiar with how you can provision most common expiration policies on your libraries with PowerShell. In some cases, more unique scenarios call for more complex solutions.

In this recipe, we'll take a look at some of the scenarios where you need to use custom action executed when the trigger for the expiration is set off.

We'll see how you can kick off a custom workflow performing one of the common actions related to document and record retention. The benefit of using PowerShell in this scenario is mainly around the flexibility when defining multiple policies on many libraries.

Let's see what is involved in using PowerShell to define custom actions for a retention policy.

Getting ready

Considering you are using a virtual development environment as described in *Chapter 1, PowerShell Scripting Methods and Custom Commands*, you already have a record center site instance provisioned and ready to use.

We'll assume you are also familiar with creating common retention policies as described in *Chapter 8, Managing Documents and Records in SharePoint with Powershell*.

In this recipe, we'll be using PowerGUI to author the script, which means you will be required to be logged in with an administrator's role on the target Virtual Machine.

How to do it...

Next, we see how more complex expiration policy can be created using PowerShell.

1. From your browser, navigate to our **SharePoint Intranet**: `http://intranet.contoso.com`

2. From the home page's **main navigation**, click the **Record Center** link.

3. On the **Quick launch** menu, click the **All Site Content** link. From the resulting page, click the **New Records** library.

4. From within the library, in the ribbon, click the **Library** tab, under the **Settings** group, click **Workflow Settings | Add a Workflow**, as shown in the following screenshot:

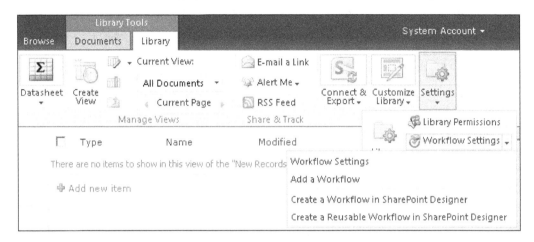

5. On the workflow configuration page, leave all of the settings as-is, except **Select a workflow template** value set to **Approval – SharePoint 2010**; set the **Name** of the workflow to **Approval**, as shown in the following screenshot:

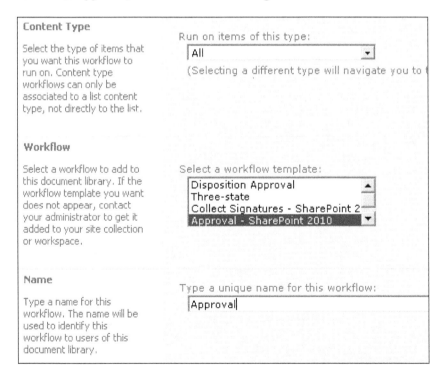

6. Accept all of the default configuration settings for the approval workflow on the next page and click **Save**.

7. Click **Start | All Programs | PowerGUI | PowerGUI Script Editor**.

8. In the main script editing window of PowerGUI, add the following script:

```
# Defining script variables
$SiteUrl = "http://intranet.contoso.com"
$RecordCenterUrl = "recordscenter"
$WorkflowName = "Approval"

# Loading Microsoft.SharePoint.PowerShell
$snapin = Get-PSSnapin | Where-Object {$_.Name -eq 'Microsoft.
SharePoint.Powershell'}
if ($snapin -eq $null) {
Write-Host "Loading SharePoint Powershell Snapin"
Add-PSSnapin "Microsoft.SharePoint.Powershell"
}

$SPSite = Get-SPSite | Where-Object {$_.Url -eq $SiteUrl}
  if($SPSite -ne $null)
  {
    Write-Host "Connecting to the Records Center at:"
$RecordCenterUrl
    $RecordsCenterWeb = $SPSite.OpenWeb($RecordCenterUrl)

  Write-Host "Connecting to a record library"
  $newRecords = $RecordsCenterWeb.Lists["New Records"];
  $worfklowInstance = $newRecords.WorkflowAssociations | Where-
Object {$_.Name -eq $WorkflowName}
  Write-Host "Creating new record library policy"
  $recordPolicy = [Microsoft.Office.RecordsManagement.
InformationPolicy.ListPolicySettings]($newRecords)
  if ($recordPolicy.ListHasPolicy -eq 0)
  {
    $recordPolicy.UseListPolicy = $true
    $recordPolicy.Update()
  }
  $contentType = $newRecords.ContentTypes["Document"]
  [Microsoft.Office.RecordsManagement.InformationPolicy.Policy]::
CreatePolicy($contentType, $null)
  $newPolicy = [Microsoft.Office.RecordsManagement.
InformationPolicy.Policy]::GetPolicy($contentType)
  $newPolicy.Items.Add("Microsoft.Office.RecordsManagement.
PolicyFeatures.Expiration",
  '<Schedules nextStageId="2" default="false"><Schedule
```

```
type="Default"><stages /></Schedule>'+
  '<Schedule type="Record">'+
  '<stages><data stageId="1">'+
  '<formula id="Microsoft.Office.RecordsManagement.PolicyFeatures.
Expiration.Formula.BuiltIn">'+
  '<number>1</number>'+
  '<property>Created</property>'+
  '<propertyId>8c06beca-0777-48f7-91c7-6da68bc07b69</propertyId>'+
  '<period>days</period>'+
  '</formula>'+
  '<action type="workflow" id="'+ $worfklowInstance.ID +'"/>'+
  '</data></stages>'+
  '</Schedule>'+
  '</Schedules>')
  $newPolicy.Update()
  $newRecords.Update()

  Write-Host "Routing rules configuration complete"
  $RecordsCenterWeb.Dispose()
  }
$SPSite.Dispose()
```

9. Click **File | Save** to save the script to your development machine's desktop. Set the filename of the script to `ProvisionWorkFlowDrivenRetentionPolicy.ps1`.

10. Open the PowerShell console window and call `ProvisionWorkFlowDrivenRetentionPolicy.ps1` using the following command:

    **PS C:\Users\Administrator\Desktop> .\
    ProvisionWorkFlowDrivenRetentionPolicy.ps1**

11. As a result, your PowerShell script will execute with an output as shown in the following screenshot:

12. Switch back to the main page of the records center and navigate to the **New Records** library.

13. From within the library, in the ribbon, click the **Library** tab, under the **Settings** group, click **Library Settings**.

14. From within the library settings, in the **Permissions and Management** category, click the **Information management policy settings** link.

15. Click the **Document** content type to open associated retention policies.

16. Take note of the newly provisioned, workflow-driven retention policy as shown in the following screenshot:

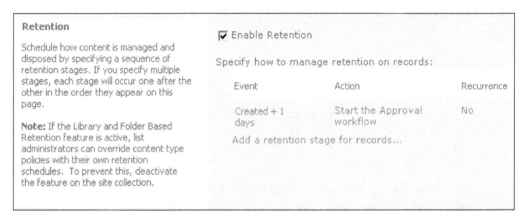

How it works...

When out-of-the-box retention actions do not satisfy your business requirements, you can launch an out-of-the-box or custom workflow as a retention action upon successful completion of all of the retention conditions.

In this recipe, we started with adding an instance of the out-of-the-box approval workflow to our record library. Although those steps were performed manually, you can automate adding the workflow to the library as we discussed in *Chapter 2, Enterprise Content Deployment and Provisioning using PowerShell*.

Next, we run our script with the following parameters.

We defined the script variables of the **Intranet** site and the URL of the records center site we have provisioned in this chapter:

```
$SiteUrl = "http://intranet.contoso.com"
$RecordCenterUrl = "recordscenter"
```

We also capture the name of the workflow instance that has been added to the library:

```
$WorkflowName = "Approval"
```

We then connect to the instance of our record center and the `New Record` library. We grab the `workflow ID` of the `Approval` workflow we previously defined:

```
$worfklowInstance = $newRecords.WorkflowAssociations | Where-Object
{$_.Name -eq $WorkflowName}
```

The preceding step is an important distinction between calling an out-of-the-box retention action and the one triggered by the workflow.

The next set of steps in the script, up to defining our custom retention formula, is exactly the same as in case of provisioning an out-of-the-box retention formula.

The difference comes when referencing the retention action for our policy:

```
'<action type="workflow" id="'+ $worfklowInstance.ID +'"/>'
```

Here, we defined the type of the action as `workflow` and `id` of the action and the workflow ID we have captured before in the script.

See also

The *Configuring a common record expiration policy* recipe in this chapter and *Using PowerShell to manage SharePoint custom and out-of-the-box workflows* recipe in *Chapter 2, Enterprise Content Deployment and Provisioning using PowerShell*.

Configuring content hub for content types used in records center

The content type hub feature in SharePoint 2010 came as a result of the necessity to share content type definitions across one or more sites in your SharePoint farm.

After all, as we have seen in *Chapter 7, Managing SharePoint Site Content in Bulk using PowerShell*, content types require provisioning of related fields and logic which are used throughout your site.

If you have several site collections in your farm, which is true even if you're using just a record center and an intranet, you will need to ensure your content types are all in sync so that routing rules on the record center site are working in sync with the metadata of incoming files.

In this recipe, we'll take a look at how PowerShell can help you with configuring a content type hub in the scenario where we have an **Intranet** site and the corporate portal.

Getting ready

Assuming you are already using a virtual development environment as described in *Chapter 1, PowerShell Scripting Methods and Creating Custom Commands*, you will have an environment with multiple sites which can take advantage of content hub capability.

In this recipe, we'll be using PowerGUI to author the script, which means you will be required to be logged in with an administrator's role on the target Virtual Machine.

How to do it...

Let's take a look at how a content type hub can be configured using a PowerShell script:

1. Click **Start | All Programs | PowerGUI | PowerGUI Script Editor**.

2. In the main script editing window of PowerGUI, add the following script:

```
# Defining script variables
$SiteUrl = "http://intranet.contoso.com"

# Loading Microsoft.SharePoint.PowerShell
$snapin = Get-PSSnapin | Where-Object {$_.Name -eq 'Microsoft.
SharePoint.Powershell'}
if ($snapin -eq $null) {
Write-Host "Loading SharePoint Powershell Snapin"
Add-PSSnapin "Microsoft.SharePoint.Powershell"
}

$SPSite = Get-SPSite | Where-Object {$_.Url -eq $SiteUrl}
  if($SPSite -ne $null)
  {
    Write-Host "Connecting to intranet"
  $RootWeb = $SPSite.RootWeb

  Write-Host "Enabling Content Type Hub feature"
  #$ContentTypeHubFeature = Enable-SPFeature "ContentTypeHub" -url
$RootWeb.Url

  Write-Host "Setting hub URL for service application"
  $managedMetadataSvcApp = Get-SPServiceApplication | Where-Object
{$_.TypeName -eq "Managed Metadata Service"}
  Set-SPMetadataServiceApplication -Identity
$managedMetadataSvcApp -HubURI $SiteUrl
```

```
Write-Host "Enabling publishing of content types"
  $managedMetadataProxy = Get-SPServiceApplicationProxy | Where-
Object {$_.TypeName -eq "Managed Metadata Service Connection"}
  Set-SPMetadataServiceApplicationProxy -Identity
$managedMetadataProxy -ContentTypeSyndicationEnabled
-ContentTypePushdownEnabled -Confirm:$false
  }


$SPSite.Dispose()
```

3. Click **File | Save** to save the script to your development machine's desktop. Set the filename of the script to SetupContentTypeHub.ps1.

4. Open the PowerShell console window and call SetupContentTypeHub.ps1 using the following command:

    PS C:\Users\Administrator\Desktop> .\ SetupContentTypeHub.ps1

5. As a result, your PowerShell script will execute with results as shown in the following screenshot:

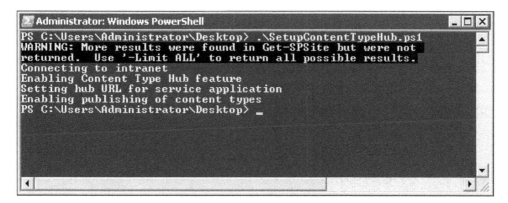

6. Now, let's switch to our **SharePoint Intranet**: http://intranet.contoso.com/

7. Click **Site Action | Site Settings**.

8. Under the **Galleries** category, click the **Site content types**.

9. Under the **Document Content Types** category, click **Document**.

10. On the resulting page, under **Settings**, click **Manage publishing for this content type**.

11. Ensure that the option for the content type publishing is set to **Publish** and click **OK**, as shown in the following screenshot:

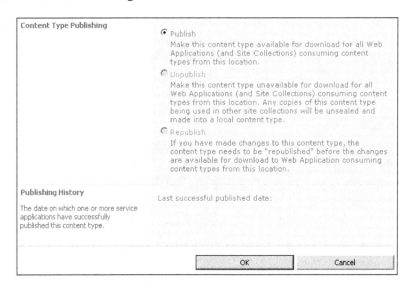

12. In your browser, navigate to another site collection in your farm, in our case `http://www.contoso.com`.

13. Click **Site Actions | Site Settings**.

14. Under **Site Collection Administration**, select **Content type publishing**.

15. Take note of how this site collection is now set to automatically receive updates about content type definition changes from within our **Intranet** site, as shown in the following screenshot:

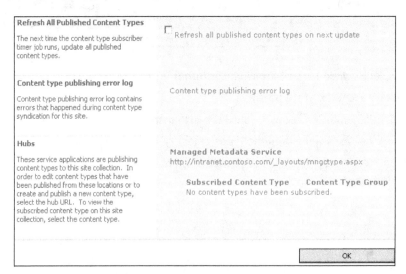

How it works...

We started by defining the URL of the site which is going to be our content type hub:

```
$SiteUrl = "http://intranet.contoso.com"
```

We loaded PowerShell SharePoint snap-in and retrieved a current site collection object.

The first step is to enable the content type hub feature on the site collection, which is going to be the hub:

```
#$ContentTypeHubFeature = Enable-SPFeature "ContentTypeHub" -url
$RootWeb.Url
```

Since the content type hub feature uses **Management Metadata Service** application, we need to create a connection to the managed metadata service application to perform additional configurations related to content type hub functionality:

```
$managedMetadataSvcApp = Get-SPServiceApplication | Where-Object
{$_.TypeName -eq "Managed Metadata Service"}
```

Next, with the connection information we have retrieved, we set the value of the content type hub to the URL of our intranet site:

```
Set-SPMetadataServiceApplication -Identity $managedMetadataSvcApp
-HubURI $SiteUrl
```

The preceding setting will make our intranet site a hub for all of the published content types.

Finally, we need to ensure all of the site collections in the farm will have synchronization set up to pull the updates to published content type definitions. To ensure that, we connect to the **Managed Metadata Service** application proxy:

```
$managedMetadataProxy = Get-SPServiceApplicationProxy | Where-Object
{$_.TypeName -eq "Managed Metadata Service Connection"}
```

Once connected, we enable content type syndication:

```
Set-SPMetadataServiceApplicationProxy -Identity $managedMetadataProxy
-ContentTypeSyndicationEnabled -ContentTypePushdownEnabled -
Confirm:$false
```

All that is left to do now is to publish content types which you want shared on all the other site collections. Once the content types are published, they are subject to a scheduled sweep by the synchronization service job which propagates content type definition changes to subscribed site collections.

See also

The *Creating basic and complex content types* recipe discussed in *Chapter 7, Managing SharePoint Site Content in Bulk using PowerShell*.

9
Administrating Web Application and Server Administration in SharePoint with PowerShell

In this chapter, we will cover:

- ▶ Configuring web application settings
- ▶ Parsing SharePoint logs using PowerShell
- ▶ Managing web application throttling settings
- ▶ Configuring sandbox solution policies
- ▶ Managing sandbox solutions on SharePoint site collections

Introduction

SharePoint web application administration and configuration involves managing multiple features and capabilities we have seen in chapters of this book. In this chapter, we'll take a look at what's involved with managing some of the most common configuration parameters in your web application and a farm.

We'll take a look at how you can troubleshoot issues with your custom and out-of-the-box functionality by using SharePoint logs and see where PowerShell can help you with getting all of the relevant information faster.

As your custom and out-of-the-box applications are used, you're likely to face an issue of managing available server resources effectively. In one of the recipes of this chapter, we'll take a look at some of the resource-throttling capabilities available in SharePoint, and how you can use PowerShell to speed up the configuration of such parameters for newly provisioned farms and environments.

The concept of sandbox solutions is new in SharePoint 2010 and has already gained a lot of popularity by truly giving SharePoint the ability to host solutions running separately for different site collections in the farm. As with any other feature, sandbox solutions have a variety of configuration options which allow you to control various parameters of execution of solution running in sandbox.

In this chapter, we'll take a look at how you can use PowerShell to configure sandbox solution policies, as well as manage the availability of sandbox solutions used on site collections in your farm.

Configuring web application settings

SharePoint has a variety of web application settings and configurations which, in typical scenarios, administrators interact with as the new site is created or on an on-going basis.

In this recipe, we'll take a look at how you can configure parameters such as SharePoint recycle bin settings, alert settings, and upload size limits. Also, we'll take a look at how you can manage whether the content on your site is opened within respective client applications or using the SharePoint 2010 Office Web Applications feature. We'll also see how you can create a site collection quota template allowing you to set initial limits for your site collections. We will then use the quota template on one of the existing site collections.

The benefit of performing the preceding configurations using PowerShell is that it allows you to script the most common environment configurations as a single set of instructions which can be used when similar environments are provisioned in your organization. From the disaster recovery standpoint, configuration scripts similar to the one we use in this recipe, can simplify recovery operation.

Let's take a look at what's involved in using PowerShell to script some of the most common configurations for SharePoint web application.

Getting ready

Considering you have already set up your virtual development environment as described in _Chapter 1, PowerShell Scripting Methods and Creating Custom Commands_, you already have installed and configured Office Web Applications feature used in this recipe.

Since, in this recipe, we'll be using PowerGUI to author the script, you will be required to be logged in with an administrator's role on the target Virtual Machine.

How to do it...

Let's see what's involved in configuring SharePoint web application settings with PowerShell:

1. Click **Start | All Programs | PowerGUI | PowerGUI Script Editor**.

2. In the main script editing window of PowerGUI, add the following script:

```
# Defining script variables
$SiteUrl = "http://intranet.contoso.com"

# Loading Microsoft.SharePoint.PowerShell
$snapin = Get-PSSnapin | Where-Object {$_.Name -eq 'Microsoft.
SharePoint.Powershell'}
if ($snapin -eq $null) {
Write-Host "Loading SharePoint Powershell Snapin"
Add-PSSnapin "Microsoft.SharePoint.Powershell"
}

Write-Host "Connecting to site"
$SPSite = Get-SPSite | Where-Object {$_.Url -eq $SiteUrl}
  if($SPSite -ne $null)
  {
    $webAppsFeatureId = $(Get-SPFeature -limit all | where {$_
.displayname -eq "OpenInClient"}).Id

  Write-Host "Enabling web apps feature"
   Enable-SPFeature $webAppsFeatureId -url $SiteUrl

  Write-Host "Changing default behavior for each library on web"
    $SPSite.RootWeb.Lists | ForEach-Object {$_.DefaultItemOpen =
[Microsoft.Sharepoint.DefaultItemOpen]::PreferClient;
   $_.Update()
   }
   Write-Host "Default application configured"

   Write-Host "Creating web application quota template"
```

```
    $QuotaTemplate = New-Object Microsoft.SharePoint.Administration.
SPQuotaTemplate
        $QuotaTemplate.Name = "Team Site"
        $QuotaTemplate.StorageMaximumLevel = 1048576
        $QuotaTemplate.StorageWarningLevel = 524288
        $AdminService = [Microsoft.SharePoint.Administration.
SPWebService]::ContentService
        $AdminService.QuotaTemplates.Add($QuotaTemplate)
        $AdminService.Update()

    Write-Host "Setting web application quota"
    $SPSite.WebApplication.DefaultQuotaTemplate = "Team Site"
    $SPSite.WebApplication.Update()

    Write-Host "Updating maximum file size upload limit"
    $SPSite.WebApplication.MaximumFileSize = 100
    $SPSite.WebApplication.Update()

    Write-Host "Updating recycle bin settings"
    $SPSite.WebApplication.RecycleBinEnabled = $true
    $SPSite.WebApplication.RecycleBinRetentionPeriod = 15
    $SPSite.WebApplication.Update()

    $SPSite.WebApplication.AlertsEnabled = $true
    $SPSite.WebApplication.AlertsMaximum = 100
    $SPSite.WebApplication.Update()

    Write-Host "Web application configuration complete"
    }
$SPSite.Dispose()
```

3. Click **File | Save** to save the script to your development machine's desktop. Set the filename of the script to `ConfigureWebApplication.ps1`.

4. Open the PowerShell console window and call `ConfigureWebApplication.ps1` using the following command:

   PS C:\Users\Administrator\Desktop> .\ ConfigureWebApplication.ps1

5. As a result, your PowerShell script will execute with the following output, as seen here:

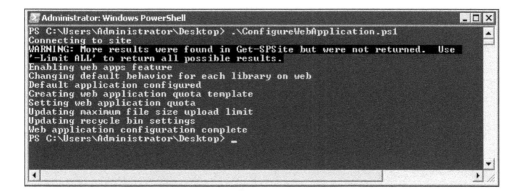

6. Now, from your browser, let's switch to our **SharePoint Intranet**:
   `http://intranet.contoso.com`

7. On the **Quick launch** menu, click the **Shared Documents** link and click any of the files created in MS Office application, such as MS Word. Observe the client application attempting to open the file, as shown in the following screenshot:

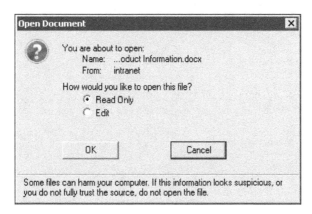

8. Now, navigate to the **SharePoint Central Administration** site by clicking **Start | All Programs | Microsoft SharePoint 2010 Products | SharePoint 2010 Central Administration**.

9. Click **Application Management | Manage web applications**.

10. Select **Intranet** web application and from the ribbon click **General Settings | General Settings**, as shown in the following screenshot:

11. Take note of how the web application settings have changed according to our configuration in the script, seen in the following screenshot:

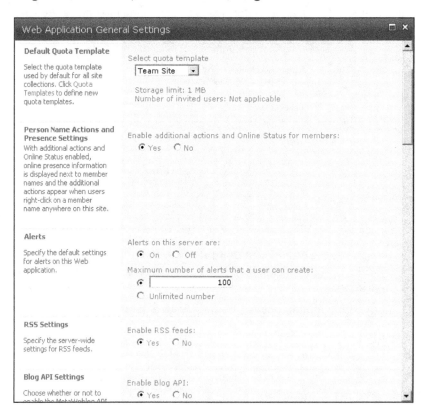

How it works...

In this recipe, we looked at how you can configure web application parameters that affect features available in the farm.

First, in our script, we defined the script variables. In this recipe, the only variable includes the URL of our intranet site:

```
$SiteUrl = "http://intranet.contoso.com"
```

Once a PowerShell snap-in has been loaded, we get hold of the instance of the current site. the first feature on the agenda will allow us to change how Microsoft Office documents are opened when clicked in the document library. With the introduction of Office Web Applications functionality, the default behavior is to open your office documents right in the browser using the applicable browser application. To change this behavior, we get a hold of the feature responsible for methods to open documents:

```
$webAppsFeatureId = $(Get-SPFeature -limit all | where {$_.displayname
-eq "OpenInClient"}).Id
```

We then enable this feature on the site with the following command:

```
Enable-SPFeature $webAppsFeatureId -url $SiteUrl
```

The last step in this configuration is to access the list or library which requires the new behavior and apply the setting using the following command:

```
$SPSite.RootWeb.Lists | ForEach-Object {
$_.DefaultItemOpen = [Microsoft.Sharepoint.DefaultItemOpen]::
PreferClient;
$_.Update()
}
```

Above, we iterate through the list collection on the site. For each list we change the default behavior to open items in the client application. An alternate option for opening application is in the browser by using the following parameter `[Microsoft.Sharepoint.DefaultItemOpen]::Browser`.

Next in our script, we create a quota template for the site collection and assign it to be used by our site collection. We start with creating new instance of the quota template:

```
$QuotaTemplate = New-Object Microsoft.SharePoint.Administration.
SPQuotaTemplate
```

We give it a name, storage maximum, and warning level:

```
$QuotaTemplate.Name = "Team Site"
$QuotaTemplate.StorageMaximumLevel = 1048576
$QuotaTemplate.StorageWarningLevel = 524288
```

Now that the quota template is created, we connect to the admin service which will help us with saving our newly created template:

```
$AdminService = [Microsoft.SharePoint.Administration.SPWebService]::
ContentService
```

To save the template, we add it to the collection of templates available in our admin service object:

```
$AdminService.QuotaTemplates.Add($QuotaTemplate)
$AdminService.Update()
```

Once the quota template is created, we can use it on the site and assign it to other site collections using the user interface or the script. Here is how we can assign the **Team Site** template to our site collection:

```
$SPSite.WebApplication.DefaultQuotaTemplate = "Team Site"
$SPSite.WebApplication.Update()
```

Among other items demonstrated in our script, we change the values for various parameters in the web application. One of the parameters we change is the maximum file size which is allowed to be uploaded to the site:

```
$SPSite.WebApplication.MaximumFileSize = 100
$SPSite.WebApplication.Update()
```

In this case, if the file exceeds the maximum capacity, it will not be uploaded to the library and the user will receive an error message. This is a handy setting but it only can be applied to all libraries in a particular web application and not to an individual library.

Here is how we specified whether the recycle bin feature is enabled on the site and what the retention period for deleted items is:

```
$SPSite.WebApplication.RecycleBinEnabled = $true
$SPSite.WebApplication.RecycleBinRetentionPeriod = 15
$SPSite.WebApplication.Update()
```

Lastly, we looked at how you can enable or disable the alerts feature on your web application and how many alerts can be sent to a user. This configuration is particularly handy if you want to optimize the usage of your outbound mail infrastructure:

```
$SPSite.WebApplication.AlertsEnabled = $true
$SPSite.WebApplication.AlertsMaximum = 100
$SPSite.WebApplication.Update()
```

See also

The *Provisioning site hierarchy during solution deployment* recipe in *Chapter 2, Enterprise Content Deployment and Provisioning using PowerShell*.

Parsing SharePoint logs using PowerShell

SharePoint has a variety of ways to extract information about issues in your farm. One of the most trusted sources to determine the cause of the particular issue is using Unified Logging Service (ULS) logs.

If your farm is set to catch detailed errors of multiple features in the system, you might run into a challenge to find the useful information from your logs purely due to the large volumes of data collected.

In this recipe, we'll take a look at how you can use PowerShell to extract useful information about issues happening in the farm.

Getting ready

Considering you are using virtual development environment as described in *Chapter 1, PowerShell Scripting Methods and Creating Custom Commands*, you're all set and your farm is configured to collect log information based on events happening in SharePoint.

In this recipe, we'll be using PowerGUI to author the script, which means you will be required to be logged in with an administrator's role on the target Virtual Machine.

How to do it...

Using the following steps, we'll take a look at how you can parse SharePoint logs easily with PowerShell:

1. Navigate to the **SharePoint Central Administration** site by clicking **Start | All Programs | Microsoft SharePoint 2010 Products | SharePoint 2010 Central Administration**.
2. Click **Monitoring** on the **quick launch** of the **Central Administration**.
3. Under **Reporting**, select **Configure diagnostic logging.**
4. In the resulting window, ensure you have ticked a checkbox beside **SharePoint Foundation** and **SharePoint Server**.
5. For **Least critical event to report to the event log**, select **Warning**.
6. For **Least critical event to report to the trace log**, select **Medium**.

7. Take note of the **Path** value for the **trace log**, as shown in the following screenshot:

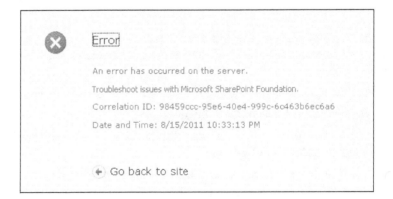

8. Click **OK** to save your settings.

9. Next, navigate to the following URL in your browser: `http://demo2010a:2010/_admin/AddEditTrustedDataSourceLocations.aspx`.

10. As a result, you should receive the following error message, this is expected:

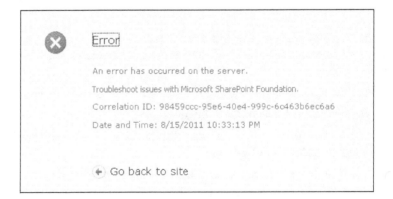

11. Take down the value of **Correlation ID** which will be used later on.

12. Click **Start | All Programs | PowerGUI | PowerGUI Script Editor**.

13. In the main script editing window of PowerGUI, add the following script:

```
# Defining script variables
$CorrelationID = "98459ccc-95e6-40e4-999c-6c463b6ec6a6"


# Loading Microsoft.SharePoint.PowerShell
$snapin = Get-PSSnapin | Where-Object {$_.Name -eq 'Microsoft.
SharePoint.Powershell'}
if ($snapin -eq $null) {
Write-Host "Loading SharePoint Powershell Snapin"
Add-PSSnapin "Microsoft.SharePoint.Powershell"
}


Write-Host "Retrieving ULS events by correlation ID"
$events = Get-SPLogEvent | Where-Object {$_.Correlation -eq
$CorrelationID}
$events | Select Timestamp, Message


Write-Host "Retrieving ULS events by area and level"
$events = Get-SPLogEvent | Where-Object {$_.Level -eq "Error" -and
{$_.Area -eq "SharePoint Foundation "}}
$events | Select Timestamp, Message


Write-Host "Retrieving ULS events by event timestamp"
Get-SPLogEvent -StartTime "08/15/2011 22:50:30" -EndTime
"08/15/2011 22:50:35"


Write-Host "Creating new ULS log file"
New-SPLogFile
```

14. Click **File | Save** to save the script to your development machine's desktop. Set the filename of the script to WorkingWithULSLogs.ps1.

15. Open the PowerShell console window and call WorkingWithULSLogs.ps1 using the following command:

```
PS C:\Users\Administrator\Desktop> .\ WorkingWithULSLogs.ps1
```

16. As a result, your PowerShell script will execute with an output as shown in the following screenshot:

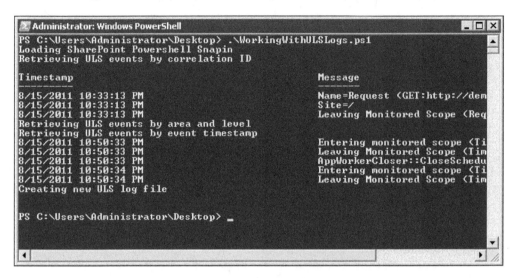

17. Now, from Windows Explorer on your server, navigate to `C:\Program Files\ Common Files\Microsoft Shared\Web Server Extensions\14\LOGS` to ensure a new log file has been created as per our script, as shown in the following screenshot:

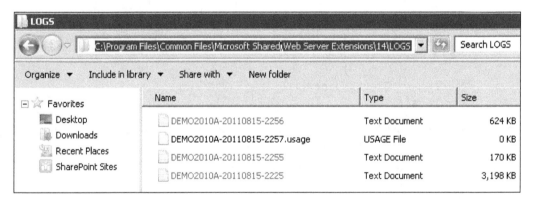

How it works...

SharePoint logs provide useful insight a into troubleshooting your farm. In this recipe, we looked at what your options are in terms of troubleshooting your farm using ULS logs more efficiently.

First, we ensured that the logging configuration in your SharePoint farm is enabled and we have detailed logging in your environment. The selected logging configuration may be different for your production environment. For our testing purposes, we turned on logging which produces moderate amounts of error and tracing messages so we have something to work with.

Next, we hit the URL of the page which, by default, expects parameters which have not been supplied. The sole purpose of this is to generate and error condition which you can see on the screen and with our new logging configuration. The error is surely going to generate a trace in the log.

Next, we execute our PowerShell script where we demonstrate how we can use PowerShell features to navigate logs more efficiently out of the box.

As always, we defined the script variables. In this recipe, the variables include a correlation token which represents an identifier which each logged condition generates. In our case, the identifier is exactly the same value which has been given to us during the error condition from the page in **Central Administration**:

```
$CorrelationID = "98459ccc-95e6-40e4-999c-6c463b6ec6a6"
```

Once a PowerShell snap-in has been loaded, we get hold of the list of events which are filtered by our correlation identifier, by using the following command:

```
$events = Get-SPLogEvent | Where-Object {$_.Correlation -eq $CorrelationID}
```

We display only a few of the returned properties, such as a time stamp and a message:

```
$events | Select Timestamp, Message
```

 Depending on the number of log files you have in your environment, this command and any other commands may take some time to execute. This is normal. One way to improve the performance of the log parsing is to delete unnecessary or old log files we captured during our log configuration earlier from their default location.

Another example of accessing information from your log is by area and the type of the event. Here is how we can retrieve all of the **Error** events which have been generated by **SharePoint Foundation** logging system:

```
$events = Get-SPLogEvent | Where-Object {$_.Level -eq "Error" -and {$_
.Area -eq "SharePoint Foundation "}}
$events | Select Timestamp, Message
```

Perhaps one of the easiest ways to narrow down events which have happened during the error condition is using a time stamp. By using a time stamp, you can get a collection of events which have taken place during your testing and narrow down exactly what caused the problem. Here is how to retrieve events that have taken place in point in time:

```
Get-SPLogEvent -StartTime "08/15/2011 22:50:30" -EndTime "08/15/2011
22:50:35"
```

Finally, the following command is used to cut the current error logging stream and start a new file where the log is written. This is very handy when all you need to do is take a copy of the file with recorded error conditions and give it to someone else for remote troubleshooting. Since log files may be quite large, by starting a new file and capturing events for the interval of time you're interested in, you can significantly improve your troubleshooting efficiency. Here is how you instruct PowerShell to start a new log file:

New-SPLogFile

Managing web application throttling settings

Each SharePoint 2010 web application instance comes with a variety of throttling settings which allows administrators to control how intensive daily farm operations are allowed to be. If you realize that certain new functionality in your site is used heavily and takes resources away from your core business functionality, such as collaboration features, you may choose to use options in this recipe to get the heavy usage under control.

In particular, this recipe will focus on setting thresholds for rendering list views and items that can be retrieved from the view. In this scenario, it's important to understand the difference between the setting of a threshold using the Central Administration option and the individual option on a view and how it impacts custom components that are being developed on a view.

We'll also take a look at how you can throttle operations related to list lookup retrieval and cascade actions performed on linked lists. In many scenarios, the handy concept of a lookup list is used on large data sets and decreases the efficiency of day-to-day user interaction.

Finally, we'll take a look at how you can manage whether user-defined workflows are allowed on the site. This ensures that if the workflow is defined first it goes through approval before it can harm data on the site.

By using PowerShell in this recipe, we'll have an understanding on how all of the configurations here can be scripted to create replicable development, staging, and production environments in a typical organization.

Getting ready

Considering you are using virtual development environment as described in *Chapter 1, PowerShell Scripting Methods and Custom Commands*, you have access to all of the web application settings for one of the default web applications available in the farm.

In this recipe, we'll be using PowerGUI to author the script, which means you will be required to be logged in with an administrator's role on the target Virtual Machine.

How to do it...

Let's see what's involved in managing SharePoint throttling settings with PowerShell using the following steps:

1. Click **Start | All Programs | PowerGUI | PowerGUI Script Editor**.

2. In the main script editing window of PowerGUI, add the following script:

```
# Defining script variables
$SiteUrl = "http://intranet.contoso.com"

# Loading Microsoft.SharePoint.PowerShell
$snapin = Get-PSSnapin | Where-Object {$_.Name -eq 'Microsoft.
SharePoint.Powershell'}
if ($snapin -eq $null) {
Write-Host "Loading SharePoint Powershell Snapin"
Add-PSSnapin "Microsoft.SharePoint.Powershell"
}

Write-Host "Connecting to site"
$SPSite = Get-SPSite | Where-Object {$_.Url -eq $SiteUrl}
  if($SPSite -ne $null)
  {
  Write-Host "Setting the List View Threshold"
   $SPSite.WebApplication.MaxItemsPerThrottledOperation = 2000

  Write-Host "Setting the List View Threshold for Auditors and
Administrators"
   $SPSite.WebApplication.MaxItemsPerThrottledOperationOverride =
5000

  Write-Host "Setting the Object Model Override"
   $SPSite.WebApplication.AllowOMCodeOverrideThrottleSettings =
$true

  Write-Host "Setting the List View Lookup Threshold"
```

```
$SPSite.WebApplication.MaxQueryLookupFields = 200

Write-Host "Allowing User Defined Workflows"
$SPSite.WebApplication.UserDefinedWorkflowsEnabled = $true

Write-Host "Setting cascade delete operation item limit"
$SPSite.WebApplication.CascadeDeleteMaximumItemLimit = 20

$SPSite.WebApplication.Update()

Write-Host "Web application configuration complete"
}
$SPSite.Dispose()
```

3. Click **File** | **Save** to save the script to your development machine's desktop. Set the filename of the script to WebApplicationThrottling.ps1.

4. Open the PowerShell console window and call WebApplicationThrottling.ps1 using the following command:

   PS C:\Users\Administrator\Desktop> .\ WebApplicationThrottling.ps1

5. As a result, your PowerShell script will execute and return results as shown in the following screenshot:

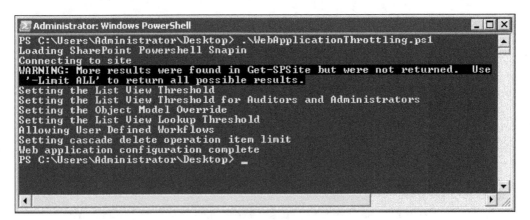

6. Now, navigate to the **SharePoint Central Administration** site by clicking **Start** | **All Programs** | **Microsoft SharePoint 2010 Products** | **SharePoint 2010 Central Administration**.

7. Click **Application Management** | **Manage web applications**.

8. Select **Intranet** web application and from the ribbon click **General Settings** | **Resource Throttling**, as seen in the following screenshot:

9. Take note of what web application settings have changed according to our configuration in the script, as shown in the following screenshot:

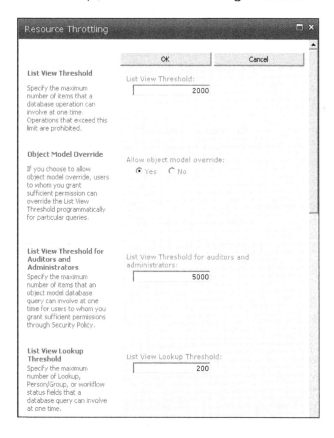

10. From the **Application Management | Manage web applications** screen, select **Intranet** web application, and from the ribbon click **General Settings | Workflow**.

11. Verify the setting for the **User-Defined Workflows** is set to **Enabled**, as shown in the following screenshot:

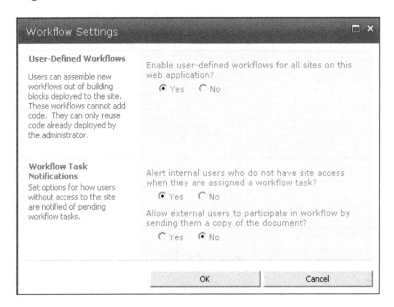

How it works...

Web application throttling settings give administrators more control over the farm usage. In some cases, you may want to throttle only high-level areas of your farm that are critical, in other cases, you may want to lock down your farm or web application on a more granular level.

In this recipe, we used PowerShell to demonstrate various throttling options available using the out-of-the-box user interface and through a script.

First, in our script, we defined our script variables. In this recipe, it's the URL of the intranet site collection for which we modify web application settings:

```
$SiteUrl = "http://intranet.contoso.com"
```

Once a PowerShell snap-in has been loaded, we get hold of the instance of the current site to get access to web application object on it.

First, we set the threshold on how many items are displayed in the view for site collections on the web application, using the following command:

```
$SPSite.WebApplication.MaxItemsPerThrottledOperation = 2000
```

The important concept to understand here is that this setting is different from the setting for an individual list view. With the list view limitation, users can still create new views to access the data they need. In cases where users are willing to wait for slow rendering of the view, they may not realize they are slowing down the entire web application with a long running operation. The following setting allows us to configure maximum number of list items allowed to be retrieved for any new or existing view on the system.

Next is the setting which defines the same list view rendering limit but this time for administrators and auditors. Since administrators and auditors typically have higher threshold limits due to the fact that they rarely execute list view operations and normally it is due to troubleshooting, they get higher priority and less limitations. Here is how this setting is defined with PowerShell:

```
$SPSite.WebApplication.MaxItemsPerThrottledOperationOverride = 5000
```

The next command demonstrates how you can set the last two settings to be overwritten for custom and out-of-the-box code, such as web parts:

```
$SPSite.WebApplication.AllowOMCodeOverrideThrottleSettings = $true
```

Typically, custom and out-of-the-box components have well thought out logic, Therefore, you may choose for your custom components to be able to retrieve more items.

Next, we are setting up how many items can be retrieved for a field which looks up values into another list. Lookup list relationship is a great feature which allows you to maintain two lists and update values from the parent list by changing referenced items in the child. However, if the number of items for the field exceeds your desired threshold, the lookup operation may slow down the execution of the operation.

Here is how we can control this setting:

```
$SPSite.WebApplication.MaxQueryLookupFields = 200
```

On a topic of lookup lists, if your lists have referential relationship, in SharePoint 2010, you can choose to perform a cascade delete operation which will delete any related child elements when parent item is deleted. Since this lookup and delete operations can take time, we use the following setting to choose how many items are allowed to be deleted with cascade delete option:

```
$SPSite.WebApplication.CascadeDeleteMaximumItemLimit = 20
```

Another useful setting we've looked at allows you to choose whether user-defined workflows are allowed on the site. Those include custom workflows created with SharePoint Designer. Here is the command which allows using of SharePoint designer workflows:

`$SPSite.WebApplication.UserDefinedWorkflowsEnabled = $true`

See also

The *Throttling items returned with external lists* recipe in *Chapter 4, Managing External Data in SharePoint and Business Connectivity Services using PowerShell*.

Configuring sandbox solution policies

The SharePoint 2010 sandbox solutions model truly allows for multiple tenants running on separate site collections to run individual pieces of custom functionality without affecting other site collections. SharePoint 2010 also has a variety of features you can use to configure how your sandbox solutions are going to run. Earlier in this chapter, in the *Configuring web application settings* recipe, we looked at how you can create custom quota templates which will be applied to new and existing web applications in your farm. One of the options available for the quota template is the ability to assign resource points to your sandbox solutions.

As your sandbox solutions become more popular in your environment, you can manage how many resources you want to allocate for some of the sandbox solutions compared to others and SharePoint will automatically take care of turning off the solution, if it exceeds its allocated limits.

If you think your users are not ready for sandbox solution, or you see a potential risk of too many solutions used, you can turn off the sandbox solution feature altogether.

In this recipe, we'll take a look at how you can configure sandbox solution options using PowerShell which allows you to script configuration along with other settings as you provision multiple environments within your organization.

Getting ready

Considering you are using virtual development environment as described in *Chapter 1, PowerShell Scripting Methods and Custom Commands*, sandbox solutions should be configured and enabled in your environment.

We'll also assume you are familiar with **Quota template** creation for the web application and have already created a **Team site** quota template as described in the *Configuring web application settings* recipe.

In this recipe, we'll be using PowerGUI to author the script, which means you will be required to be logged in with an administrator's role on the target Virtual Machine.

How to do it...

Using the following steps, we'll see what it takes to configure SharePoint sandbox solution policies with PowerShell:

1. Click **Start | All Programs | PowerGUI | PowerGUI Script Editor**.

2. In the main script editing window of PowerGUI, add the following script:

```
# Defining script variables
$SiteUrl = "http://intranet.contoso.com"

# Loading Microsoft.SharePoint.PowerShell
$snapin = Get-PSSnapin | Where-Object {$_.Name -eq 'Microsoft.
SharePoint.Powershell'}
if ($snapin -eq $null) {
Write-Host "Loading SharePoint Powershell Snapin"
Add-PSSnapin "Microsoft.SharePoint.Powershell"
}

Write-Host "Connecting to site"
$SPSite = Get-SPSite | Where-Object {$_.Url -eq $SiteUrl}
  if($SPSite -ne $null)
  {
  Write-Host "Accessing web application quota template"
    $AdminService = [Microsoft.SharePoint.Administration.
SPWebService]::ContentService
    $QuotaTemplate = $AdminService.QuotaTemplates["Team Site"]
  $QuotaTemplate.UserCodeMaximumLevel = 200
    $QuotaTemplate.UserCodeWarningLevel = 100
  $AdminService.Update()

  Write-Host "Setting web application quota"
  $SPSite.WebApplication.DefaultQuotaTemplate = "Team Site"
  $SPSite.WebApplication.Update()

  Write-Host "Enabling execution of sandbox solutions"
  Start-Service -Name SPUserCodeV4

  Write-Host "Web application configuration complete"
  }
$SPSite.Dispose()
```

3. Click **File | Save** to save the script to your development machine's desktop. Set the filename of the script to `ConfigureSandbox.ps1`.

4. Open the PowerShell console window and call `ConfigureSandbox.ps1` using the following command:

   PS C:\Users\Administrator\Desktop> .\ ConfigureSandbox.ps1

5. As a result, your PowerShell script will execute with an output as shown in the following screenshot:

6. Now, let's navigate to the **SharePoint Central Administration** site by clicking **Start | All Programs | Microsoft SharePoint 2010 Products | SharePoint 2010 Central Administration**.

7. From the **Quick launch** of **Central Administration,** click **Application Management**.

8. From **Site Collections,** click **Specify quota templates**.

9. From **Template Name,** select and existing template provisioned named **Team Site** and ensure the section **Sandboxed Solutions With Code Limits** has values as specified in our script, as shown in the following screenshot:

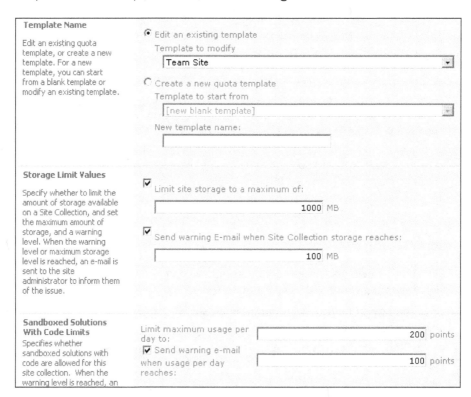

10. Now, from the home page of your **Central Administration**, click **System Settings | Manage services on server**.

11. Ensure the **Microsoft SharePoint Foundation Sandboxed Code Service** is started as specified in our script.

How it works...

SharePoint sandbox solutions introduce an entirely new set of features along with the configurations which allow administrators to have a better control over how sandbox solutions are used on their farm.

We started with defining the script variables for our script which includes the URL of our intranet site:

```
$SiteUrl = "http://intranet.contoso.com"
```

We then connect to the root site of our main site collection to work with its associated web application. As we have seen in the recipe *Managing web application throttling settings*, you can create a quota template where the site which uses the quota template can inherit configurations from. Here is how we modified our existing quota template with the configuration values for managing sandbox solution.

We connect to administration service first:

```
$AdminService = [Microsoft.SharePoint.Administration.SPWebService]::
ContentService
```

We then get hold of the existing quota template provisioned in the previously referenced recipe. Our quota template is called **Team Site**.

We then update the resource points for sandbox solutions. The resource points are calculated by the amount of resources a particular custom solution is using. When the threshold you specify is reached, the solution is shut down. Here is how resource points are assigned in our script:

```
$QuotaTemplate.UserCodeMaximumLevel = 200
$QuotaTemplate.UserCodeWarningLevel = 100
$AdminService.Update()
```

Just as before, we update the site collection `DefaultQuotaTemplate` property by specifying the quota template with the quota template we would like to use:

```
$SPSite.WebApplication.DefaultQuotaTemplate = "Team Site"
$SPSite.WebApplication.Update()
```

Finally, we ensure that sandbox solutions are enabled on the site by starting up sandbox service host by using the following command:

```
Start-Service -Name SPUserCodeV4
```

Similar to starting the service, you can stop the service, which will disable any sandbox solutions from being activated or used.

When the sandbox host service is stopped, the user interface involved in interacting with sandbox solutions is disabled.

See also

The *Configuring web application settings* and *Managing sandbox solutions in SharePoint site collections* recipes in this chapter.

Managing sandbox solutions in SharePoint site collections

As we've seen in the previous recipe, sandbox solutions give your users the flexibility to run applications within the scope of their site collection without affecting other site collections. Depending on the policies you have established, your users may run sandbox applications which cost significant resources to the system. In this case, you wouldn't want to restrict resource points for all of the sandbox solutions as we discussed in *Configuring sandbox solution policies*, because all of the solutions will be affected. In an organization where you have just a few site collections, you can instruct your users to avoid using the problem solution. However, in case you're running multiple site collections and you have many users allowed to deploy sandbox solutions to their site collections, you can choose to block a particular sandbox solution from being deployed and used on the farm.

In this recipe, we'll take a look at how PowerShell can help you with blocking a particular sandbox solution regardless of where on the farm it's deployed or what is the filename of the solution.

Getting ready

Assuming you are already using virtual development environment as described in *Chapter 1, PowerShell Scripting Methods and Creating Custom Commands*, you will have site collections allowing you to deploy sandbox solutions.

Since in this example we will be using a sample sandbox solution called `Solution1.wsp`, we will assume you will have an existing sandbox solution provided to you with the same name. If you're familiar with the Visual Studio development environment, this should not be a problem for you as you can create a new solution in a few minutes. Alternatively, you can download one of the freely available SharePoint sandbox solutions from `http://www. codeplex.com`.

In this recipe, we'll be using PowerGUI to author the script, which means you will be required to be logged in with an administrator's role on the target Virtual Machine.

How to do it...

Next, we see how you can manage sandbox solutions in your site collections using PowerShell:

1. Ensure you have a sandbox solution file available at the following path:

   `C:\Users\Administrator\Desktop\`

2. Ensure the solution name is `Solution1.wsp` as that's the name assumed further in the script.

3. Click **Start | All Programs | PowerGUI | PowerGUI Script Editor**.

4. In the main script editing window of PowerGUI, add the following script:

```
# Defining script variables
$SiteUrl = "http://intranet.contoso.com"
$SolutionName = "C:\Users\Administrator\Desktop\Solution1.wsp"

# Loading Microsoft.SharePoint.PowerShell
$snapin = Get-PSSnapin | Where-Object {$_.Name -eq 'Microsoft.
SharePoint.Powershell'}
if ($snapin -eq $null) {
Write-Host "Loading SharePoint Powershell Snapin"
Add-PSSnapin "Microsoft.SharePoint.Powershell"
}

Write-Host "Connecting to User Solutions Host"
$UserCodeSvc = [Microsoft.SharePoint.Administration.
SPUserCodeService]::Local

Write-Host "Retrieving sandbox solution signature"
$Signature = [Microsoft.SharePoint.Administration.SPUserCodeServic
e]::GetSolutionSignatureFromFile($SolutionName)

Write-Host "Creating blocked solution object"
$BlockedSolution = New-Object Microsoft.SharePoint.UserCode.
SPBlockedSolution -ArgumentList ($SolutionName), ($Signature),
("Solution Blocked")
```

```
Write-Host "Blocking the solution"
$UserCodeSvc.BlockedSolutions.Add($BlockedSolution)
$UserCodeSvc.Update()

Write-Host "Solution blocking complete"
```

5. Click **File | Save** to save the script to your development machine's desktop. Set the filename of the script to ManageSandbox.ps1.

6. Open the PowerShell console window and call ManageSandbox.ps1 using the following command:

   PS C:\Users\Administrator\Desktop> .\ ManageSandbox.ps1

7. As a result, your PowerShell script will execute with results as shown in the following screenshot:

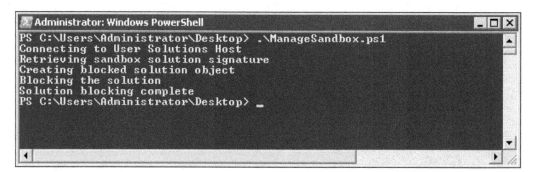

8. Now, let's navigate to the **SharePoint Central Administration** site by clicking **Start | All Programs | Microsoft SharePoint 2010 Products | SharePoint 2010 Central Administration**.

9. From the **Quick launch** of **Central Administration,** click **System Settings**.

10. From the **Farm Management**, click **Manage user solutions**.

11. Ensure the solution from your desktop is listed under the **Blocked Solutions** list, as shown in the following screenshot:

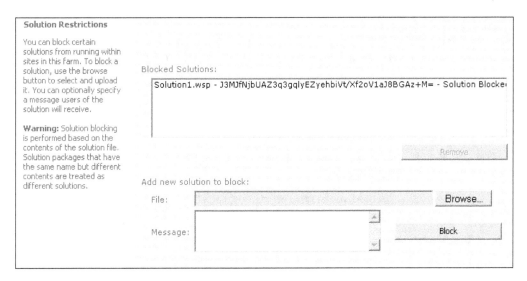

12. Next, let's navigate to our **SharePoint Intranet** site collection: `http://intranet.contoso.com`.

13. Click **Site Actions | Site Settings**.

14. Under **Galleries**, click **Solutions**.

15. From the ribbon, click the **Library** tab, then click the **Upload Solution** ribbon button.

16. Upload the solution from the desktop to the solution library.

17. Try activating the solution to see that it's blocked and you cannot activate it, as shown in the following screenshot:

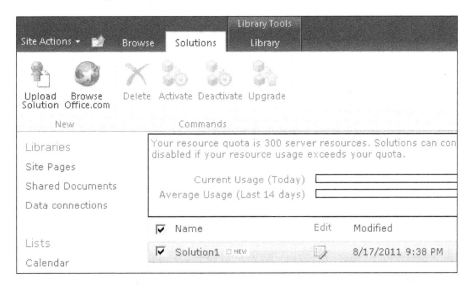

How it works...

We started by defining the location of our solution to be blocked:

```
$SolutionName = "C:\Users\Administrator\Desktop\Solution1.wsp"
```

We loaded PowerShell SharePoint snap-in used to perform SharePoint related PowerShell commands.

The first step is to connect to the Sandbox Service Host, which supplies methods and objects used to work with sandbox solutions:

```
$UserCodeSvc = [Microsoft.SharePoint.Administration.
SPUserCodeService]::Local
```

Next, we need to retrieve the solution hash which will uniquely identify the solution as well as its integrity. As per TechNet, here is how solution hash helps with identifying the solution:

Each sandboxed solution is identified by a hash result of the solution code. If the solution code is changed and redeployed, it will be seen as a new sandboxed solution and will be allowed to run even if the original is still blocked.

The following command is used to extract the hash from the solution we are about to block:

**$Signature = [Microsoft.SharePoint.Administration.SPUserCodeService]::
GetSolutionSignatureFromFile($SolutionName)**

The only parameter is the location of the solution.

Next, we need to create an instance of an object which will represent a blocked solution:

```
$BlockedSolution = New-Object Microsoft.SharePoint.UserCode.
SPBlockedSolution -ArgumentList ($SolutionName), ($Signature),
("Solution Blocked")
```

The three arguments required to describe our blocked solution include the:

- ▸ Path to the solution
- ▸ Hash of the solution which we determined earlier
- ▸ Message shown to users if the solution is attempted to be activated

Blocking the solution is just a matter of adding our newly created blocked solution object to the collection of blocked solutions, as follows:

```
$UserCodeSvc.BlockedSolutions.Add($BlockedSolution)
```

Finally, to save all of the changes we perform the update on the Sandbox Code Host:

```
$UserCodeSvc.Update()
```

There's more

In some cases, you may have solutions which are already added and activated on the system. In this case, the functionality delivered by the solution will be blocked. For example, if you have a web part which runs from within a solution. If that solution has just been blocked, the web part will not function, and if users try to add a new instance of it, they will get an error message which the administrator has specified when they blocked the solution.

In some cases, the solution which provisions files to the site, such as modules provisioning master pages or stylesheets, can also be blocked. In this case, the functionality associated with the solution has already been executed and files have made it into the server. In this case, when the administrator blocks the solution, the files will not be retracted from the site.

In the event that a blocked sandbox solution has a feature with an event receiver on it, if such feature has not been activated, when activation is attempted, the user will receive an error with an error message specified by administrator during solution blocking.

See also

The *Configuring sandbox solution policies* recipe in this chapter.

Index

Thank you for buying
Microsoft SharePoint 2010 and Windows PowerShell 2.0: Expert Cookbook

About Packt Publishing

Packt, pronounced 'packed', published its first book "*Mastering phpMyAdmin for Effective MySQL Management*" in April 2004 and subsequently continued to specialize in publishing highly focused books on specific technologies and solutions.

Our books and publications share the experiences of your fellow IT professionals in adapting and customizing today's systems, applications, and frameworks. Our solution-based books give you the knowledge and power to customize the software and technologies you're using to get the job done. Packt books are more specific and less general than the IT books you have seen in the past. Our unique business model allows us to bring you more focused information, giving you more of what you need to know, and less of what you don't.

Packt is a modern, yet unique publishing company, which focuses on producing quality, cutting-edge books for communities of developers, administrators, and newbies alike. For more information, please visit our website: www.PacktPub.com.

About Packt Enterprise

In 2010, Packt launched two new brands, Packt Enterprise and Packt Open Source, in order to continue its focus on specialization. This book is part of the Packt Enterprise brand, home to books published on enterprise software – software created by major vendors, including (but not limited to) IBM, Microsoft and Oracle, often for use in other corporations. Its titles will offer information relevant to a range of users of this software, including administrators, developers, architects, and end users.

Writing for Packt

We welcome all inquiries from people who are interested in authoring. Book proposals should be sent to author@packtpub.com. If your book idea is still at an early stage and you would like to discuss it first before writing a formal book proposal, contact us; one of our commissioning editors will get in touch with you.

We're not just looking for published authors; if you have strong technical skills but no writing experience, our experienced editors can help you develop a writing career, or simply get some additional reward for your expertise.

Microsoft Exchange 2010 PowerShell Cookbook

Manage and maintain your Microsoft Exchange 2010 environment with Windows PowerShell 2.0 and the Exchange Management Shell

Mike Pfeiffer   [PACKT] enterprise

Microsoft Exchange 2010 PowerShell Cookbook

ISBN: 978-1-84968-246-6   Paperback: 480 pages

Manage and maintain your Microsoft Exchange 2010 environment with Windows PowerShell 2.0 and the Exchange Management Shell

1. Step-by-step instructions on how to write scripts for nearly every aspect of Exchange 2010 including the Client Access Server, Mailbox, and Transport server roles

2. Understand the core concepts of Windows PowerShell 2.0 that will allow you to write sophisticated scripts and one-liners used with the Exchange Management Shell

3. Learn how to write scripts and functions, schedule scripts to run automatically, and generate complex reports

Microsoft SharePoint 2010 Administration Cookbook

Over 90 simple but incredibly effective recipes to administer your SharePoint applications

Peter Serzo   [PACKT] enterprise

Microsoft SharePoint 2010 Administration Cookbook

ISBN: 978-1-84968-108-7   Paperback: 288 pages

Over 90 simple but incredibly effective recipes to administer your Microsoft SharePoint 2010 applications

1. Solutions to the most common problems encountered while administering SharePoint in book and eBook formats

2. Upgrade, configure, secure, and back up your SharePoint applications with ease

3. Packed with many recipes for improving collaboration and content management with SharePoint

Please check **www.PacktPub.com** for information on our titles

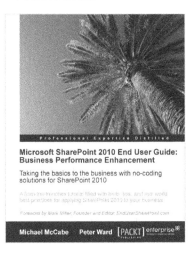

Microsoft SharePoint 2010 End User Guide: Business Performance Enhancement

ISBN: 978-1-84968-066-0   Paperback: 424 pages

A from-the-trenches tutorial filled with hints, tips, and real world best partices for applying Sharepoint 2010 to your business

1. Designed to offer applicable, no-coding solutions to dramatically enhance the performance of your business

2. Excel at SharePoint intranet functionality to have the most impact on you and your team

3. Drastically enhance your End user SharePoint functionality experience

Microsoft SharePoint 2010 Power User Cookbook

ISBN: 978-1-84968-288-6   Paperback: 344 pages

Over 70 advanced recipes for expert End Users to unlock and apply the value of Microsoft SharePoint 2010

1. Discover how to apply SharePoint far beyond basic functionality

2. Explore the Business Intelligence capabilities of SharePoint with KPIs and custom dashboards

3. Take a deep dive into document management, data integration, electronic forms, and workflow scenarios

Please check **www.PacktPub.com** for information on our titles